angles on psychology

for
Edexcel
AS Level

Third Edition

endorsed by
edexcel

Matt Jarvis
Julia Russell
Dawn Collis

Folens

© 2008 Folens Limited, on behalf of the authors.

United Kingdom: Folens Publishers, Waterslade House, Thame Rd, Haddenham, Buckinghamshire HP17 8NT.

www.folens.com

Ireland: Folens Publishers, Greenhills Road, Tallaght, Dublin 24.

Email: info@folens.ie

Project development: Rick and Samantha Jackman (Jackman Publishing Solutions Ltd)

Layout artist: GreenGate Publishing Services

Illustrations: Barking Dog Art, Alex Machin

Cover image: © 2008 Jupiterimages Corporation

First published 2008 by Folens Limited.

British Library Cataloguing in Publication Data. A catalogue record for this publication is available from the British Library.

ISBN 978-1-85008-298-9

Contents

Introduction

This is the third edition of the hugely successful *Angles on psychology*, previously published in 2000 and 2004. This edition of *Angles* is tailor-made to the needs of students and teachers taking on the new 2008 AS psychology from Edexcel. We know that many students have in the past found *Angles* useful for other A-level specifications as well. If you are studying AQA spec A, you might like to know that we now have a book, *Exploring psychology*, for this specification. You can see details of this at this at: http://www.folens.com/page.cfm?&webpageid=74.

Matt and Julia were both heavily involved in the development of the 2008 psychology specifications, Julia at Edexcel and Matt as part of the Major Stakeholders Group that advised all the Awarding Bodies. This means that we have been in an excellent position to develop a textbook that really meets the changing needs of psychology students and their teachers. Since the last round of specifications were written, psychology has been reclassified as a science A-level. For psychology students this means a whole new emphasis on how science works or research methods. In a change from previous years this will no longer be assessed by coursework. Instead students will undertake a series of practicals, on which exam questions can be asked.

As well as updating our content, our major task in writing the third edition of *Angles* has been to keep as many of the popular features of the last edition as possible, while making some changes in line with the requirements of the new specification.

- **Classic research:** this feature identifies the studies named on the specification to be studied in detail. Some of these are compulsory and some are optional – this is clear in each boxed feature.
- **What's new?** Although much of the research we quote is very up-to-date, the *What's new?* feature allows us to flag up examples of current research that are particularly interesting in themselves or which are particularly useful as examples of methodological choices or issues flagged up in *How science works*.

- **Media watch:** this feature takes newspaper articles reporting real events and invites you to use the psychology you have been studying to explain why these events might have happened.
- **How science works:** this is perhaps the biggest change from the previous two editions. The Edexcel AS spec now fully integrates research methodology into the approaches. We have placed the *How science works* boxes in the relevant chapters, linked to the rest of the chapter content.
- **Interactive angles:** this is an interactive feature that gives you thinking, research or revision tasks to make sure you deeply process and fully understand the material you are studying.
- **Over to you:** for each psychological approach you study at AS level you are required to undertake a piece of practical work. *Over to you* introduces you to this task.
- **For & against:** these are summaries of the major strengths and weaknesses of theories.

If you have seen previous editions of *Angles* you'll be pleased to know that our basic principles haven't changed. We structure the book closely around the Edexcel specification so you won't waste a lot of time reading material you don't need to know. However, we also make an effort within the demands of the specification to provide you with as much interesting, up-to-date and relevant material as possible to study. This is because motivation is incredibly important in learning; we want you to share the authors' love of psychology, work hard at it and do well. Happy angling!

Dedications

To Em, with love

To Clare, Sam & Ellie

chapter **1**

Studying psychology

In this introductory chapter we look briefly at some of the things you should know a little about before going too much further with studying psychology. We define psychology and explain why it comprises so many approaches. We also explain the differences between the key terms of theory, study and research method. Crucially, we introduce you to evaluating psychological material and try to prepare you for thinking critically about the theories, studies and research methods you will come across throughout this book. Finally, we explain our ideas about the place of a book like this in studying psychology, and offer some advice on where else to look for information on psychology.

What is psychology?

Psychology is often defined as the 'science of mind and behaviour'. By this we mean that it is the study of how people (and sometimes animals) behave, and how their minds work. The subject matter of psychology is extremely wide-ranging, covering everything from why pilots crash planes (Chapter 2) to why a minority of men like to dress as babies (Chapter 4). One thing you need to get used to immediately if you are going to study psychology is the range of different approaches we can bring to bear on the subject. Chapters 2–6 introduce you to five particularly important approaches to psychology. These are briefly summarised in Table 1.1.

Table 1.1 Five major approaches to psychology

Approach	Description	Examples of real life applications
Social	Concerned with how people interact, and how individuals, groups and society and culture at large influence us.	Understanding and tackling genocide.
Cognitive	Concerned with the workings of mental processes such as thinking and memory, which we use to make sense of information.	Understanding and improving the accuracy of eyewitness testimony.
Psychodynamic	Concerned with the influence of the unconscious mind i.e. mental processes of which we are not normally aware.	Understanding the process and benefits of psychotherapy.
Biological	Concerned with the relationship between biological processes, in particular the workings of the brain and psychological functions.	Understanding drug treatments for mental illness.
Learning	Concerned with how we learn behaviours, for example by associating different events together and observing others.	Understanding the effect of media violence on aggression.

Some psychologists work very much within a framework of one particular approach. Thus social psychologists may think very much in social terms and bring social-psychological theory and research to bear on a range of problems. Others draw freely on a range of approaches and are said to be eclectic.

Theories, studies and research methods

There are many technical terms to learn as you study psychology. Before you go any further it is worth being absolutely clear about three terms in particular. As examiners we have seen many students who knew their stuff well fail to achieve what they should have, because in the exam they wrote about a theory when the question asked for a study or a study when the question required a research method. *All* psychology will make more sense when you are clear about the distinction between theories, studies and research methods.

What is a theory?

A theory is an *explanation* for a psychological phenomenon. Some theories (for example Freud's theory, see p. 83) are very ambitious, aiming to explain almost everything about human nature. Others are much narrower, seeking to explain something very specific. For example, the multi-store model of memory (p. 52) just aims to show that human memory involves more than one system.

It is important to remember that, although there are usually several different theories concerned with a phenomenon, our task is *not* to choose the correct theory and discard the others. Often, different theories are concerned with different aspects of the same broad area. For example, in Chapter 3 we look at three theories of memory. Each of these focuses on a different aspect of memory and they thus complement one another.

What is a study?

A study is any exercise where data (information) is gathered and analysed. This is a quite different idea to a theory. There is a huge range of studies, and you will encounter more studies than anything else as you learn about psychology. Some studies aim to test a theory. Others just gather information about a psychological phenomenon. A classic example of a study is Hofling *et al.*'s investigation of nurses' obedience to doctors (p. 19). This involved gathering two types of data from nurses. First, they were asked how they thought they would behave if ordered by a doctor to do something that would harm a patient. Secondly, they were actually put in that position and their behaviour recorded. Studies should tell us something useful. For example, Hofling *et al.*'s (1966) study showed how nurses tended to follow doctors' orders unquestioningly and that this obedience could sometimes pose a danger to patients.

What is a research method?

Studies make use of one or more research methods, techniques for gathering and/or analysing data. You will come across a range of research methods in this book, some being particularly associated with specific approaches to psychology. For example surveys are associated with social psychology. This is not to say that they are only used in social psychology, or that social psychologists rely entirely on them, just that they have an important role in that area.

interactive
angles

Look up each of the following and identify them as a theory, a study or a research method.

1. Milgram's idea of agency (p. 21).

2. Case studies of brain-damaged patients (p. 85).

3. A case of adult baby syndrome (p. 98).

4. Little Albert (p. 165).

5. Freud's explanation for dreaming (p. 86).

Learning to think critically about psychological material

Assessments in psychology (such as exams) test two main abilities. First, you have to be able to describe psychological material, for example theories and studies, clearly, accurately and in sufficient detail. If you have learned the material and you understand the question, this is quite a straightforward task. However, there is another more difficult skill to develop; the evaluation of psychological material. This means to be able to explore its strengths and weaknesses and identify any other issues attached to it. If you are studying A-level then you need to be aware that evaluation is up to 35% of AS-level marks and up to 48% of A2 marks. The ability to evaluate is what really distinguishes students who achieve grades A, C and E. Get it sussed now!

Evaluating theories

Although we help you in this book with discussion sections and 'for and against' summary boxes, try to avoid simply learning these evaluations parrot-fashion. Try instead to ask yourself the following questions every time you encounter a theory.

1. **What sort of evidence is this theory based on?** If a theory is derived from a few unrepresentative cases it might not apply well to everybody. If it is based on laboratory studies then it may not explain people's behaviour in real-life situations.
2. **Is this theory testable?** If it is difficult to test then this is a weakness.
3. **Is there supporting evidence?** Have you found studies that could be used to support the theory or does it seem to be based just on speculation?
4. **Is there conflicting evidence?** Are there in fact studies that suggest that the theory is incorrect or at least limited in what it can explain?
5. **Is the theory useful?** By that we mean, does it have applications in understanding or intervening in a real-life situation?
6. **Is the theory socially sensitive?** By this we mean, is the theory likely to offend people, perhaps because it places blame on someone for a psychological phenomenon, or because it identifies something undesirable about human nature?
7. **Is there something important that this theory cannot explain?** A common limitation of theories is the inability to explain all aspects of the phenomenon, for example why people vary so much individually.

interactive
angles

Turn to Milgram's agency theory (p. 21). Ask all seven questions of the theory. Some will be more applicable than others, but by going through them all you should be able to compile quite a detailed evaluation.

Evaluating studies

There are so many studies in a book like this that it is impossible to include evaluations of all of them. However, you can get into the habit of asking yourself the following questions whenever you encounter a study.

1. **Has this study been conducted ethically?** By that we mean, have participants been put at risk, taken advantage of, had their privacy invaded or in some other way had their rights violated. See p. 16 for a detailed account of the British Psychological Society code of ethics.

Figure 1.1
Rodin's *The Thinker*

2. **Are the findings socially sensitive?** Do the findings of the study risk offending people because they place blame on particular people or justify discrimination against a vulnerable group?

3. **Has the study involved a representative group of people?** If, as is often the case the researcher used their own students as participants, how representative are students of the population? Have both men and women, and people of a good range of ages participated?

4. **Has it been carried out in an artificial or a natural environment?** If the study was carried out in a laboratory can we be sure that participants behaved as they would in their own surroundings?

5. **Are the tasks given to participants like those they would encounter in real life?** A common limitation of research is to put participants in situations or give them things to do that bear little resemblance to their real lives.

6. **How good are the measures used to record the results?** For example if the study used a questionnaire, was it a standard one widely accepted by psychologists or did the researchers make it up for the study? It is time-consuming and difficult to standardise a measure. Unless there is evidence that this has been done properly in the study it is generally better to use a standard existing measure.

7. **Do the findings of this study conflict with those of other studies?** If so, think about how the findings are different, and try to explain why they differ. You might be able to suggest which study was better designed and which results we should accord more importance to.

interactive angles

Turn to Milgram's famous study of destructive obedience (p. 13). Ask all seven questions about Milgram's study. Again, some will be more important than others, but see how detailed an evaluation you can build.

7

Of course in some cases there are specific criticisms you might want to make about a theory or study. For example, you might wish to quote what another psychologist has said about it. That is fine, but don't rely on learning specific criticisms for every theory and study – it is too much information.

Other sources of information about psychology

Although we have put this book together with a lot of care, the last thing you should do is accept everything we say. That may sound a little odd! However, it is important to realise that all writers in psychology see things slightly differently. When we cover a theory like Freud's (p. 83), what we are doing is summarising a few key ideas out of several decades of work. It is inevitable that every writer will select slightly different material and present it slightly differently. Ultimately this means that if you study psychology to a high level you should read the original material rather than rely on textbooks like this. If you are studying at a relatively introductory level then that is a little harsh, and you will need to rely on people like us to give you a fair picture of the field. However, it is *always* worth reading a range of books rather than just one. Apart from anything else it is valuable to see how different writers have different opinions about psychology. There are many good general psychology texts about and we don't need to go plugging the competition! We can advise you on a couple of other sources of good information though.

Journals

There is a huge variety of journals where new research is published. Most of these are very advanced and difficult to read, but a few are well worth considering even if you are new to psychology; *Psychology Review* is aimed specifically at pre-degree level students, and carries articles by leading experts pitched at people fairly new to studying psychology. *The Psychologist* is rather more advanced, but unlike most journals, is pitched at those without a detailed knowledge of specialist areas in psychology, and it can therefore be fairly readable for students new to the subject. The British Psychological Society also publishes *Psych-Talk*, a newsletter put together by student members. This contains articles by university students and interviews with experts. Like *Psychology Review* it should be relatively easy to read.

The Internet

There is a huge range of material on psychology available online. Beware of some pitfalls however. Much of the material on the web is generated by amateurs and contains serious inaccuracies. Even some of the material on sites designated .ac.uk (British universities and colleges) or .edu (American universities) has been posted by students and can be unreliable. We would advise using the Internet in three main ways:

1. When you see a news story that grabs your interest because it relates to some psychology you have studied, try putting key words into a general search engine such as Google. Some newspapers and broadcasters have their own search engines to locate material they have publicised, and these can also be searched. The BBC, *The Guardian* and the *Times Educational Supplement* all have such search facilities.

2. There are organisations that have good web pages and have links to other good sources of information. The British Psychological Society and the American Psychological Association are perhaps the best general sources of information and links, but of course there are sites devoted to areas within psychology. There are for example institutions devoted to key figures such as Freud and Milgram (see for example the Freud Museum, the British Psychoanalytic Society and www.stanleymilgram.com). You can easily locate all these by means of a Google search. In addition the British Psychological Society publishes a regular research digest, summarising some very up-to-date studies of use to A-level students. You can subscribe to this at http://bps-research-digest.blogspot.com/.

3. There are some online databases that give access to summaries of the latest psychological research. The best known of these are PsycINFO and MEDLINE. Unfortunately you are unlikely to gain access to these without a password, which is difficult and expensive to obtain. However, have a go at tracking down PUBMED. This is a medical database not password protected, and gives access to some good psychological material.

interactive angles

Try some Internet searching now. Take a leading figure in psychology such as Stanley Milgram, who is best known for studying obedience.

1. Locate and look at the Stanley Milgram website.

2. Locate *The Guardian* and BBC websites and search there for recent articles mentioning obedience.

3. Locate the British Psychological Society website and see what Milgram or obedience-related links you can find.

4. Locate PUBMED and input 'obedience' as a search term.

Conclusions

There are quite a few things you should know about psychology before embarking on studying it. Be aware that there are different approaches to psychology, and that each treats the subject as something slightly different. Know your key terms. In particular be clear about the difference between a theory, a study and a research method. Rather than learn evaluation of every theory and study parrot-fashion, develop your skills of critical thinking and learn to evaluate all psychological material whenever you encounter it. Finally, seek information from a variety of sources and don't worry when they present the same idea differently, or when different writers have different opinions on a topic. In particular learn how to use the Internet effectively.

what's ahead

By the end of this chapter I should know about:

- the social approach to psychology
- Milgram's studies of human obedience, in particular the original study and one variation
- later studies of human obedience including that of Hofling *et al.* (1966) and one study conducted in a different country
- the agency theory of obedience
- prejudice and discrimination
- the social identity theory of prejudice
- one study of prejudice; *either* Sherif *et al.* (1961), Tajfel (1970) *or* Reicher & Haslam (2003)
- applying social-psychological ideas to explain real life situations

In addition I should understand:

- the survey method
- hypothesis-writing
- the distinction between quantitative and qualitative data
- ethical issues in research
- sampling techniques
- issues of reliability, validity and subjectivity

where does the social approach take us?

→ Killing people: is it normal?

↖ Football: would you help a Chelsea supporter in trouble?

← Obedience: a train guard says 'Give up your seat.' Would you?

↘ Virtual reality: why do we feel guilty about harming an avatar?

↙ Iraq: why do some psychologists defend troops who abuse Iraqi prisoners?

The social angle

The social approach to psychology is concerned with the ways in which people affect one another. We are affected at all times by the social situation in which we find ourselves. The social situation is the result of the influence of individuals, groups and of our wider culture and society. An example of the influence of individuals on us is in obedience. This occurs when we obey a direct order from another individual in a position of authority. Groups also affect us. For example, we respond differently to people according to the nature of the groups to which they belong, and we tend to display favouritism towards members of groups to which we also belong. We also tend to conform to the behaviour of a group in which we find ourselves.

The influence of other people on us is not limited to the individuals and groups we encounter directly. Our culture exerts more subtle influences of which we might not normally be aware. Culture is a set of beliefs and norms that characterises a group of people. This group can be as small as a single family, however the term 'culture' is more often used in relation to a larger group such as the society in which we live or our ethnic group. Our culture will affect our response to individuals and groups. For example, our culture will affect who has the authority to give us orders. It *may* also affect our general tendency for obedience. Our culture will also affect our attitudes to particular groups.

Obedience

Obedience means to follow direct orders from an individual who is in a position of authority over us. Technically, obedience is distinct from *compliance*, which means going along with suggestions or instructions, and *conformity*, which means to adopt the attitudes and behaviours of those around us. Although we like to think of ourselves as free and independent, most of the time a degree of obedience is probably a good thing. If we didn't usually obey road signs and traffic lights there would be carnage every time we took to the streets, and if as students we didn't do what our teacher says (some of the time anyway!) we would probably make little headway with our studies. However, there is a downside to our tendency for obedience; when we are ordered to do something immoral we frequently obey, even if this causes us distress and we bitterly regret doing so later. This phenomenon is known as **destructive obedience**.

The attention of psychologists turned to destructive obedience following the Holocaust of the 1940s, in which the Nazis and their collaborators obeyed unquestioningly when ordered to perform monstrous acts, including the extermination of several million Jews, Romanies, Communists and Trade Unionists. Stanley Milgram was one of an international network of researchers committed to investigating the psychology underlying the Holocaust with the intention of preventing anything similar happening again. Early attempts to explain the Holocaust focused on the idea that there was something distinctive about German culture that had allowed the Holocaust to take place. Milgram initially set out to test the idea that the German people were unusual in their response to orders from authority figures, but he quickly found that people in general are surprisingly obedient to people in authority.

Figure 2.1
Ordinary Germans obeyed orders that led to millions being killed in extermination camps

what's that?

- **Obedience:** following the direct orders of a person in a position of authority over us

- **Destructive obedience:** following orders that lead to the harming of another person or people

The Milgram studies of obedience

The original study

Milgram (1963) set out to investigate how obedient people would be in a situation where following orders would mean breaking participants' moral code and harming another person. In his original study, Milgram advertised for volunteers to take part in a memory experiment for a fee of $4.50. When the 40 participants (males aged 20–50) arrived at the university, the participants were told they would be either a teacher or a learner. They were then introduced to 'Mr Wallace', a mild-mannered and pleasant middle-aged man as a fellow participant (in fact he was a stooge working for Milgram). By fiddling an apparently random procedure, Milgram ensured that the participant was always the teacher and 'Mr Wallace' was always the learner.

The learner was then strapped into a chair and wired up to a shock generator. This was demonstrated by giving the participant a mild shock. The participant then took their place in front of the shock machine. Mr Wallace and the participant were positioned on each side of a screen so that they could hear but not see each other. An experimenter was in the room, in clear view of the participant. The experimenter issued orders to the participant that whenever Mr Wallace gave a wrong answer he was to give him an electric shock. Of course Mr Wallace did not receive real shocks, but there was no way for the participant to realise this. Following each mistake the level of the 'shock' appeared to increase by 15 volts. The shock levels on the machine were labelled from 0 to 450 volts and also had signs saying 'danger – severe shock' and, at 450 volts "XXX". The experimenter ordered participants to continue giving increased shocks whilst the learner shouted and screamed in pain then, after 300 volts, went silent. When participants protested they received a series of verbal prods:

- 'Please continue' or 'please go on'
- 'The experiment requires that you continue'
- 'It is absolutely essential that you continue'
- 'You have no choice, you *must* go on'

Figure 2.2
Milgram's shock apparatus

Figure 2.3
Milgram's participants were clearly distressed at what they were doing

To Milgram's great surprise, all the participants gave Mr Wallace at least 300 volts (more than you would receive from the mains supply in Britain), and 65% went the distance, giving the full 450 volts to an apparently dead Mr Wallace. The average maximum voltage given was 368.25 V. The distribution of maximum shocks is shown in Table 2.1. Most of the participants protested and some wept and begged in their distress, obviously believing that they had killed Mr Wallace. However, interviews revealed that most people did not feel that they could stop when ordered to continue by the experimenter. The minority of participants who defied the experimenter showed particular signs of stress as they agonised over their decision, however, this disappeared once they had made their decision to disobey. This dramatic study demonstrates the power of authority over our behaviour. What is particularly remarkable about the results is that participants were clearly very upset by what they had to do, but *saw no alternative except to obey*.

Table 2.1 The distribution of maximum voltages given by participants

Voltage	Number of Ps giving this as a maximum
15–60 V	0
75–120 V	0
135–180 V	0
195–240 V	0
255–300 V	5 (at 300 V)
315–360 V	8
375–420 V	1
420 V+	26

how **science** works

Research Methods

Quantitative and qualitative data

In any psychological study we gather and analyse data. 'Data' simply means information. We can collect this information in two forms, quantitative and qualitative. Quantitative data comes in the form of numbers. Qualitative data is any information *not* in the form of numbers, for example verbal information such as notes from observers or interview transcripts. Milgram's study is a really good example of how we can use both quantitative and qualitative data. It also shows how misleading one can be without the other. Milgram's quantitative data comes in the form of the percentages of participants giving various voltages and the mean voltage given. The headline figures are the 100% of participants giving 300 V and the 65% giving 450 V. Taken in isolation this quantitative data would suggest that people are quite willing to harm a stranger when under orders.

However, a closer look at the qualitative data reveals a quite different picture. Records of observers and transcripts of interviews with participants reveal the enormous distress and conflict they went through when obeying the orders. Taken alone these observations and interviews might also be misleading as they would suggest that people would *not* be willing to harm someone when ordered to. Taken together however the qualitative and quantitative data show that people experienced great distress at receiving destructive orders but that they nonetheless felt unable to disobey them.

This example illustrates the strengths and weaknesses of qualitative and quantitative data. Quantitative data can be crude and misleading, and can fail to capture the subtleties of what is being studied. In this case the subtleties are what the participants felt. On the other hand qualitative data can be vague and fail to show the key trends. In this case knowing how Milgram's participants responded emotionally is important but possibly not quite as important as knowing that the majority would inflict a potentially lethal voltage on the learner.

Variations in the procedure

Over the next few years following the original study, Milgram conducted a number of variations on the original procedure. These included varying the location of the study, the directness of the participant's involvement in harming Mr Wallace and the appearance of the experimenter. Findings are summarised in Table 2.2.

Table 2.2 Variations in the Milgram procedure and results

Rank order of obedience	Condition	% giving 450 V
1	Victim is silent throughout	100
2	Standard procedure	65
3	Procedure in run-down office block	48
4	Victim in same room	40
5	Orders phoned in	20.5
6	Experimenter has no lab coat	20
7	Fellow participants disobey	10
8	Teacher has choice of voltage	2.5

Over the past four decades these variations have been replicated many times by other psychologists. Lüttke (2004) has reviewed these studies and concluded that only some of Milgram's findings have proved reliable. In particular two variations have very significant effects on obedience rates; the proximity of the victim (obedience falls when the victim is near and visible) and the presence of obedient or disobedient co-participants. We can look in detail at Milgram's study of the latter.

Classic research

Compulsory

Milgram S. (1965) 'Liberating effects of group pressure'

Journal of Personality and Social Psychology 1, 127–34.

Aim: to test whether the rate of obedience in the Milgram procedure would be affected by witnessing rebellious or obedient fellow participants.

Procedure: 80 male participants aged 20–50 took part in one of two conditions. Those taking part in each condition were matched for age and occupation with those in Milgram's original procedure. Milgram's original procedure served as a control condition. In one of the experimental conditions the participant worked with two rebellious stooges. At 150V one refused to give any further shocks and at 210V the other also refused. In the second experimental condition two obedient stooges gave shocks without protest and offered mild rebukes when the participant expressed displeasure with the procedure.

Findings: in the baseline condition all 40 participants gave at least 300V and 26 (65%) gave the full 450V. In the rebellious stooge condition 50% refused to carry on past 150V, and only 6 of the 40 (15%) gave the full 450V. In the obedient stooge condition 29 participants (72.5%) went to 450V.

Conclusion: the behaviour of fellow participants made a difference to the rates of obedience. The presence of rebellious stooges had a much larger effect on participants than that of obedient stooges; the majority felt able to refuse orders once one or both the others had done so.

Discussion of Milgram's studies

Milgram's studies were of great practical value as they showed that we have a surprising tendency towards destructive obedience. This in turn helps us to understand historical events, such as the Holocaust, in which large numbers of people obeyed orders that required them to breach the moral codes by which they normally lived. Milgram's procedure was easy to replicate, and by and large replications have reproduced similar results. The exceptions to this are in variations in which the experimenter changed his appearance and in which the location was moved to a less respectable setting. Most replications have not found that these variations made much difference to obedience rates (Lüttke, 2004).

There have been other methodological criticisms of Milgram's work. He carried out his studies under laboratory conditions and gave participants a task that they do not normally come across in everyday life. Thus the situation in which participants found themselves was in some ways quite artificial. However, many features of the experiment reproduced quite accurately the features of destructive obedience in real life. As a scientist running an experiment, the experimenter was in a position of legitimate authority and, dressed as a scientist and based in a university laboratory, he had the trappings of authority. In some ways this made him comparable to a military commander with a title and uniform. On the other hand, some features of Milgram's procedure differed from the situations in which destructive obedience takes place in real life. For example, the experimenter assured participants that although the shocks were painful, Mr Wallace would come to no real harm. That is very different to, say, the position of a Nazi concentration camp guard who could have no doubt that his charges would die as a result of his actions.

Ethical issues in research

All scientists have to take account of the ethics (i.e. the moral implications) of their research. This is particularly true of psychologists, who deal with people and are committed to their welfare. Some psychologists criticised Milgram on the basis of the ethics of his studies. In response to these concerns Milgram's application to join the American Psychological Association was briefly suspended and he was investigated. However, he was soon reinstated after investigators concluded that he had taken care to check the welfare of each participant following the procedure, and that his work was sufficiently important to justify his methods. Below is a summary of the British Psychological Society's (2006) ethical guidelines.

1. **Introduction:** it is important that the public can have confidence in the profession of psychology, and researchers must remember that how they treat participants will affect public perceptions of all psychologists.
2. **General:** psychologists must always consider the ethical implications of their research. Foreseeable threats to the well-being, dignity, health and values of participants should always be eliminated. They should only conduct research in areas where they are competent.
3. **Consent:** researchers must take reasonable steps to obtain *real* consent from participants. Real consent is consent freely given from a participant who fully understands what they are agreeing to. Researchers should not use payment or their position of power over participants to persuade them to consent to activities.
4. **Deception:** deceiving participants should be avoided whenever possible. Participants should be informed of the purpose of the investigation as soon as possible. It is not acceptable to deceive participants when it is likely that they will object or become distressed when debriefed.
5. **Debriefing:** whenever participants are aware that they have taken part in a study they should receive a full explanation of the research as soon as possible. Researchers should also ensure that the participants' experiences were not distressing and that they leave the study in at least as positive a mood as they entered it.
6. **Withdrawal:** participants should be made aware of their right to withdraw from a study at any point. Payment does not alter a participant's right to withdraw. When debriefed, participants have the right to withdraw their data.
7. **Confidentiality:** unless agreed with participants in advance, their individual results and any personal information obtained in a study should be completely confidential.
8. **Protection:** participants should be protected from harm, including stress. This means that they should be exposed to no more risk than they would normally encounter in their usual lifestyle.
9. **Observation:** observational studies risk breaching privacy. In observations where participants are unaware they are being observed they should only be observed in places and situations where they would expect people to observe them.

10. **Advice:** If a researcher sees signs of a physical or psychological problem the participant is unaware of, but which might threaten their future well-being, they should inform them. Where participants seek professional advice the researcher should be cautious.
11. **Colleagues:** where colleagues are conducting research that falls foul of one or more of the above principles, it is important to inform them and to try to persuade them to alter their conduct.

exercise

No such guidelines existed in the 1960s when Milgram's studies were carried out so he did not breach them as such. However, Milgram was criticised on the basis of some of these issues. Go through Milgram's procedure and assess which issues he might have been picked up on.

interactive angles

Visit http://home.swbell.net/revscat/perilsOfObedience.html. This contains transcripts of some of Milgram's conversations with his participants over the several studies he ran.

1. Read the transcripts. Do any participants buck the trend and act less obediently, as Milgram expected most people to? How obedient are they?

2. Look at Mr Batta's transcript. What is unusual about his behaviour? How could you explain this?

what's new?

Obedience experiments in virtual reality

Milgram's procedure is not normally run nowadays because of the serious ethical issues it raises. It is one thing to run a study when we do not know what will be found and when the results have profound implications for real life. Now, however, we do have a pretty good idea what we would find were we to run the study again, so there is not sufficient reason to do so. This leaves us with a problem, however. It *might* be that Milgram's findings were simply a product of their time, and that people would not respond the same way nowadays. Until recently there seemed to be no way to test this, but an international team of researchers has now developed an ingenious solution; they ran the study in virtual reality.

Slater *et al.* (2006) aimed to find out whether people in a Milgram-type situation would respond to destructive orders in virtual reality in the same way as they would in real life. Thirty-four volunteer participants were recruited by advertisement from staff and students at University College London. The Milgram experiment was recreated with participants acting as teacher and interacting with a 'learner' avatar (shown in Figure 2.4). In 23 cases the participant had the full visual experience of virtual reality. In 11 they communicated with the avatar by text. As in the Milgram procedure the avatar was given word pairs to learn. An experimenter ordered the participant to give a series of 20 ascending shocks whenever the avatar got an answer wrong. The avatar exhibited distress when 'shocked'. To assess their responses to the stress of the situation participants had their skin conductance and heart rate monitored.

The results of this study were very much in line with those of Milgram's. Seventeen of the 23 participants (73.9%) obeyed the orders and gave all 20 shocks. However, skin conductivity, heart rate and interview responses all indicated that they suffered stress as a result of hurting the avatar. This shows that participants respond to destructive orders in virtual reality in much the same way as they do in real life. It also provides strong support for Milgram's study and suggests that Milgram's findings were not just a product of his time but generalise to the twenty-first century.

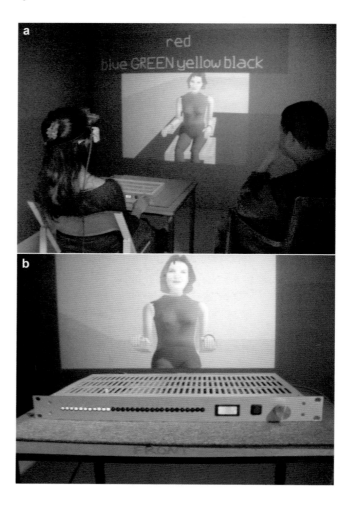

Figure 2.4
The virtual reality apparatus and avatar used in the Slater *et al.* (2006) study

interactive angles

You can read the Slater *et al.* study in full at; http://www.plosone.org/article/fetchArticle.action?articleURI=info%3Adoi%2F10.1371%2Fjournal.pone.0000039. Hear an audiofile of the study discussed on Radio 4's *Today* programme here: http://www.plos.org/cms/comment/reply/174

How convincing do you find this type of research?

Studies like Slater et al.'s are fascinating because they appear to show that we respond to people in virtual reality in much the same way as we do real people. This is important because it suggests that our social behaviour is automatic rather than consciously thought out. However, the situation is *not* real, and we should be cautious about the extent to which we can apply any findings from virtual reality to real life.

Other approaches to studying obedience

Other studies, including those carried out in real-life settings, have confirmed that people have a remarkable tendency to obey those in authority. One real-life setting where a degree of obedience is necessary for smooth running is in medicine. In a classic field experiment, Hofling et al. (1966) demonstrated that nurses would obey doctors even when doing so would be likely to endanger patients.

Classic research

Compulsory

Hofling, C.K., Brotzman, E., Dalrymple, S., Graves, N. & Pierce, C.M. (1966)

'An experimental study in nurse–physician relationships'

Journal of Nervous and Mental Disease 143, 171–80.

Aim: To see whether nurses would obey a doctor when doing so would breach hospital regulations and endanger the lives of patients. A secondary aim was to see whether nurses were aware of how obedient they tended to be.

Procedure: Boxes of capsules labelled 'Astroten' were placed with other medicines in 22 hospital wards of American hospitals. In the capsules was glucose, harmless to most patients, however the label identified the maximum safe daily dose as 10mg. A researcher calling himself 'Dr Smith from the psychiatric department' telephoned nurses on duty on each ward and instructed them to give a patient 20mg of Astroten. Although written authorisation was normally required before nurses were allowed to give drugs, Dr Smith said that he was running late and would get there and sign the necessary authorisation shortly. Meanwhile 22 other nurses not involved in the field experiment were interviewed and asked whether, if a doctor telephoned when they were on duty and instructed them to administer more than the maximum safe dose, they would do so.

Findings: 21 of the 22 nurses interviewed said that they would not obey the doctor's instructions, yet 21 of the 22 nurses told by telephone to give a large dose of Astroten did so. When questioned later, 11 of these nurses said that they had not noticed the discrepancy between the maximum dose and the dose they were told to give. The other ten did notice it but judged that it must be safe if the doctor ordered them to give it.

Conclusion: Although the nurses believed that they would not obey a doctor unquestioningly if they were ordered to do something that breached regulations and endangered patients, in fact they did just that.

Figure 2.5
In Hofling's study, nurses were surprisingly obedient to doctors

More recent research has continued to demonstrate our tendency for obedience. Influenced by early studies such as that of Hofling et al., some research still focuses on the doctor–nurse relationship. Krackow & Blass (1995) gave 68 American nurses a questionnaire asking them about the last time they had disagreed with a doctor's order. Two factors emerged as influencing the nurses' decision whether to obey or disobey. The most important factor was the authority of the doctor; most nurses obeyed the order because they recognised the doctor as a legitimate authority with a right to make the decision. However, their responses were also influenced by the seriousness of the consequences to the patient. Where these were serious the nurses were more likely to take responsibility for the decision themselves and challenge the order.

Culture and obedience

Recall that when Milgram began his research it was hypothesised that something distinctive about German culture may have contributed to the widespread destructive obedience that characterised the Holocaust. Although Milgram abandoned this idea it has remained an interesting question whether obedience varies as a product of culture. For ethical reasons we cannot now replicate Milgram's procedure with different populations in order to tell whether they differ in their obedience. This makes it hard to draw direct comparisons between cultures. However we can draw on other sources of research to address the culture question. The Slater *et al.* (2006) study (What's new? p. 17) is one such source of evidence – in fact this is as close as we can get nowadays to Milgram's procedure. This study was carried out in the UK some 40 years after Milgram's study, so the culture of participants is quite different. However, the results are very much in line with those obtained by Milgram using 1960s American men. This suggests that obedience may not vary according to culture. Another classic obedience study conducted in a different decade and country was by Meeus and Raaijmakers (1986) – see Classic Research.

Classic research

Optional

Meeus, W.H.J. & Raaijmakers, Q.A.W. (1986)

'Administrative obedience: carrying out orders to use psychological-administrative violence'

European Journal of Social Psychology 16, 311–24.

Aim: To investigate destructive obedience in the everyday situation of a job interview. Specifically, to see to what extent people will obey orders to psychologically abuse a job interviewee.

Procedure: 24 Dutch people took part in the study. They were asked to interview applicants for a job. In fact the 'interviewee' was a stooge, rather like Mr Wallace in the Milgram studies. Participants were told that the job required the ability to handle stress, and that they must therefore cause the applicant stress during their interview. They were told to make a series of 15 cutting comments to interviewees, ranging from 'your answer to question 9 was wrong' (the mildest) to 'according to the test it would be better for you to apply for lower functions' (the harshest). The stooges showed signs of increasing distress throughout the interview, appearing to finish it in a state of despair. In one condition an experimenter who gave the order sat in on the interview. In a control condition the experimenter was not present.

Findings: In the experimental condition, where the experimenter who had given the order sat in, 22 of the 24 participants (92%) made all 15 stressful comments. In the control condition none did. When interviewed participants said that they had not considered the questions fair, but that the stress suffered by the 'interviewees' was the responsibility of the experimenter not themselves.

Conclusion: People in an everyday situation like a job interview will generally obey orders to abuse a stranger psychologically. Rates of obedience were higher than in the Milgram study, as we might expect as people believed they were upsetting rather than physically hurting someone.

Figure 2.6
Participants in the Meeus & Raaijmakers study obeyed orders to deliberately cause stress to job interviewees

Like the Slater *et al.* (2006) study, the Meeus & Raaijmakers study was conducted in a very different culture from that of the Milgram experiments. The results, however, were very similar. The results of both these studies suggest that obedience may not vary much between cultures.

There are, however, other ways of investigating possible cultural differences in obedience. Cross-cultural surveys do suggest that there are some cultural differences in attitudes to obedience. Hamilton & Sanders (1995) presented participants from the USA, Japan and Russia with stories of crimes set in the workplace, some of which were the orders of superiors and some of which were the actor's own idea. When questioned about how responsible the actor was, respondents attributed little responsibility to them when they were acting under orders, but a lot of responsibility when they acted independently. Some cultural differences emerged, with the American respondents attributing more responsibility to criminals following orders than those from Russia and Japan. This suggests that Russian and Japanese cultures place more emphasis on obedience than American culture.

Studies like this have the advantage that they are direct cross-cultural comparisons. Unlike when we use the Slater *et al.* study we do not have to compare findings in different studies to make a judgement about cultural differences. However, studies like this look at *attitudes* to obedience, *not* obedient behaviour. Attitudes are perhaps not a valid measure of obedience in the way the behavioural measures used by Milgram and Slater are.

interactive angles

Compare the original Milgram study with either the Slater *et al.* or the Meeus and Raaijmakers study. Think about the precise aims of the studies, the sample they used, the environment the studies were conducted in and the measures of obedience they used. How similar are the results?

Explaining obedience: agency theory

Milgram (1974) proposed that our tendency to obey people in authority is a way of maintaining a stable society. In order to live in complex societies we need social rules. Sticking to these rules means that at least some of the time we have to give up some of our free will. Milgram proposed that in order to accomplish this we have developed two social states:

- In the **autonomous state** we are free to act as we wish, including how our conscience dictates.
- However in our **agentic state** we surrender our free will and conscience in order to serve the interests of the wider group. When we are in an agentic state we see ourselves as primarily the agents of those in authority and only secondarily as individuals.

We are socialised into developing the capacity for the agentic state during childhood. In school, we learn to put aside our individual wishes in favour of maintaining order, and so putting the good of the class as a whole first. Milgram believed that, like children in the classroom, we are all constantly subordinating our own needs and wishes to those of society. We can see this tendency in our job-related behaviour. If asked, most people would probably say that they work for their own benefit and would not go out of their way for their employers. In reality however, once people are in a job and they identify

what's that?

- **Autonomous state:** the state in which we have free will
- **Agentic state:** the state in which we give up our free will in order to serve the needs of society

what's that?

- **Moral strain:** the unpleasant sensation resulting from pressure to obey orders to commit an immoral act

themselves as part of an organisation, they have a tendency to put the needs of their employers above their own.

An important aspect of the agentic state is the strategies we use to deal with **moral strain**. Moral strain results when we have to do something we believe to be immoral in order to function as an agent of authority, and so benefit society. Milgram suggested that we use defence mechanisms (see Chapter 4) to avoid the distress of having to perform acts we would normally find abhorrent. *Denial* was found to be particularly common in participants in the Milgram studies, and in the Holocaust, as perpetrators refused to confront what they were doing.

Discussion of agency theory

Agency theory explains a wide range of social behaviours, ranging from how we act at work to the way in which peaceful people can go to war, and of course how 'normal' people become involved in atrocities such as the Holocaust. The idea of moral strain explains Milgram's finding that the minority of dissenters in his studies showed signs of stress while deciding whether to obey but not after making the decision to disobey.

Agency theory is also supported by studies showing that we attribute less responsibility to actors following orders than people acting of their own free will. In one study Blass (1996) showed students an edited film of Milgram's study and questioned them about the relative responsibility of Milgram and his participants in administering shocks. Participants identified Milgram in the role of authority figure and attributed responsibility for the treatment of Mr Wallace to him rather than the participant. This supports agency theory because the participants were apparently seen as being in an agentic state and therefore not to blame for their actions. In a follow-up, Blass and Schmitt (2001) showed students the same footage and questioned them about why Milgram had such power over his participants. Agency theory would predict that the main factor was Milgram's position of legitimate authority. In fact participants identified two main factors; legitimate position as a scientist and expertise. This partially supports agency theory.

A limitation of agency theory is that it does not neatly explain individual differences in obedience or in the ability of leaders to command obedience from subordinates. Remember that a significant minority of Milgram's participants held their ground and did not obey him. Also, studies of charismatic leadership have revealed that some people are particularly skilled at gaining obedience regardless of the legitimacy of their position of authority. A further problem is that agency theory does not explain the findings of other lines of research such as Hofling's study of nurses. Recall (p. 19) that although the majority of Hofling's nurses did obey the doctor, half did not notice that they exceeded the maximum dose and half thought it must be safe if the doctor gave the order. None exhibited any sign of going into an agentic state or suffering moral strain.

Eight years for US soldier who abused prisoners

Jamie Wilson
The Guardian Friday 22 October 2004

A US soldier at the centre of the Abu Ghraib prisoner abuse scandal was yesterday sentenced to eight years for sexually and physically abusing detainees. Staff Sergeant 'Ivan Chip' Frederick, 38, who admitted carrying out a mock electrocution of a detainee, was also given a reduction in rank, forfeiture of pay and a dishonourable discharge. Frederick, an army reservist from Buckingham, Virginia, pleaded guilty at the court martial on Wednesday to eight counts of abusing and humiliating Iraqi detainees.

It was the longest sentence in the three convictions so far related to the abuses at Abu Ghraib, exposed in April with the publication of photographs and video showing US soldiers abusing naked Iraqis. Frederick's lawyer, Gary Myers, called the sentence excessive and said he intended to appeal to seek a reduction. Frederick, a military policeman who is a prison officer in civilian life, acknowledged his part in the abuse but also blamed his chain of command, telling the court prisoners were forced to submit to public nudity and degrading treatment "for military intelligence purposes". During the court martial, Chief Warrant Officer Kevin Kramer, a military intelligence soldier called as a witness, referred to an email from the US command in Baghdad telling him to order his interrogators to be tough on prisoners. "The gloves are coming off, gentlemen, regarding these detainees," said the email. It added that the command "wants the detainees broken". Frederick, who was in charge of the night shift at the 'hard site' facility at Abu Ghraib, west of Baghdad, said military intelligence soldiers and civilian interrogators told guards how to treat detainees. That included stripping detainees, depriving them of sleep or taking away their cigarettes, Frederick said. Investigators wanted detainees "stressed out, wanted them to talk more," he added.

"Give me an image of the all-American boy, and it's this young man," said a San Francisco-based doctor, Philip Zimbardo. "He is a wonderful young man who did these horrible things."

1. Using ideas from agency theory, explain why Frederick might have participated in the maltreatment of prisoners.
2. Google Philip Zimbardo. Where might his view that individuals in Frederick's situation are not to blame have come from?

Figure 2.7
Social psychologist Philip Zimbardo defends individuals in Frederick's position

For & Against
agency theory

FOR   the idea that obedience serves the function of allowing complex human societies to develop makes sense, that is, it has face validity. It also neatly explains a range of real-life situations in which people obey orders, in particular orders that go against their moral code.

FOR   agency theory explains neatly the results of the Milgram studies, in which people obey destructive orders but suffer stress as a result.

FOR   there is direct support for agency theory from studies such as Blass (1996), which show that people do not see those obeying orders as responsible for their actions.

AGAINST   the idea of an identifiable agentic state has proved very difficult to pin down. Simply saying that someone is in an agentic state because they obey and that they obey because they are in an agentic state is circular logic.

AGAINST   agency theory does not explain individual differences in obedience, for example why some people did not obey Milgram. Nor does it explain easily why some people carrying no more authority are so skilled at commanding obedience.

AGAINST   agency theory does not explain the findings of Hofling *et al.* Although the nurses overwhelmingly obeyed the order, they gave different reasons for doing so and showed no signs of moral strain.

what's that?

- **Prejudice:** making judgements about people based on their membership of a group rather than their individual nature
- **Discrimination:** treating people differently according to their group membership

Prejudice

The word **prejudice** can be broken down to *pre* (meaning before) and *judice* (meaning judgement). To be prejudiced then means to *prejudge* someone, in other words to make a judgement about them before knowing anything about them as an individual. A prejudice is an extreme attitude towards a group that causes us to prejudge individuals based only on their membership of that group. Like all attitudes, prejudices consist of three elements:

- **The cognitive element**: this involves the beliefs held about the group. These beliefs will be in the form of *stereotypes*, common but oversimple views of what particular groups of people are like.
- **The affective element**: this involves the feelings experienced in response to the group. If we are prejudiced against a group we may experience anger, fear, hate or disgust when we encounter a member of that group.
- **The behavioural element**: this consists of our actions towards the object of our prejudice. Behaving differently towards people based on their membership of a group is called **discrimination**. Our actions against members of a group against which we hold a prejudice can range from avoidance and verbal criticism to mass extermination.

We can illustrate these three elements with the example of prejudice against university students. Stereotyped views of students might include that they are lazy and spoilt, that they make inconsiderate neighbours and that they are heavy drinkers. People who subscribe to those stereotypes are likely to feel angry (and perhaps jealous!) in response to students. The resulting behaviour will probably include verbally criticising students and avoiding places where students congregate. In a minority of people with strong anti-student views, behaviour extends to physical violence.

Figure 2.8
What stereotyped views might you hold about these students?

interactive angles

Complete the following table by identifying the cognitive, affective and behavioural components of prejudice against the following groups. This should help you understand the different forms prejudice can take towards different groups.

	Stereotypes	Emotional responses	Nature of discrimination
Goths			
Blonde women			
Trekkies (Star Trek fans)			

The targets of prejudice

Prejudice is universal. However much value we might place personally on being tolerant of human diversity, we are bound to have stereotyped views about some groups and to prefer the company of some groups over others. In a review of recent surveys Sagger & Drean (2001) report that 64% of British people admit to feeling 'less positively' about at least one minority group. Although prejudice is universal, and perhaps to some extent inevitable, it is important not to lose sight of the terrible harm it causes to minority groups. The stress of suffering racism appears to be the direct cause of significantly worse health in members of minority ethnic groups (Gee *et al.*, 2006). Women are still paid less than men (Hellerstein *et al.*, 2002) and 75% of gay school pupils suffer homophobic bullying severe enough to lead them to truant or fake illness to avoid going to school (Stonewall, 2005).

Racism

The most extensively studied prejudice is racism. Racism exists in a range of cultures and situations, including between Tamils and Sinhalese in Sri Lanka and Albanians and Serbs in the former Yugoslavia. It is tempting to believe that in twenty-first-century Britain we have outgrown racism. However, surveys show that this is not the case. In a MORI poll in 2001, 18% of respondents said they were less positive about minority ethnic groups and 43% said they knew someone who had racist views.

Sexism

Worldwide, women are probably the group that suffers the most discrimination. Sexism takes a range of forms. At its most extreme there are still societies in which adultery by women (though not by men) is punishable by death, and in which women cannot travel alone, own property or vote. In Europe and the USA sexism is likely to be more subtle. For example, women are likely to experience *benevolent sexism*, a patronising attitude in which men are not hostile towards women, but treat them as incapable of independence or performing tasks. Women are also likely to encounter the 'glass ceiling' in their career. This means that women, like minority ethnic groups, are much less likely to be promoted beyond a certain level at work.

what's new?

Research into homophobia

Until recently psychological research involving gay people has centred on explaining *why* they are gay. Recently, however, the emphasis has changed, and psychologists are making more effort to conduct research that is of potential benefit to lesbians and gay men. One focus in such research has been gay people's experiences of homophobia. Homophobia is of particular concern to psychologists for two reasons. First, unlike racism and sexism, homophobia is a largely socially acceptable prejudice. Whereas most people holding racist and sexist views are wary of voicing them in public, people have no such qualms about making anti-gay comments. Secondly, gay people are particularly likely to suffer extreme forms of discrimination, including hate crimes, commonly in the form of violence. We can look in detail at two quite different survey studies that cast light on homophobia.

In the first of these studies, Bergan-Gander & von Kurthy (2006) investigated gay people's experiences at work. This was an exploratory study so no specific hypothesis was tested. Unstructured interviews were conducted with two gay men and three lesbians. A snowball sampling method was used; the first participant identified suitable other participants who they felt would not be distressed by the study. Interviews lasted between 25 and 75 minutes. The opening question was the same for all respondents: 'I would like you to tell me about what you do in your everyday life. So for instance, in your work, your home and your social life and how you feel that they are influenced by your sexual orientation.' Open-ended questions such as 'have you experienced any difficulty in your everyday life because of your sexual orientation?' were used as prompts. Interviews were recorded and analysed for common themes. Five themes emerged from the interviews. These were issues around socialising with colleagues, issues of coming out, heterosexism at work (for example clients asking about an opposite sex partner), discrimination (for example one respondent was told they would not progress at work if they gave away their sexual orientation on an application form) and personal relationships (being gay affected friendships etc.). This study shows how gay people have particular stresses to cope with in the workplace.

In the second study, Koh & Ross (2006) compared the frequency of stress and mental health problems suffered by lesbians, heterosexual and bisexual women. A secondary aim was to see whether being 'out' affected rates of stress and mental health problems. At 33 American Health Centres, 1304 participants were given an anonymous questionnaire; 637 respondents were heterosexual, 143 bisexual and 524 lesbian. The questionnaire contained closed questions asking about sexual orientation, 'out status' and stress and mental health problems. It was found that bisexual women and lesbians reported more stress than did heterosexuals. If a bisexual woman was out she was twice as likely to suffer an eating disorder than a heterosexual woman. Bisexuals who were out were more than twice as likely to have contemplated suicide in the previous year. Lesbians reported more depression than did heterosexual or bisexual women. This study shows that bisexuals and lesbians suffered more stress and mental health problems than heterosexual women. Not being out was also associated with stress and mental health problems in lesbians.

how science works

Research Methods

Psychologists use surveys when we need to know what people think or feel about an issue or how they have experienced an event or condition. The only way to get at this sort of information is to ask people. Surveys do this, either by means of questionnaires or interviews. Interviews are spoken whereas questionnaires are written.

Open and closed questions

Whether asked in an interview or questionnaire, questions can be open or closed. Closed questions require a fixed response. It might for example be in the form of yes [ ] no [ ], or:

strongly agree [ ], agree [ ], don't know [ ], disagree [ ], strongly disagree [ ].

The advantage of closed questions is that they can be analysed quantitatively. For example a survey of men and women might ask them whether they have suffered sex discrimination, using a yes/no format. This will allow us to say that x% of men and x% of women report being discriminated against because of their gender. An example of a published survey using closed questions is the Koh & Ross study (above). Respondents had to specify their sexual orientation: heterosexual [ ] lesbian [ ] bisexual [ ] and their out status something like this: yes [ ] no [ ].

Open questions do not require a fixed response and a well-phrased open question encourages an extended answer. An example of a published survey using open questions is the study by Bergan-Gander & von Kurthy (p. 26). This used the open question 'I would like you to tell me about what you do in your everyday life. So for instance, in your work, your home and your social life and how you feel that they are influenced by your sexual orientation' to start each interview. Open questions generate qualitative data, for example in the form of common themes that emerge in respondents' answers. For example in the Bergan-Gander & von Kurthy study the interview transcripts would have been read and the major issues each person talked about identified as themes.

Themes that cropped up in several participants' responses would be identified as major themes.

Survey structure

Interviews can be structured to a greater or lesser extent. Unstructured interviews typically start with the same opening question and may have some common prompts. However beyond this the content of the interview is left very much to the interviewee. Unstructured interviews are most useful when we are investigating something that has not been well studied before. This is because they allow respondents to identify themes that we might not have thought of had we been structuring the interview. Unstructured interviews necessarily have open questions and so can only be analysed qualitatively. Structured interviews involve all respondents being asked the same questions in the same order. This generates quantitative data. Semistructured interviews ask the same questions of each respondent but they are more open questions, and respondents can 'go off on one' when a particular question sparks their interest or 'touches a nerve'.

In principle, questionnaires can also be structured to a greater or lesser extent. In practice however, they lend themselves best to being highly structured. More often than not we use questionnaires when we are primarily interested in quantitative data, and interviews when we are mostly interested in qualitative information. Of course we *can* gather both quantitative and qualitative data by either method. You may have seen questionnaires that have a number of fixed response questions designed to gather quantitative data, then a box at the end saying something like 'please tell us anything else you wish to about this topic'. This will gather qualitative data but is less effective than an interview because we don't have a person offering us prompts.

Hypotheses in surveys

Some survey studies are conducted to test specific hypotheses. An hypothesis is a testable statement that predicts the outcome of a study. For example Koh and Ross (2006) predicted that lesbians and bisexual women would suffer more stress and mental health problems than heterosexual women. Other studies are said to be *exploratory* in nature. Such studies just aim to gather information on a topic. An example of such an exploratory study is the one by Bergan-Gander & von Kurthy (2006). Studies like this do not test a particular hypothesis. They look instead for the sort of themes that emerged from interviews. Sometimes exploratory studies like this can lead to hypotheses that can be tested in further studies.

Explaining prejudice

Social psychologists have often found that where two groups exist, they tend to show in-group favouritism, that is they discriminate in favour of members of their own group and against the members of the other (out) group. Muzafer Sherif *et al.* (1961) demonstrated this in a classic field experiment – see Classic Research.

Classic research

Optional

Sherif, M., Harvey, O.J., White, B.J., Hood, W.R. & Sherif. C.W. (1961)

Intergroup conflict and co-operation: the Robber's Cave experiment

Norman, University of Oklahoma Press.

Aim: To investigate relations between groups. Specifically to see whether strangers brought together into a group with common goals will form a close group, and to see whether two such groups brought into contact and competition will become hostile towards each other.

Procedure: Twenty-two 12-year-old boys took part in the study. All were white American lower-middle-class protestants. All were psychologically well adjusted. They were transported in two groups to the Robber's Cave National Park in Oklahoma. At the camp the two groups lived separately. For five days (stage I) each group was given tasks to carry out together in order to help them bond. Each group was given a name (Eagles and Rattlers) to further strengthen their group identity. Over the next four days (stage II) friction between the groups was encouraged by means of competitions between the groups for attractive prizes like penknives. In stage III, designed to reduce tension between the groups, they were brought together, initially to watch films and then to take part in joint problem-solving activities. In one of these activities the water supply was blocked by 'vandals', and the two groups worked together to remove the blockage. In another, the groups had to pool their money to pay for a film all the boys wanted to watch. In a third activity the groups worked together to free a truck apparently stuck in mud.

Findings: In stage I the boys bonded within their groups and, although they had not met the other group, each group expressed dislike of them. In stage II competition led to immediate hostility. The Eagles refused to eat with the Rattlers. When together the groups shouted insults at each other and were reported by observers to get close to physical violence. Both groups raided the others' huts and burned their flags. Early activities in stage III, which just involved getting the groups together without competition, did not reduce hostility, however the joint problem-solving tasks did. Following these, both groups opted to share a bus home and the Rattlers spent a $5 prize won in one of the competitions on drinks for both groups.

Conclusion: Some hostility was observed between the groups as soon as they were aware of each other. Once competition was introduced this became more intense. This suggests that competition is a factor in leading to discrimination between groups, but that some discrimination takes place even without competition. However, when groups work together on cooperative tasks that benefit both of them, prejudice and discrimination can be reduced.

Figure 2.9
The Rattlers' banner

Sherif's study has a number of strengths. It was conducted outside the laboratory and looked at a number of key variables in prejudice and discrimination; group identity, competition and cooperation. It does, however, have weaknesses. The sample was taken from a single ethnic, religious and socio-economic group at a particular period in American history. We cannot necessarily generalise findings to other populations or times. Most importantly the design is *pre-experimental*, that is it compares before and after conditions rather than comparing results with those in a control condition. It would be extremely useful to know – and we cannot from this design – how much hostility between the groups would have developed without competition, and whether continued contact without competition or cooperation would have led to a decline in this hostility.

Social identity theory

Social identity theory is one of a group of theories that share the assumption that prejudice can be explained by our tendency to identify ourselves as part of a group, and to classify other people as either within or outside that group. This means that we tend to make sharp judgements of people as either one of 'us' or 'them'. The exact nature of the groups we see ourselves as belonging to varies widely according to our individual experience and the culture we live in. However our tendency to think of ourselves as belonging to one or more groups is a fundamental part of human nature. A key aspect of social identity theory is that being a group member is important to us, to the extent that we will discriminate against out-groups even when there is no logical reason, for example competition. Studies like the Robber's Cave experiment are of little use in judging this principle, because they include both the formation of in-groups *and* competition – it is therefore hard to separate out the effects of group identity without competition. Tajfel and Turner's theory was based instead on a series of laboratory experiments called the 'minimal group studies'. A key feature of minimal group studies is that two groups are created in the absence of competition. One such study is reported in Classic Research.

Classic research

Optional

Tajfel, H. (1970)

'Experiments in intergroup discrimination'

Scientific American 223, 96–102.

Aim: Previous studies had clearly established that two groups in competition would show prejudice towards one another. The aim of this study was to see whether two clearly identifiable groups not in competition would still favour their own group over the other.

Procedure: Two experiments were set up, using 14- to 15-year-old British schoolboys as participants. The first is reported here. Sixty-four participants were told that the researchers were investigating vision. They were shown clusters of dots on a screen and asked to estimate the number of dots. They were divided into two groups, (underestimators

and overestimators), supposedly on the basis of their number-estimates. In fact they were randomly divided into two groups. The boys were then given the task of allocating points to each other, choosing which one of a pair of boys should receive points for their estimates of the numbers of dots. They were told that points could later be converted into money. The participants did not know which individuals they were allotting the money to but they *did* know which group each boy was in. In one condition, the choice was between two boys in the in-group, in the second condition the choice was between two boys in the out-group and in the third group it was between one boy from the in-group and one from the out-group.

Findings: The boys overwhelmingly chose to allocate points to boys who had been identified as in the same group as themselves, either overestimators or underestimators. This occurred irrespective of the accuracy of the boys' estimates.

Conclusion: In spite of the fact that there was no direct competition between the two groups, participants consistently displayed favouritism towards those who were identified as being in the same group as themselves, and against those identified as in a different group.

Based on the minimal group experiments, Tajfel and Turner (1979) proposed that there are three cognitive processes involved in evaluating others as either one of 'us' or 'them'. Social categorisation takes place when we categorise other people as members of particular social groups. Categories we all tend to subscribe to involve gender, race and social class. Others are more relevant to some people than others, for example football supporting and cat loving. We tend to adopt the identity of the group we have categorised ourselves as belonging to. This is called social identification, and it is the feature that distinguishes social identity theory from other theories of in-group favouritism. We tend to follow the behavioural norms of our in-group. There is also an emotional significance to identification with a group, and one's self-esteem becomes bound up with group membership. If our self-esteem is to be maintained our group needs to compare well against other groups. This is assessed in a process of social comparison. Hostility between groups is thus not only a matter of competing for resources like jobs, but also the result of competing identities.

Social identity and group status

Typically, when there is more than one group, there is inequality between them. One group may be larger, financially better off or for some other reason have a superior position. Members of the dominant group would have a positive group identity. Both groups are likely to show some favouritism to members of their own group, but clearly the dominant group has more power to oppress the others. They may or may not do this according to the norms and values of the dominant group. Members of less dominant groups, known as subordinate groups, *may* act together against the dominant group. This is called collective action. However, whether collective action actually takes place depends on two factors. First, if groups are seen as *permeable*, that is people can move from one to another, members of subordinate groups are less likely to work collectively against the dominant group. Collective action becomes more likely once groups become impermeable. Second, if the status of the dominant group is seen as unfair or changeable, members of subordinate groups are more likely to act together against the dominant group. In a recent but already classic experiment, Reicher & Haslam (2006) demonstrated the circumstances in which a group placed in a socially inferior position might take collective action. They used a prison scenario, with participants taking on the roles of either prisoners or guards. This is described in Classic Research (p. 32).

Classic research

Optional

Reicher, S. & Haslam, S.A. (2002)

'Learning from The Experiment'

The Psychologist 15, 344–5.

Reicher, S. & Haslam, S.A. (2006)

'Rethinking the psychology of tyranny: the BBC Prison Study'

British Journal of Social Psychology 45, 1–40.

Aim: To investigate how two groups with unequal status and power behave towards one another. Specifically to test the hypotheses that a dominant group will quickly display a strong group identity, but that a subordinate group will only develop a strong identity and act collectively against the dominant group once boundaries between groups become impermeable and the power inequality appears unfair and changeable.

Procedure: Fifteen male participants were selected from 332 applicants. All were assessed by clinical psychologists for aggression and stability. They were also police-checked and their good character testified to by referees. Five were randomly selected to be guards. The remaining ten were given the role of prisoners. They lived in a prison environment (see Figure 2.10) for ten days. Guards were given routines and rules to enforce. They had more comfortable accommodation and better facilities than the prisoners. At the start of the experiment the guards were told that they had been selected as guards because they were the trustworthiest. Prisoners were told that one of them would be promoted on day 3 to become a guard. This created a condition of high group permeability and high fairness. However on day 3 after the promotion prisoners were told there would be no more promotion, creating a condition of low permeability. Three days later they were told that in fact there was no difference in the characters of prisoners and guards. This created a condition of low fairness. Each morning all participants rated their identification with their own group (prisoner or guard) and with the other group.

Findings: For the first three days the prisoners were dissatisfied with their living conditions but focused on being promoted to guard rather than working together to improve their conditions. For the first two days while group permeability was high the guards identified more strongly with their group than did the prisoners.

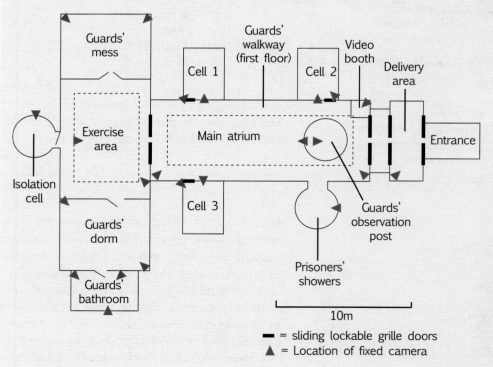

Figure 2.10
The prison layout

= sliding lockable grille doors
= Location of fixed camera

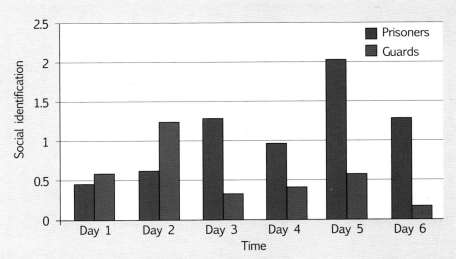

Figure 2.11
Identification scores of prisoners and guards

Figure 2.12
Prisoners and guards at a stand-off in Reicher and Haslam's study

However, once the prisoner was promoted on day 3 and group permeability dropped, the group identity scores of prisoners outstripped those of the guards, remaining higher for the rest of the study (see Figure 2.11). On day 4 three prisoners defied three guards, demanding better food. The guards could not agree on how to respond, so came off worse in the confrontation. The prisoners' confidence increased steadily and on day 6 they broke out of their cells and occupied the guards' quarters. Prisoners and guards then decided to form a commune and govern together. This initially worked well, however four participants became dissatisfied and proposed a new and very harsh regime.

The study was halted at this point to avoid the possibility of violence.

Conclusions: The dominant group (the guards) quickly showed high levels of group identification. The subordinate group (the prisoners) had low levels of identification as long as group permeability was high but this increased sharply when group permeability was reduced. Collective action quickly followed on day 4. By day 6 this was successful, and the inequalities between groups were scrapped. However, the new equal regime soon broke down. These findings are as predicted by social identity theory.

Figure 2.13
Members of youth subcultures like these Emos are likely to take on the behavioural norms of Emos

Discussion of social identity theory

Social identity theory explains a whole host of social phenomena involving in-group favouritism, ranging from racism to the sense of togetherness we get from following a football club or being part of a subculture. Studies have investigated all of these areas. Verkooijen *et al.* (2007) demonstrated the importance of social identification with subcultures in a study of drug taking in Danish teenagers. Six thousand 16- to 20-year-olds were sent a survey asking about their subcultural affiliations and use of alcohol, tobacco and cannabis. Those who identified themselves as part of skater, hip-hop, techno and hippie groups were particularly likely to use drugs whilst those identifying with nerdy, sporty and religious groups were least likely. This suggests that the individuals took on the drug-related norms of their subculture.

Sampling

Consider the Verkooijen *et al.* (2007) study. Although 6000 is an impressive sounding figure, it is actually around 2% of Danish 16- to 20-year-olds. There is plenty of scope therefore to pick 6000 people that do not really represent the target population. If we want a clear picture of drug use in Danish teenagers it is important that our sample is representative. The process of selecting participants is called sampling. Psychologists use a number of different sampling procedures:

- **Opportunity sampling**: this involves asking whoever is easily available. Participants might end up being classmates, friends or whoever happens to be available in the college canteen.
- **Self-selecting (or volunteer) sampling**: this involves seeking volunteers, either by word of mouth or advertising.
- **Snowball sampling**: this involves recruiting an initial participant who in turn recruits further participants.

Opportunity, self-selecting and snowball methods are unlikely to produce a representative sample. However, they have important advantages. Opportunity sampling allows us to recruit large numbers of participants very quickly and easily. It is therefore the most commonly used sampling procedure in student practicals. Self-selecting samples are useful when our target population is hard to locate, for example people claiming to have been abducted by aliens. Snowball sampling is likewise used when we need to recruit a hard-to-reach population. The snowball method is also used when the topic of research is very sensitive and one participant can recommend another who is resilient enough to undergo the study without being unduly upset. An example of this is the Bergan-Gander & von Kurthy study (p. 26). In addition to these unrepresentative sampling methods there are a range of ways we can obtain participants more representative of their target population.

- **Systematic sampling**: this involves selecting every nth person on a list. We can choose n by dividing the population size by the sample size. So if we have a school population of 1000 and we want a sample of 50, 1000/50 = 20 so we could simply go down the list of pupils and select every twentieth person. Another systematic method is to take everyone in a target population with a particular birthday. This is in fact what Verkooijen *et al.* did.
- **Random sampling**: the technical definition of a random sample is one in which every member of the target population has an equal chance of being selected. This is *not* true in an opportunity or systematic sample. In an opportunity sample taken from the college library, students who never go to the library will never be selected. In a systematic sample selected by birthday those with a different birthday have no chance of selection.
- **Stratified sampling**: in a stratified sample we try to ensure that as many as possible of the types that characterise the target population are represented by the proportions of the sample. So if our target population is 60% female 40% male, so will be our sample. There is however a random element to stratified samples. Every member of the target population within the bounds of the proportions has an equal chance of selection. So if the sample is 40% male then every male has an equal chance of making it into the 40% of males in the sample.

These sampling methods are generally more complex and time consuming than the non-representative methods. In particular stratified sampling is a lengthy procedure.

However these techniques *are* likely to produce representative samples. Stratified samples are likely to be the most representative, so there is a trade-off between the time taken to select a sample and its representativeness. In social psychology it is particularly important to have a representative sample. In the Verkooijen study, for example, it was important that a representative group of skaters, nerds, etc. was obtained because an unrepresentative sample might have included a large number of particularly druggy nerds or unusually health-conscious hippies. This would have distorted the results.

Many studies show that, as social identity theory would predict, people show in-group favouritism. Poppe & Linssen (1999) demonstrated this on a national level in a survey of 1143 Eastern European teenagers. Respondents were asked to rate a range of European nationalities for their morality and efficiency. Although some national stereotypes were upheld – the English were judged to be most moral, the Italians the least efficient and so on – generally the youth of each country judged their own nation to be both more moral and more efficient than any of their neighbours.

A further series of studies has demonstrated that the in-group out-group distinction affects behaviour towards those in trouble. People are more likely to help those in difficulty if they are part of the in-group. Levine *et al.* (2005) carried out an experiment on football supporters. Fans were invited to a secluded part of the university campus where they witnessed a stranger fall and apparently injure themselves. In one condition the person having the accident wore their team colours whilst in another condition they wore neutral colours, or those of a rival football club. Football fans were much more likely to help someone wearing their team colours.

media
watch

Football Violence Is Down

Sky.com/news
Updated: 15:33, Saturday 21 October 2006

Figure 2.14
These football fans have a strong identity

Football banning orders have been slapped on a record number of hooligans. Home Office figures show there were 3387 yobs subject to the orders, which prevent them attending domestic and international matches. A total of 995 were imposed during the year, making a net total rise of 7% year-on-year after allowing for orders that have expired. Meanwhile, arrests for football-related offences have dipped by 7% to 3462 — the third consecutive season to see a fall. Leeds United gained the unenviable title of the club with the most banning orders. An extra 20 orders imposed on its fans during the year brought its total to 115, following an even larger rise last year. Portsmouth were second with 110, followed by Cardiff City (last year's highest, falling from 152 orders to 109), Stoke City (108) and Manchester United (106). Leeds United has the worst record. Stoke City also gained the largest number of orders in the year — 58.

Home Office Minister Vernon Coaker said: "I am very encouraged by the new figures. A 7% decrease in football-related arrests coupled with a 7% increase in football banning orders shows that tough legislation and targeted policing continues to be effective. However, we are not complacent. Football disorder remains a lingering menace, and will not be tolerated."

Sports Minister Richard Caborn said: "The thrill of watching football from the terraces without fear of violence is the right of the genuine majority fans and should not be compromised by the tiny minority of thugs intent on causing trouble."

1. Explain, using ideas from social identity theory, why people might take part in football violence.
2. Why, according to social identity theory, might certain clubs become associated with particularly high levels of violence?

Clearly, then, there is plenty of evidence to support social identity theory. However, there is also evidence to suggest that it does not provide a complete explanation of group relations or prejudice. Early minimal group studies suggested that the categorisation of people into groups and comparison of these groups was always sufficient to create in-group favouritism. However, recent studies have challenged this. Dobbs & Crano (2001) conducted a minimal group study with different conditions, some of which involved having to explain *why* fewer points were allocated to out-group members. In the condition where the person allocating the points was in the majority group and had to justify their decision, there was much less in-group favouritism than in the control condition. However, when the allocator was in the minority and had to justify discriminating against the majority out-group, in-group favouritism increased. This suggests that in-group favouritism is actually a more complex business than indicated by the original studies.

A closer look at the minimal group studies also tells us that individual participants differed considerably in the extent to which they favoured the in-group over the out-group. Platow *et al.* (1990) assessed individual differences in responses to the minimal group situation and concluded that participants assessed as highly competitive showed greater in-group favouritism than those assessed as highly cooperative. The latter tended to favour fair distribution of resources rather than the interests of the in-group. Although social identity theory has proved useful in understanding relations between groups, studies such as Platow's show clearly that social identity alone is not sufficient to explain prejudice in its entirety.

For & Against
social identity theory

FOR
there is clear evidence from the minimal group studies, for example Tajfel (1970), that being part of a group is sufficient to lead to prejudice against people not within that group. This suggests that social identity rather than competition between groups is responsible for prejudice.

FOR
there is evidence from surveys (e.g. Poppe & Linssen, 1999) and experiments (e.g. Levine *et al.*, 2005) to show that people show in-group favouritism.

FOR	there is evidence from studies such as Verkooijen *et al.* (2007) to show that people's behaviour changes to conform with that of groups with whom they identify. This supports the idea of social identification.
FOR	social identity explains a wide range of real-life phenomena, ranging from support for football teams to racism, and can be applied to a wide range of social situations.
AGAINST	some contemporary minimal group studies, for example Dobbs & Crano (2001), show that under some circumstances people show much less in-group favouritism than was suggested by early studies such as that of Tajfel.
AGAINST	social identity theory does not neatly explain individual differences in prejudice. A closer look at the results of the minimal group studies shows wide variations in the degree to which people discriminate against the out-group.

how science works

Research Methods

Reliability and validity

In psychological research we constantly have to measure things, so we are very concerned with how well we measure them. In everyday life we normally use the word 'accuracy' when we talk about how well something is measured. We want to be sure when we buy a kilo of vegetables that the scales are accurate; otherwise we might not get what we paid for. When we are talking about weighing scales defining accuracy is quite straightforward. Do the scales say 1kg when there is really 1kg there? The sort of things we are trying to measure in psychology (for example when we carry out surveys) are rarely this clear-cut because there is no absolute measure like perfectly accurate weighing scales to refer to. All we can do is *estimate* how accurate our measures are. There are two ways of estimating accuracy: reliability and validity.

Reliability

Reliability means consistency. If a survey tool such as a questionnaire or interview procedure is reliable then it will consistently obtain the same results. There are various ways we can assess reliability:

- **Test–retest reliability**: we can administer our survey to the same people on two occasions. If there is a strong relationship between the results on the two occasions this indicates good reliability.
- **Split-half reliability**: we can alternatively split a survey into two smaller tests. If the two halves of the survey indicate the same thing this is also an indicator of good reliability.
- **Inter-rater reliability**: if two or more interviewers conduct the same interview with the same respondents and obtain similar results this indicates good reliability.

Validity

Validity is the extent to which we are measuring what we are setting out to measure. We can the judge the validity of a measure such as a questionnaire or interview procedure in the following ways:

- **Face validity**: we can make a crude judgement about validity by simply looking at whether our survey appears to measure what it sets out to. Are the questions about the correct topic?
- **Content validity**: we can ask a panel of experts to look at our questionnaire or interview items and judge whether they are appropriate to investigate what we want to find out about.
- **Concurrent validity**: we can compare the findings of our survey with those obtained by other already existing measures. If they show the same thing then our survey has concurrent validity. Say for example we survey attitudes to football violence. If our survey shows that those who are self-confessed hooligans or have criminal records for football violence have really pro-violent attitudes then this validates our survey.
- **Predictive validity**: we can see whether the results of our survey predict people's behaviour in the future. Sticking with our football violence example, if someone who shows strongly pro-football violence attitudes in our survey goes on to receive convictions for football violence then our survey has good predictive validity.

Subjectivity and objectivity

Another issue we need to consider when evaluating survey methods is subjectivity. We are subjective when we consider something from our own perspective. The opposite of subjectivity is objectivity. We are objective when we see what is really there, unaltered by our own biases. When we survey people, asking about their experiences, views, opinions, feelings and so on we are *always* asking for subjective data because we are asking people to describe something from their own point of view. This is perfectly acceptable – people's opinions and feelings are important in their own right, particularly in social psychology. However, it is possible to fall into the trap of asking for subjective information when what you actually want is objective data. Say you wanted to know about racist views. It is important to know about people's own views on race, what they think of particular views and how particular views make them feel. You would use a survey method. Subjectivity here is not a weakness of the method – on the contrary it is a strength. However, say we wanted to know something more factual – for instance how many people expressing racist views would help a member of a minority ethnic group in trouble. If we were to address this by asking people as part of a survey we would only find out about people's *beliefs* about their racist behaviour. This subjective data would tell us very little about how people actually behave confronted by a real situation. To find out about this we would need to employ a different method. We could for example set up an experiment in which people encountered someone from a different ethnic group in trouble. Observing their behaviour in this situation gives us much more objective data because the information will be 'real' rather than someone's opinion or perception.

You have now explored a selection of ideas, theories, studies and research methods from the social approach to psychology. We have come across a number of real life issues that can be examined using a social-psychological perspective. The aim of this section is to show in some detail how we can take an issue of real world importance and apply social psychology to understand it. We will do this for you with one issue then challenge you to do the same with a different situation.

The social psychology of genocide

Background

Genocide is defined as a systematic effort to wipe out a group of people. Stop for a moment and consider what a staggering thought that is: that people will make the decision and follow it through to devote their time, energy and resources to purging another group of human beings from the planet. The classic instance of genocide was the Holocaust, and this inspired much of the research we have looked at in this chapter concerning both obedience and prejudice. However, be in no doubt that genocide still takes place. In the 1990s genocide took place in Rwanda, Iraq and the former Yugoslavia. At the time of writing there is a situation developing in the Darfur region of Sudan that may meet the criteria to be acknowledged as genocide. One of the most important questions social psychologists can address is why do ordinary people willingly take part in genocide?

Figure 2.15
Genocide still takes place today

Revealed: why evil lurks in us all

Martin Bright
The Observer 17 December 2000

Psychologists have struggled for decades to explain why ordinary people participate in atrocities such as the Nazi Holocaust or the Stalinist purges. Now experiments carried out in Britain reveal that most people obey authority unquestioningly and would also walk past an injured stranger who did not come from their ethnic or social group. The findings will shake the long-held British belief that this country is immune from the kinds of tyranny found in other parts of the world.

Research carried out at Lancaster University on football supporters found that they failed consistently to come to the aid of an injured supporter from a rival team. Secret cameras filmed individual Manchester United fans as they ignored a Liverpool fan played by an actor as he writhed on the floor. When the actor wore a Manchester United shirt the supporters helped him in 80% of cases.

A separate experiment — again filmed with a secret camera — shows the majority of people on a train complying with a stranger's order to give up their seat. When the stranger is accompanied by a man in a uniform not a single passenger chooses to disobey.

Dr Mark Levine, the psychologist who developed the football fan experiment, said: "These are ordinary people. If you ask people whether they would help a stranger in distress, they say they would. But in reality, they just don't do it."

Colonel Bob Stewart, former commander of UN forces in Bosnia, said his experiences in the Balkans left him in no doubt that, given the right circumstances, similar human rights atrocities could be committed in Britain. "What makes a man go for a drink with his neighbour one moment and shoot him the next? We still don't understand what causes normally good people to go over the edge. Until we do, there is the possibility that it will happen."

1. Do the experiments reported in this article fit in with the previous research you have studied?
2. To what extent do you agree with Colonel Stewart that we don't yet fully understand the psychological processes involved in genocide?

Applying social-psychological ideas to understanding genocide

Although genocide is incomprehensible to the layperson, having studied some social psychology you may begin to get more of a handle on the phenomenon. Just to take some relatively simple examples of social-psychological concepts we can show how obedience, agency, in-group favouritism and social identity may all contribute to genocide.

In-group favouritism and social identity

Perhaps the first process that needs to take place before genocide can take place is the categorisation of people into 'them' and 'us'. Whenever we can identify someone as a member of a different group from our own we tend to exhibit in-group favouritism, that is we favour members of our own group. According to social identity theory we do this to protect our self-esteem, which is tied up with the status of our group relative to others. This means that we have a tendency to put down out-groups in order to boost the status of the in-group. Although this does not normally lead to genocide it is perhaps a necessary condition for it to take place.

Obedience and agency

The research of Milgram and others has clearly shown that people have a remarkable tendency to follow orders, even when doing so breaches their personal moral beliefs. Looking in particular at Milgram's research, we should face the uncomfortable truth that if ordered by someone we accepted to be in a position of authority to commit an atrocity, we would probably do it. Agency probably also contributes to genocide. Interviews with Nazis and participants in more recent instances of genocide (e.g. Peters & Richards, 1998) reveal that when people commit atrocities they tend to believe that they are serving the interests of their community. Even if they find their tasks repulsive they believe that they must carry them out.

Thinking critically

It is clear that obedience, agency, in-group favouritism and social identity are potential influences on genocide. However, there is a lot we don't know. Which of these factors are the most important? Is there one particular factor that is always necessary for genocide to occur? These things remain unclear. In any case, thinking more broadly for a moment, are psychological factors the most important ones in genocide? Historians, political scientists and economists have a range of alternative ways to explain genocide that do not involve social-psychological factors at all. Although it is always important to think critically and consider these questions, it does seem likely that social psychology will remain very important in understanding genocide.

exercise

Key

Look at the following two extracts from newspaper articles. The first is concerned with an atrocity committed in the Second World War. The second describes a more recent plane crash.

1. Do as you're told

Nicci Gerrard *The Observer Review* 12 October 1997

CP Snow wrote that 'more hideous crimes have been committed in the name of obedience than have ever been committed in the name of rebellion'.

In the early hours of 13 July 1942, the 500 men of the German Reserve Police Force Battalion 101 — middle-aged family men, too old for the army, barely trained and stationed in Poland — were addressed by their leader, Commander Trapp. In a voice shaky with distress he told them of their next assignment: to seek out and kill the 1800 women and children in the nearby village of Jozefow. Then, astonishingly Trapp told them he knew what a repugnant task some might find it, and that anyone could stand out with no punishment and no reprisals. Out of 500, only 12 men stood out.

During that terrible day, a further 10–20% managed to evade their duty; many more became distressed but continued to carry out the orders. Quite a few exhibited no signs of distress. A few seemed to enjoy themselves.

2. *Russian pilot obeyed wrong instructions.*

Barrie Clement *The Independent* 9 July 2002

Figure 2.16
Some avoidable plane crashes can be explained using social psychology

The Russian pilot involved in a mid-air crash last week that killed 71 people was given conflicting orders by Swiss air traffic control and his automatic warning system, German investigators said yesterday.

Ground staff told the pilot to dive to avoid an oncoming cargo plane, but the TCAS on-board crash-avoidance device ordered the plane to climb. The pilot of the Tupolev 154 airliner, Alexander Gross, obeyed the second command from controllers to descend and 30 seconds later crashed into a Boeing 757 freight jet.

Voice recorders recovered from fragments of the two planes scattered across the Swiss-German border showed that the on-board system on the Boeing had told its pilot to dive. The systems are designed to communicate so that aircraft are sent in opposite directions to avoid a collision. If the Russian pilot had obeyed the machine rather than the air traffic controller, the disaster might have been avoided.

Explain using ideas, theories and studies from social psychology why each of these incidents might have taken place.

over to you

Your practical exercise for the social approach is to conduct a survey study of your own. If you have read this chapter thoroughly you will by now know quite a lot about surveys. You can carry out this task individually or in small groups. The survey should be related to a topic you have studied as part of the social approach. Suitable examples include the following:

- non-psychology students' beliefs about how participants would respond in the Milgram procedure or the Hofling study
- how people judge guilt in individuals acting independently or following orders (see Hamilton and Sanders (1995), p. 21)
- attitudes to the human rights abuses at Abu Ghraib
- attitudes to smoking and drinking in different youth subcultures
- students' experiences of age discrimination from older people.

You can be asked questions about this task in your exam, so make sure you clearly understand the following as you design your survey:

1. What are you aiming to find out in your survey?
2. Are you going to test a particular hypothesis?

3. Will you use an interview or questionnaire method?
4. How will you gather both quantitative and qualitative data?
5. Will you use open or closed questions (probably both as you want quantitative and qualitative data)?
6. How structured will your questionnaire or interview schedule be?
7. What response format will you use (e.g. yes/no, strongly agree/agree/don't know/disagree/strongly disagree)?
8. What is your target population? What sampling procedure will you use? How many people will you survey?
9. What ethical considerations does your survey raise? How will you deal with these to make it as ethical as possible?
10. When your survey is constructed, how could you establish its reliability and validity?

Make sure that when you have carried out your survey you keep a record of your answers to all these questions and a record of your findings and conclusions as part of your social approach notes.

Conclusions

Social psychology is concerned with how and why humans interact with and influence one another. We have looked in particular at two aspects of social interaction, obedience and prejudice. A feature of human social behaviour is our tendency for obedience to authority. Milgram has explained this in his agency theory as an innate tendency, which helps us form stable societies. Prejudice is another important feature of human interaction. Social identity theory provides us with a good basis from which to study and understand prejudice, although it does not neatly explain individual differences in prejudice. We have applied social-psychological theory and research to understanding real life issues, most importantly genocide. We have also learned about research methodology, with particular regard to survey methods. Surveying can gather both quantitative and qualitative data. As a method it requires particularly careful thought about sampling procedure and about issues of reliability and validity. Like all psychological research, survey methods also require careful thought about ethical issues.

what do I know?

1. Describe and evaluate one study from the social approach.

2. Discuss agency theory as an explanation for human obedience.

3. Explain the key features of the survey method.

4. Explain what is meant by reliability and validity.

5. Using an example explain how psychologists might obtain a representative sample.

6. Describe and evaluate social identity theory.

7. Use ideas from the social approach to explain **one** key issue in psychology.

what's ahead

By the end of this chapter I should know about:

- the cognitive approach to psychology
- levels of processing theory
- *either* the multi-store model of memory *or* reconstructive memory
- cue dependency as an explanation for forgetting
- repression as an explanation for forgetting
- two studies of memory or forgetting, including Godden & Baddeley (1975) and *either* Peterson & Peterson (1959), Craik & Tulving (1975) *or* Ramponi *et al.* (2004)
- applying ideas from the cognitive approach to explaining real life situations

In addition I should understand:

- the experimental method and experimental design
- independent, controlled and dependent variables
- issues of experimental control and the operationalisation of variables
- issues of objectivity, reliability and validity
- issues of experimenter effects and demand characteristics
- measures of central tendency (averages) and dispersion
- the use of graphs to show information

where does the cognitive approach take us?

← Mobiles: do they wreck or boost your memory?

↖ Childhood memories: did you visit Disneyland and meet Bugs Bunny as a child?

↙ Exams: does chewing gum improve your performance?

↑ Rude words: easier or harder to remember?

↘ Divers: do they remember better on land or in the water?

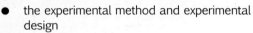

chapter **3**

The cognitive approach

what's that?

- **Memory:** the processes by which we store and retrieve information

- **Information processing:** the processing by which information is taken in by the senses, analysed and responded to

The cognitive angle

Cognitive psychologists are concerned with the internal operations of the mind. These are collectively called cognitive processes (or *cognition*). Cognitive processes include perception – the ways in which we take in information via the senses and make sense of it, **memory** – the processes of storing and retrieving information, and thinking – the mental manipulation of information that allows us to have ideas, hold opinions and decide on courses of action. Cognitive psychologists think of the mind as a system for handling information. We constantly receive information from the external environment, interpret it in the light of existing information in our memory and think about it. We then respond to the information, for example with an opinion, an emotional response or sometimes with action.

Many cognitive psychologists find it helpful to think of the mind as operating in the same way as a computer. Like a computer the mind handles information; it has an input of information from the senses, throughput of information in the form of memory, thinking and language, and an output in the form of decision making, speech and action. In some ways of course, the mind is *not* like a computer. We are much more fallible and slower at searching for information. On the other hand we are much better at using mental shortcuts to locate information. Despite these differences, the workings of a computer can serve as an *analogy* to understand the human mind. We can thus think of ourselves as having hardware (the nervous system), and of acquiring programming through experience.

Memory

Memory is absolutely fundamental to living. In the course of a day we have to store vast amounts of new information and retrieve even more already stored information. We have to recall who we are, recognise the faces of everyone we meet and retrieve all the relevant information about the person, remember how to move and to communicate. We also have to refer back to information from our past experiences and recall technical information such as psychological theories! In this chapter we look at a number of case studies of people who, through accident or illness, have lost one or more aspects of their memory function. To lose just one aspect of memory, such as the ability to store new memories of events, can be severely disabling, yet this is only a fraction of what we are constantly doing with our memory. In this chapter we are concerned with two main theoretical issues. First, how does memory operate? Second, how and why do we forget things? We are also concerned with the very practical issue of eyewitness memory. How accurate are the recollections of eyewitnesses about crimes they have seen? How can we explain the sort of mistakes witnesses make?

Theories of memory

There are a number of theories of memory, that is explanations for how memory operates. There is no single correct explanation for how memory works; each of the following theories of memory explains a different aspect of memory functioning. Levels of processing theory aims to explain why some things are better remembered than others. The multi-store model is concerned with different memory stores while the reconstructive memory model is mostly concerned with what happens when we retrieve information from memory.

The levels of processing (LOP) approach

Craik & Lockhart (1972) produced an influential approach to explaining how memory operates. Their aim was to explain why some things are better remembered than others. They suggested that how well a piece of information is remembered depends on how it is processed. Memory is thus a by-product of the general processing of information in the mind. Information can be processed deeply or shallowly. Craik (1973) defined depth of processing as the amount of meaning that was extracted from the information. Information that is deeply processed, that is thought deeply about, is likely to be remembered. Craik & Lockhart suggested three levels at which information is processed.

- Structural processing, i.e. processing information about what things look like.
- Phonetic processing, i.e. processing information about what something sounds like.
- Semantic processing, i.e. processing information about what something means.

Semantic processing is the *deepest* form of **information processing**, that is it involves the most cognitive work. Material that is semantically processed is likely to be the best remembered. Structural processing is the *shallowest* form of information processing and is likely to result in the least material being remembered. This was demonstrated in a classic study by Craik and Tulving (1975).

Classic research

Optional

Craik, F.I.M. & Tulving, E. (1975)

'Depth of processing and the retention of words in episodic memory'

Journal of Experimental Psychology 104, 268–94.

Aim: The aim was to test whether words that were processed for their meaning would be better remembered than words that were processed for information about their appearance or sound.

Procedure: Several variations on the procedure were reported. In the first, 20 students were individually given reading lists of 40 1–2-syllable words. They were asked whether each word was written in capitals (structural), whether it rhymed with another word (phonetic) or whether it was part of a category or fitted a gap in a sentence (semantic). To control for other factors affecting how memorable each word might be, the questions and words were rotated so that each participant received a different combination. At this point participants were unaware that the experiment was concerned with memory, so were not expecting to be tested. Later they were tested for either their recall of the words (in which they were asked to remember as many of the words as possible) or recognition (in which they chose the words from a selection).

Findings: In all the experiments participants remembered the words best that had been processed semantically. In the first experiment 96% of words that had been processed for whether they would fit into a sentence were recognised. Memory was worst for words that had been processed structurally, for example only 18% of words were recognised after they had been processed for capital letters.

Conclusion: Depth of processing affects how well words are remembered. Semantic processing, that is thinking about the meaning of the words leads to their being remembered best.

how **science** works

Research Methods

The experimental method

Historically the experiment has been the most commonly used research method in cognitive psychology. The idea in an experiment is to create a situation in which a single variable is altered whilst all others remain constant, so that the effect of this variable on the variable or variables that we are measuring for our results can be seen. Experiments can be carried out in a laboratory or in a more natural environment (field experiments). The differences between laboratory and field experiments are discussed in detail on p. 67.

Independent and dependent variables

The variable that we alter in an experiment is called the independent variable (or IV). The variable that we measure in our results is called the dependent variable (DV). In Craik and Tulving's experiment for example the independent variable is how deeply each word is processed. The dependent variable is how well the words are remembered. When we design a study we need to think about exactly how these variables will be put into practice or operationalised. Craik & Tulving operationalised their IV of how deeply words were processed as the type of question participants were asked about each word. Their DV was operationalised as the percentage of words recalled or recognised.

Comparing conditions

In an experiment we set up different levels of our IV. Each level of the IV has its own condition. In Craik and Tulving's study for example there are three levels of the IV: structural processing, phonetic processing and semantic processing. There are hence three conditions. The results of an experiment come in the form of a measurement of the DV for each condition.

The simplest way to show these results is with a bar chart. A bar chart showing the results for one of Craik and Tulving's experiments is shown in Figure 3.1.

Looking at this bar chart you can clearly see that the percentage of words recognised after they had been presented with a question asking whether they fitted into a sentence was greater than that after they had been presented with a question about whether they rhymed with another word or whether they were upper or lower case.

Figure 3.1
A bar chart showing Craik and Tulving's results

Hypotheses

An hypothesis is a statement predicting our results. In some types of research we are simply exploring what takes place under particular circumstances and we are not testing a particular hypothesis. However, the aims of experiments are generally quite specific – we are testing an idea by saying that if it holds true it predicts a particular outcome. For example, Craik & Tulving were testing the idea of levels of processing by saying that it predicted that a greater proportion of deeply processed words would be recalled. If you browse some original journal publications you will find that most hypotheses are either mentioned in passing or implied rather than stated explicitly. However, trainee researchers (that's you!) are required to go through the formal process of stating an experimental hypothesis (H_E) and a null hypothesis (H_0).

The experimental hypothesis states the difference you expect to find between your conditions if the idea you are testing holds true. For example an experimental hypothesis for Craik and Tulving's study might read something like:

H_E: More words will be recalled after being analysed for meaning rather than appearance or sound.

This is an example of a *directional* hypothesis. When we are entirely clear about what should happen in an experiment we sometimes use directional hypotheses like this. However, if we are less sure about the direction of our findings we can use a *non-directional* hypothesis, which would read more like this:

H_E: There is a difference in the number of words recalled after being analysed for appearance, sound and for meaning.

As well as the experimental hypothesis, we need to be clear about the null hypothesis. The null hypothesis states that any difference between conditions is so small that there is a high probability that it is due to chance. It is rare to see a null hypothesis explicitly stated nowadays in a research journal, however the idea is important because when you come to carry out statistical tests on your results (which you will in Unit 2) what these tests tell you is the likelihood that the null hypothesis is correct. A null hypothesis is best phrased something like this:

H_0: Any difference in the number of words recalled after being processed for appearance, sound and for meaning is due to chance.

Experimental control: situational variables

In an experiment it is important to know as far as possible that any differences in the results in different conditions are due to our IV. This means that we need to keep as many other factors constant as we can. Craik & Lockhart ensured that each word was presented for the same time (0.2 seconds) and that every question was asked about each word. These factors that are kept constant are called controlled variables. The major advantage of being in a laboratory setting is that a range of situational variables can also be controlled. This means that the situation is kept as constant as possible for each participant. Thus temperature and lighting can be kept constant, and distracting stimuli such as people walking past can be eliminated altogether. This is harder in a field experiment.

❝❞ Discussion of the levels of processing approach
There is a large body of evidence from experiments like that of Craik and Tulving to suggest that generally material that is processed for meaning is better remembered. There is also support from neuroscience for the idea that processing information semantically does involve more cognitive work than other forms of processing. Nyberg (2002) examined brain-scanning studies looking at information processing and memory. He concluded that activity

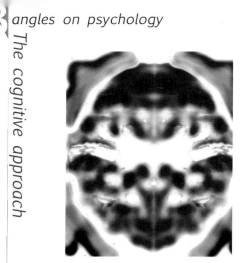

Figure 3.2
The brain is more active when material is being deeply processed

in the frontal and temporal lobes of the brain is greater when information is semantically processed. This suggests that these regions are doing 'more work' when information is processed for meaning.

The LOP model has a number of practical applications in helping people to remember information better by processing it more deeply. In clinical practice patients with impaired memory can sometimes be taught to use deep processing to improve their memory. Gardiner *et al.* (2006) describe the case of Jon, a young man with early-onset developmental amnesia (memory loss normally associated with old age). Jon had poor memory for events. The researchers gave him a selection of study tasks to either review or carry out. Unusually, carrying out the tasks did not improve his memory of them, however when the tasks were highly meaningful he did remember them relatively well. In educational practice, there is evidence to suggest that 'deep learning', that is approaches to learning that involve deeply analysing material for meaning improves memory of that material – see What's new?

what's new

Deep learning will improve your psychology grades

Figure 3.3
Deeply processing your psychology will help you remember it

An important practical application of levels of processing research has been in the teaching and learning of psychology. Studies of both A-level and undergraduate psychology students have shown that those who report ways of studying that involve deeply processing information tend to do better in their exams. Learning strategies that involve only shallow processing of information include looking at only one textbook and rote learning. 'Deep' learning involves wider reading, critical thinking and applying knowledge to real-life situations. We can measure the extent to which we use deep and shallow learning by questionnaires, for example ASSIST (Entwistle & Tait, 1996). You can see ASSIST at http://www.tla.ed.ac.uk/etl/questionnaires/ASSIST.pdf. Diseth & Martinsen (2003) assessed learning strategies in Norwegian psychology undergraduates and found that low levels of surface learning were associated with higher exam marks. Jarvis (2006) found similar results in a study of AS-level psychology students. High levels of deep learning and low levels of shallow learning strategies correlated positively with AS exam marks. There is an important lesson in this for psychology students; read around psychology and get stuck into any tasks your teacher sets you. Don't rely on rote-learning for your exams.

An interesting finding in recent levels of processing research has been the fact that LOP effects are much stronger in cases where people deliberately try to recall things they have learned as opposed to when they are simply primed by previously learned material to be able to recall something. This type of remembering is called involuntary retrieval or *priming*. An example of priming takes place when we learn a word like chair, then it comes to mind in response to seeing the word *table*. Associations like this can be strong, as in chair–table, bread–butter and so on or weaker, as in diamond–jewel. We can define an association as strong when one word primes the other in most participants, and weak when this happens less frequently. A recent study by Ramponi *et al.*

(2004) has looked at the effects of age and levels of processing on priming with strong and weak associated words. We can look at this study in detail in Classic Research.

Classic research

Optional

Ramponi, C., Richardson-Klavehn, A. & Gardiner, J.M. (2004)

'Level of processing and age affect involuntary conceptual priming of weak but not strong associates'

Experimental Psychology 51, 159–64.

Aim: To investigate the extent to which deep processing and age influence how well words are recalled under voluntary and involuntary conditions.

Procedure: Forty-eight older adults with a mean age of 71.67 years and 48 students with a mean age of 23.81 years took part in the experiment. The design involved repeated and independent measures. Each participant encountered prime words under each level of processing and with weak and strong associations between word pairs (repeated measures). However, participants could only be in older or younger groups (independent measures). Six lists of 28 word pairs were presented to each participant, under different LOP conditions. For the structural task participants had to say which word had more letters sticking up. For the phonetic condition they had to say which had more syllables. For the semantic task they had to identify which word had a more pleasant meaning. Recall was then tested under intentional and involuntary conditions. In the intentional condition participants were shown one word of each pair and asked to recall the associated word. In the involuntary condition they were asked to think of the first word that came to mind in response to one word from each pair.

Findings: As expected, semantic processing resulted in better recall in the intentional recall condition regardless of whether the associations between words were weak or strong. Similarly, younger people intentionally recalled more words than older people regardless of the strength of the association. However, where the association between two words was strong and recall was involuntary, neither levels of processing nor age made any difference to the number of words recalled.

Conclusion: The effect of levels of processing holds true under most conditions but there are exceptions. Where two words are strongly associated with one another, one word will trigger the involuntary recall of the other regardless of how they were processed at the time of learning.

Although the levels of processing approach has proved very useful in helping us understand memory, the model in its classic form has its limitations. One problem is that other factors also affect how well words are remembered, independent of how deeply they are processed. Information that is particularly unusual or carries a lot of emotional significance also tends to be remembered well. Reber *et al.* (1994) carried out an experiment with secondary school and university students, in which words high or low in emotional content were presented in ways that led to their being processed deeply or shallowly. Words without emotional significance were recalled best when they were semantically processed, but how the words were presented had no effect on the emotional words, which were recalled as well as the semantically processed non-emotional words. This suggests that the emotional content of information acts as an influence on how well it is remembered independently of the level of processing.

For & Against

the levels of processing approach

FOR   there is experimental support for the idea that information processed for meaning is better remembered than structurally or phonetically processed material. The classic example is Craik & Tulving's (1975) study that showed that when words were analysed for whether they would fit into a sentence they were much better remembered than when they were identified as upper or lower case.

FOR   there is also support for the levels of processing approach from brain scanning studies. These show that when material is semantically processed, there is more brain activity than when it is more shallowly processed. This extra brain activity may equate to deeper processing.

FOR   the levels of processing approach has important practical applications. For example, in education, students who read around their subject and clarify their understanding (i.e. they process the information deeply) tend to do better in exams than those who process the material more shallowly by minimal reading and rote learning.

AGAINST   other factors also affect how well material is remembered, independent of depth of processing. For example, Reber *et al.* (1994) showed that emotional content of words affected recall independent of depth of processing. This suggests that levels of processing is not a complete explanation for how memory works.

AGAINST   the effect of levels of processing on recall does not hold true under all conditions. For example Ramponi and her colleagues have found that where there are strong associations between words, one will trigger the recall of the other regardless of how the word pairs were processed when they were learned.

The multi-store model

The multi-store approach to memory is concerned with identifying different memory stores. Atkinson & Shiffrin (1968) proposed an early multi-store model, which suggested that there are three types of information store. Initially, information is stored for a fraction of a second at the sensory organs in a *sensory register*. Information that is attended to whilst in the sensory register passes on to short-term memory (STM), which holds a few items and lasts a few seconds. Material that is rehearsed in short-term memory is subsequently passed on to long-term memory (LTM). The processes of sensory registration, short-term and long-term memory can be shown in Figure 3.4.

Figure 3.4
Atkinson & Shiffrin's model

Material that we attend to is held for a few seconds in short-term memory. At this stage it is kept in acoustic form (i.e. what is stored is the *sound* of words). The capacity of short-term memory is small, approximately seven items. Material that is *rehearsed*, that is repeated back, remains in short-term memory long enough to be transferred to long-term memory. Otherwise it is lost when new information comes in and displaces it. Words that are not rehearsed are lost on the first-in-first-out (FIFO) principle. A classic study by Peterson & Peterson (1959) tested how long information remains in short-term memory.

Classic research

Optional

Peterson, L.R. & Peterson, M.J. (1959)

'Short-term retention of individual verbal items'

Journal of Experimental Psychology 58, 193–8.

Aim: To test the duration of short-term memory by measuring the retention of items in STM when rehearsal is prevented for differing lengths of time.

Procedure: Twenty-four students were tested on their recall of test items presented one at a time. The items were trigrams, meaningless three-consonant syllables (e.g. CHJ). No two trigrams presented one after the other contained any of the same letters. Each participant was shown a trigram then given standard instructions to count backwards in threes or fours until a flashing light appeared in front of them. They then had to recall the trigram. There were various fixed times between the experimenter saying the syllable and the light signalling recall (3, 6, 9, 12, 15 and 18 seconds). Each participant was tested on each of these intervals once in each block of six trials.

Findings: As the delay between hearing the trigram and reporting it increased, the ability to recall it decreased. This relationship can be seen in Figure 3.5.

Conclusion: When rehearsal is prevented items in short-term memory are lost quickly, lasting a maximum of approximately 28 seconds.

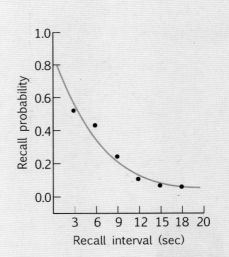

Figure 3.5
The decline of recall of words from short-term memory. From Peterson & Peterson (1959)

Long-term memory is rather different to short-term. It has an unlimited capacity and information may last a lifetime, although some things are forgotten relatively quickly. Information is held in semantic rather than acoustic form. This means that what is stored is the *meaning* rather than the sound of items. Unlike later models of memory, the Atkinson & Shiffrin model does not identify separate storage systems for different types of information.

"" Discussion of the multi-store model

The multi-store model has been of enormous use in understanding memory, and most psychologists support the existence of separate short- and long-term memory. However, we now know rather more about the way both short- and long-term memory work, and it appears that both systems are more complex than those proposed by Atkinson & Shiffrin.

Evidence for separate STM and LTM

There are two types of evidence for the existence of separate short- and long-term memory systems. First there are laboratory experiments. Glanzer & Cunitz (1966) carried out a study on recall of words from the beginning, middle and end of a list of words. They found that people recalled more words from the beginning (the primacy effect) and the end of the list (the recency effect), and fewest words from the middle. This suggests that the early words in the list had been transferred to long-term memory, while those late in the list were still in short-term memory. We would expect that words in the middle would be least likely to be available because they were in the middle of being transferred from STM to LTM. The primacy–recency effect disappeared if recall of the list was delayed by 30 seconds, meaning that all the words that were going to be transferred to long-term memory had been.

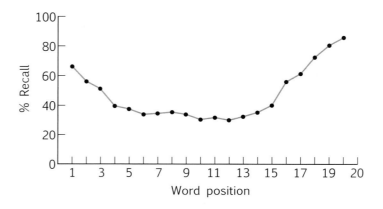

Figure 3.6
The primacy and recency effects, as found by Glanzer & Cunitz

Figure 3.7
Mobile phones may affect short-term but not long-term memory

Another line of experimental research that suggests that short- and long-term memory are two distinct systems involves stimulating one system but not the other. A recent study by Smythe & Costall (2003) looked into the effect of mobile phones on short- and long-term memory. Sixty-two students were randomly allocated to one of three conditions. In one condition they held an active mobile phone to their ear. In a second condition they held an inactive phone and in the third they had no phone. Each group was given the memory task of learning words arranged into a pyramid for three minutes. To test short-term memory they were given a task of reading a newspaper (to prevent rehearsal) then tested for recall of the words. To test long-term memory they returned a week later and were tested again. In both cases they were given three minutes to recall the pyramid of words. In male participants the group with the active phone made fewer errors in the short-term memory task (mean 12.9 errors as opposed to 23 with an inactive phone). There was no such difference in recall a week later. In females there was no difference in short- or long-term recall. These findings suggest that, as short- and long-term memory responded differently to the mobile phone, they must be separate systems.

The results of an experiment: central tendency, dispersion and distribution

When we compare the results in each of our experimental conditions we don't want to have to make sense of every participant's individual score. What we are most interested in is whether on average people score more in one condition than another. For example, in the Smythe & Costall (2003) study on the effect of mobile phones on memory we can see that participants exposed to an active mobile made on average 12.9 errors as opposed to 23 errors for those holding an inactive phone. A more technical term for 'average' is *central tendency*. Like many memory researchers Smythe & Costall used the mean as a measure of central tendency. The mean is calculated by adding up all the scores in the condition and dividing the total by the number of participants. There are alternative measures of central tendency however. The median is the midpoint of ranked scores. To find a median, simply put all the scores for a condition in rank order and find the mid-point. If you have an odd number of scores the median will be the score that has an equal number of scores on each side of it. If there is an even number of scores the median is the mid-point between the two scores that have an equal number of scores on each side of them. The mode is the third measure of central tendency. This is the most frequently occurring score in a condition.

exercise

Look at the following (made up) dataset and work out the mean, median and mode for each condition.

(1) No. words recalled without mobile	4	6	5	6	9	7	6	3	5
(2) No. words recalled with mobile	4	9	5	11	6	12	9	9	8

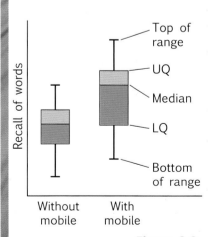

Figure 3.8
A box and whiskers plot

Although in an experiment the first thing we look for is a difference in the average results in each condition, there are other things we might want to know. For example are the results equally spread out in each condition? The technical term for this is the *dispersion* of the results. The simplest measure of dispersion is the range. This is simply the interval between the highest and lowest numbers. For example the ranges in the above dataset are 3–9 and 4–12. This can be expressed as a single number if you wish: highest–lowest + 1. 9 – 3 + 1 = 7 and 12 – 4 + 1 = 9. A quick and easy way to show dispersion on a graph is by means of a box and whiskers plot. This is like a bar chart but as well as showing the median for each condition it also shows the range and upper and lower quartiles. The quartiles are the ¼ and ¾ points along the ranked scores. The lower quartile is thus halfway from the lowest score to the median and the upper quartile halfway from the median to the highest score. The length of the whisker between these quartiles is a measure of how dispersed the results are.

Looking at this box and whiskers plot we can see two things. First, on average people remembered considerably more words when exposed to a mobile phone. Second, there is more variation in the number of words remembered when exposed to a mobile. This would suggest that mobile phones affect some people more than others. These are both important. One final thing we might want to know about our results is their *distribution*. Distributions can be shown on various types of graph. The simplest of these are histograms and frequency polygons. The principles of these two graphs are the same. We are plotting scores against how frequently they occur. The graphs below show the distribution of scores for condition 2 of our made-up data set. The graph on the left is a histogram and the one on the right a frequency polygon.

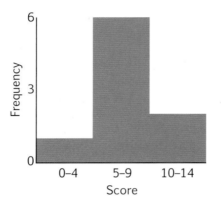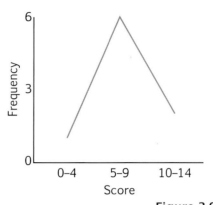

Figure 3.9
Two ways of displaying distributions

Additional evidence for separate short- and long-term stores comes from cases of brain-damaged patients who have sustained damage to either short- or long-term memory but in whom the other system remains intact. We can look at one classic case, that of HM, in detail.

REALpeople

The case of HM

HM is a patient who suffered severe epilepsy as a young man. In 1953, at the age of 27 years he had major surgery in an attempt to relieve the epilepsy. Large areas of the temporal lobes on both sides of his brain were removed. This had a profound effect on his memory. Since the day of the operation HM has been virtually unable to form new memories for facts or events, although he can still learn new motor skills. He shows only mild difficulty in recalling events for 11 years prior to the operation and no difficulty in recalling events from before the age of 16. Most interestingly, in spite of his severe difficulty in forming new long-term memories his short-term memory is relatively normal. HM was found to be able to retain the normal seven items in short-term memory, although unlike most of us he could not extend this by rehearsal. HM has a severely damaged long-term memory but a largely intact short-term memory. This is powerful evidence to suggest that short- and long-term memory are in fact separate systems.

Figure 3.10
The coloured regions show the area removed from HM's brain

interactive angles

You can read more about HM at this website: http://www.brainconnection.com/topics/?main=fa/hm-memory. You can also read a recent publication by Suzanne Corkin, who has studied HM, here. http://homepage.mac.com/sanagnos/corkin2002.pdf.

Further evidence for separate short- and long-term memory comes from studies of Prader-Willi syndrome (PWS). This is a genetic condition with multiple physical and psychological effects, ranging from short stature and obesity to learning difficulties and behavioural problems. Studies have shown that individuals with Prader-Willi syndrome have normal long-term memory but poor short-term memory. In one study Conners *et al.* (2000) compared nine patients with PWS with a control group of nine participants not suffering the condition. The two groups were matched closely for age and IQ. Relative to IQ, long-term memory in the PWS group was strong and short-term memory weak. If long-term memory but not short-term can be impaired (as in HM) and short-term memory can be impaired without long-term memory problems (as in PWS) this is a powerful argument for saying they are separate systems.

how science works

Research Methods

Experimental design

One of the important decisions to make when designing an experiment is whether to allocate your participants to separate conditions or whether they should all take part in all conditions. There are three ways to approach this problem:

Independent measures designs

Take the Smythe & Costall (2003) study of the effect of mobile phones on memory (p. 54). They allocated participants to one of three conditions. This sort of experimental design is called an *unrelated, independent measures* or *between groups design*. When we design an experiment in this way we make the assumption that if we randomly allocate participants to conditions then there is a very good chance that the people in each group will be fairly similar. Participants can vary in a number of ways – these ways are called *participant variables*. For example the people in one condition might have better memories than those in another. This is important as we need to be as sure as possible that any differences in the DV in each condition are due to the IV we are studying and not to the different participants. In practice this is difficult, and independent measures designs always have the problem that results can be affected by differences in the groups.

Repeated measures designs

An alternative approach to designing the experiment is to have all participants take part in each condition. This is called a *repeated measures, unrelated* or *within groups design*. For example Craik & Tulving (1975) had all of the participants answer structural, phonetic and semantic questions about their words. This has the advantage that there are no differences between the participants in different conditions to confuse results. In other words participant variables do not affect results. There are potential problems however, for example order effects. If all participants do one particular condition first then another it may be that they get bored or fatigued so do better in the first, or it may be that they get better with practice so do better in the last condition. Another problem can be that when participants see all the conditions they realise the aim of the study. If this happens their own views about what 'should' happen may creep in and affect results. Craik & Tulving got around both these problems by mixing up the three conditions. This is not always possible, however. What we can usually do is to make sure that participants do conditions in different order. This is called *counterbalancing*.

Matched pairs designs

A way to get around the difficulties in independent and repeated measures designs is to use matched pairs. This means that we use two or more groups (one for each condition), but for every participant in one group we have one in each other group that is matched for all relevant variables. For example in the Conners *et al.* (2000) study (p. 57), each participant with Prader-Willi syndrome was matched for age and IQ with a participant without the syndrome. This meant that the researchers could be reasonably sure that any differences in the short-term and long-term memory of the two groups were due to the syndrome and not to general differences between the individuals. The major limitation of using matched pairs designs is the time taken to find matched participants. In addition it is hard to be sure we have matched them on all the relevant characteristics.

Mixed designs

Where experiments involve more than one independent variable, sometimes the best designs are a blend of repeated and independent measures. For example, Ramponi *et al.* (2004) looked at the effect of levels of processing and age on memory (p. 51). To eliminate individual differences in memory they gave the same participants different tasks requiring structural, phonetic and semantic processing (repeated measures). However, in order to look at the effects of age they needed to do this with older and younger people. By definition this required two groups of older and younger people, so this part of the design was independent measures.

how
science
works

Research
Methods

Experimenter effects and demand characteristics

When conducting any psychological research we seek to be objective. In other words we try to see what is really there rather than what we expect to find or would like to find. This is called being objective. The opposite of objectivity is subjectivity, which means looking at things from our personal point of view. The problem with being subjective in designing or carrying out an experiment is that our own opinions can end up biasing our results through experimenter effects and demand characteristics.

Experimenter effects occur when the experimenter has a strong expectation of what their study will show. This can unconsciously affect how they communicate with participants and so affect the results. The best experiments involve standard instructions, so that all participants are spoken to in the same way, and either single blind or double blind procedures. In a single blind procedure participants do not know which condition they are taking part in. In a double blind procedure the experimenter has someone else to actually speak to the participants who does not know which condition they are administering. This means they cannot unconsciously give away clues about what is expected to happen.

Demand characteristics are any features of the experiment that give away to participants what the study is about. Once participants are aware of this their own opinions about what should happen will affect the results. Generally repeated measures designs create more problems of demand characteristics because participants see all the conditions for themselves. This can make it obvious what the study is about and therefore potentially alter the results. However, even in independent measures designs like that used by Smythe & Costall in their mobile phone study, demand characteristics can be a problem. Ethically, participants had to know that the study concerned mobile phones even though they were unaware of the hypothesis. Those without a phone scored lower than those with an inactive phone. The authors suggest that these participants realised they were a control group because of the lack of a phone and so attended less to the task.

The nature of short- and long-term memory

Although there is considerable support for the existence of separate short- and long-term memory systems, it appears that the way Atkinson & Shiffrin thought of short-term memory is flawed. Gelkopf & Zakai (1991) tested whether information is lost from short-term memory on a first-in-first-out basis as Atkinson & Shiffrin (1968) suggested. One hundred and twenty students were presented with a list of 28 words and given three minutes to rehearse and recall them. If words were lost from STM on a FIFO basis we would expect that words from the beginning of the list would be poorly recalled but this was not the case, showing that words are not in fact displaced in this way. There is also some question as to whether words in short-term memory are in fact encoded in semantic as well as acoustic form (i.e. their meaning is processed as well as the sound). This is demonstrated by the case of FK.

REALpeople

The case of FK

FK is a male patient who suffered brain damage from carbon monoxide poisoning at age 29. He has suffered damage to long-term memory and has difficulty in recalling facts although he has a relatively normal ability to recall events. FK has particular difficulty remembering the meanings of particular words, though not all. A list of 'known' words, the meaning of which he did understand, was established along with a list of 'unknown' words, the meaning of which he did not understand. FK was then tested on reading tasks involving the known and unknown words. He made many errors in pronunciation of the unknown words though not of the known words. Reading involves short-term memory. If there were no semantic processing of words in short-term memory we would expect no difference in FK's ability to pronounce known and unknown words. In fact FK has considerable difficulty pronouncing words the meaning of which he does not know. This suggests strongly that information in short-term memory is processed semantically.

Most importantly, there appears to be more than one system of short-term memory, responsible for handling different types of information. If STM were a single system as suggested by Atkinson and Shiffrin, we would expect that introducing a new task involving visual information would disrupt the ability of STM to handle verbal information and vice versa. However if there are separate visual and verbal systems we would expect an additional visual task to have little impact on verbal STM. Seitz & Schumann-Hengsteler (2000) tested this in a recent study. Twelve students were given multiplication sums to perform while either listening to irrelevant speech (verbal disruption) or tapping items on a map (visuo-spatial disruption). Listening to irrelevant speech but not the visuo-spatial task spoiled performance on the sums. This suggests that there are separate short-term memory systems to handle visual and verbal information.

It also seems that there is more than one system of storage in long-term memory. Recall the cases of Jon, HM and FK. HM has had impaired memory for events and facts encountered since his operation, but no problem learning new motor skills. FK has difficulty in recalling some *factual* information such as word meanings, but no problem recalling *events*. In Jon's case the reverse is true. These cases suggest that there are at least three different storage systems in long-term memory, and indeed most cognitive psychologists support the existence of three separate long-term memory systems. *Semantic* memory is the system responsible for memory of facts. Episodic memory contains our memory for events whilst *procedural* memory deals with our motor skills, that is memory of how to do things. There is strong evidence from numerous cases like Jon, HM and FK that in fact semantic, episodic and procedural memories are separate long-term memory systems.

For & Against
the multi-store model

FOR there is evidence from experiments to suggest that short- and long-term memory are in fact separate systems as the model proposes. For example, Smythe & Costall (2003) found that mobile phone use appears to stimulate short-term but not long-term memory.

FOR HM sustained severe damage to long-term memory but kept a relatively normal short-term memory. If one memory system but not the other is damaged this suggests they must be at least partly separate.

AGAINST it is now widely believed that there is more than one short-term memory system designed to handle different types of information. This is shown by studies such as that of Seitz & Schumann-Hengsteler (2000) in which verbal information but not a motor task interfered with the ability to do sums.

interactive angles

Compare the multi-store and levels of processing approaches. Think about what each theory emphasises, how each explains what material is best remembered, and compare the evidence for each.

AGAINST there is evidence, for example from the case of FK, to suggest that material in short-term memory is analysed for meaning, and not just for sound. This suggests that the Atkinson & Shiffrin (1968) view of short-term memory is wrong.

AGAINST there is also strong evidence, for example from the cases of Jon, HM and FK, to suggest that there are several separate stores of long-term memory, for example for facts, events and skills. Each of these cases has damage to one or more of these memory systems but not to the others.

The reconstructive memory approach

This is another very different approach to understanding memory. Whereas levels of processing and multi-store approaches emphasise what happens when information is initially processed and stored, the reconstructive memory approach is more concerned with what happens when information is stored and retrieved from memory. To the layperson, memory operates in much the same way as a DVD player; we keep in some form a complete, sequential record of everything that has happened to us. When we remember something, what we are effectively locating is the right videoclip and playing it back. However, Bartlett (1932) suggested that memory was more of 'an imaginative reconstruction' of past events; influenced by our attitudes and our responses to those events at the time they occurred (1932: 213). Retrieval of stored memories thus involves an active process of *reconstruction*. Whenever we try to recall an event, we actively piece it together using a range of information.

Bartlett developed the *serial reproduction* method of studying reconstructive memory. This is somewhat like the children's game of 'Chinese whispers'. One person tells another a story and they tell it to a third person and so on. This replicates under laboratory conditions the process in which information is passed from one person to another in real life. Bartlett famously used the Native American story, *The War of the Ghosts* in serial reproduction studies because it was unfamiliar and different in cultural origins to the participants.

An edited version of *The War of the Ghosts*	One night two men from Egulac went down the river to hunt seals, and while they were there it became foggy and calm. Then they heard war-cries, and they thought 'maybe this is a war-party '.They escaped to the shore, and hid behind a log. Now canoes came up, and they heard the noise of paddles and saw one canoe coming up to them. There were five men in the canoe and they said: 'What do you think? We wish to take you along. We are going up the river to make war on the people.' … So one of the young men went and the other returned home … the young man went ashore to his house and made a fire. And he told everybody and said: 'Behold I accompanied the ghosts and went to fight. Many of our fellows were killed and many of those who attacked us were killed.' … When the sun rose he fell down. Something black came out of his mouth. His face became contorted. The people jumped up and cried. He was dead.

Bartlett found that once it had been reproduced through six people the story changed in particular ways. It was shorter, typically around half its original length. The details that were left out tended to be those specific to Native American culture, so the story became more like an English story. Bartlett also used stories like *The War of the Ghosts* in his *repeated reproduction* procedure. In repeated reproduction the same participant retells the story on a number of occasions. The results were the same. After a number of re-tellings the story became shorter and more anglicised.

Schemas and stereotyping

Bartlett (1932) proposed that the reason for the changes in stories like *The War of the Ghosts* during serial and repeated reproduction was the fact that remembering involves looking at units of memory called *schemas*. We each have a schema for every aspect of the world, consisting of all the information we have related to it. When we reconstruct memories we activate the relevant schemas and make use of the information in them. For example, when trying to recall *The War of the Ghosts* we might make use of our ghost-schema, war-schema and death-schema. When Bartlett's participants remembered the story, they scanned all the relevant schemas for more information and eliminated information that did not fit into their understanding of ghosts, war and so on.

One way of thinking about the effect of reproduction on *The War of the Ghosts* is to say that the story became increasingly *stereotyped*. In other words it increasingly fitted in with the participants' preconceived ideas about what a story involving ghosts and war should be like. This may be much the same process that operates when we stereotype people. In a classic study of stereotyping, Allport & Postman (1947) showed white participants a picture in which a scruffy white man armed with a cut-throat razor was arguing with a black man in a suit. Descriptions of the scene were passed on to other participants through serial reproduction. After a few reproductions the descriptions changed so that the black man was usually described as holding the razor. Presumably the participants accessed their 'black-schema' and 'white-schema' and the information they found there required that they distort the scene to make it logical to them.

Figure 3.11
Because of their schemas for black and white people, participants in Allport & Postman's study remembered this scene with the black man holding the razor

Discussion

The idea that memory involves reconstruction is widely accepted in psychology. There is a wealth of evidence to show that we both interpret new information and reconstruct past information in the light of our schemas. One way of testing the role of schemas is to see whether memory is distorted in such a way as to make it more stereotyped. In one study by Carli (1999), 135 undergraduates read a story and were asked to reproduce it. In one condition the story ended abruptly without a conclusion and in the other it ended with a rape scene. In the second condition, participants tended to distort the story more they did in the first. These distortions tended to be consistent with the theme of rape, thus the rapist was described in threatening terms prior to the rape.

Further support for the role of schemas in retrieval comes from the fact that memory does not appear to be distorted when we have a new experience. This is because there are no existing schemas containing information to distort the memory. This was demonstrated by Wynn & Logie (1998) in a repeated reproduction task in which undergraduate students were asked to recall their first week at university. There was no decline in the accuracy of their recollections – as we would expect as they had no pre-existing schemas containing stereotyped accounts of starting university.

Although reconstruction probably does occur, this approach to memory is primarily concerned with the retrieval of information, and tells us little about how memories are stored. It is therefore not mutually exclusive with the multi-store model, which emphasises different storage systems or the levels of processing model, which emphasises the different ways in which information can be processed prior to storage.

For & Against

reconstructive memory

FOR   many studies have shown that our memory is inaccurate, and in particular that it distorts in line with existing schemas. This strongly suggests that memory involves a process of reconstruction using all the available information we have.

FOR   there is clear evidence that memories become more stereotyped following reproduction – as we would expect if retrieval involves accessing schemas. For example Carli (1999) showed that students asked to reproduce a story ending with a rape began to describe the rapist as threatening before the event. This supports the idea that memory is reconstructive.

AGAINST   reconstruction is a retrieval process, and there are other important aspects of memory that are not explained by the reconstructive memory approach. For example, the approach does not address the range of memory systems, as does the multi-store approach, nor the effect of the form in which information is taken in, as does the levels of processing approach.

media watch

No thanks for the memory ... it was only a TV advert.

Tim Radford
The Guardian 5 September 2001

Future generations of Britons will wistfully recall their wholemeal Hovis childhoods, that first Werther's original Toffee from cuddly Grandpa, and those festive meals around a Bisto gravy Sunday roast — even though they might never have experienced them.

Elizabeth Loftus, a psychologist from the University of Washington, told the [British] Association [of Science] yesterday that commercial advertisers could be unwittingly implanting false memories in unsuspecting viewers.

She and colleagues had studied a Walt Disney TV advertising campaign called 'Remember the magic'. This used imagery that evoked family outings and what seemed to be home movies of people shaking hands with Mickey Mouse. She wondered if these ads had triggered 'memories'

in viewers who might never have been to Disneyland or shaken hands with Mickey Mouse.

So she tested volunteers with her own 'Disneyland advert' in which someone shook hands with an impossible character — Bugs Bunny, created by Warner Brothers [not Disney]. She found she was right — some of the volunteers who saw her film were more likely to believe they had in fact met Bugs Bunny at Disneyland.

She found that Ovaltine, Alka Seltzer and Maxwell House had begun to dig into their vaults for nostalgic film of 40 years ago. In one study, US adults 'remembered' drinking Stewart's root beer from bottles in their youth, although the bottles had only been in production for 10 years.

1. Explain this phenomenon using the idea of reconstructive memory.
2. Think of some other adverts that have made use of 'retro' imagery. Can you accurately remember whether the scenes they portrayed really existed?

Figure 3.12
People can become convinced they met Bugs Bunny at Disneyland. This is impossible!

Comparing the approaches

The multi-store, levels of processing and reconstructive approaches to memory are very different and may seem quite difficult to reconcile with one another. However, there is plenty of support for the basic principles of each approach. Rather than choose which is the 'best' approach, it is more useful to reflect on what each has taught us. From the multi-store approach we have learned that memory involves a number of separate processes, some of which fall under the heading of 'short-term memory' and others under the umbrella of 'long-term memory'. The levels of processing approach reminds us that memory is only one aspect of the mind's processing of information, and that we store information while we are doing other things with it. The reconstructive memory approach has taught us much about the accuracy of retrieval and the relationship between memory for events and our existing knowledge.

Forgetting

We have all had the experience of not being able to remember a fact or event. This is forgetting. One of the basic questions cognitive psychologists have to answer is why we forget information. There have been several theories put forward to explain forgetting. Some theories propose that memories are forgotten because they have been permanently lost from the brain. These are called *availability theories*. The simplest availability theory is trace decay, the idea that the physical trace left in the brain of a memory disappears over time. Other approaches (collectively known as accessibility theories) work on the basis that memories still exist, but that we have trouble retrieving them. With regard to long-term memory, *accessibility theories* have rather more credibility than availability theories. We can look here at two accessibility theories of forgetting, cue-dependency (also called retrieval failure) and repression.

Cue-dependency

This is probably the most common reason why we forget things (Eysenck, 1998). We have all experienced the 'tip of the tongue' phenomenon, in which we know we know something but are temporarily unable to retrieve it. Endel Tulving (1972) proposed that forgetting takes place when we have the information we are seeking in our memory, but we lack the necessary cues to access it. Cues are additional pieces of information that guide us to the information we are seeking, rather like the contents page of a book.

In a classic experiment, Tulving & Pearlstone (1966) demonstrated that we can remember more words if we have access to the categories from which the words are taken. Participants were read lists of words, that fell into categories, for example dogs. The category names, for example 'dog', were included as well as a few examples of each category. In one condition the participants recalled the words without cues (free recall) and in the other they were given the category titles as cues (cued recall). In the cued condition the participants remembered more words. The category titles are a form of *semantic cue*. The word 'semantic' refers to the meaning of words, thus a semantic cue is one which works because its *meaning* triggers recall.

State and context cues
It is a well-known phenomenon that if you return to somewhere you haven't been for a while (such as your old school) the familiar sights, sounds and smells

will bring a flood of memories rushing back. This is because this distinctive sensory information serves as cues to retrieve old memories that had lain dormant for years. This type of cued retrieval is known as *context-dependent*, that is it depends on cues from the external environment (context). Context-dependent recall was demonstrated in a fascinating study by Godden & Baddeley (1975).

Classic research

Compulsory

Godden, D.R. & Baddeley, A.D. (1975)

'Context-dependent memory in two natural environments: on land and underwater'

British Journal of Psychology 66, 325–31.

Aim: To see whether words would be better remembered when recalled in the same environment than in a very different environment. In this case the two environments were a beach and under the sea.

Procedure: Eighteen divers were given word lists to learn. These were presented either on the beach or 15 feet under the sea. They were then asked to recall the words. In one condition the participants were in the same location as they were when they learned the words, and in another condition they were in the other location. To control for the possibility that any decline in accuracy of recall was due to the disruptive change from land to sea or vice versa, participants were also given a recognition test on the words.

Findings: Overall, whether words were presented on land or underwater did not affect the accuracy of recall. However, lists learned underwater were recalled considerably better when recalled underwater and those learned on the beach were similarly better recalled on the beach. In fact 40% more words were forgotten if recall took place in a different environment. In the recognition test, changing environment had no effect.

Conclusion: Recall was considerably better if the context was the same as when information was learned. This suggests that context cues enhanced recall. The fact that recognition was unaffected by a change in environment suggests that the change itself was not responsible for the decline in accuracy of recall.

Physiological cues, that is the state we are in when we learn something, can work in much the same way. Recall is said to be *state-dependent* if it requires a physiological cue for recall. When we are in a particular state at the time of learning information then that physiological state can act as a cue to help us retrieve that information. Emotional states can act as state cues, thus if we are excited or afraid when we encode information we find it easier to retrieve that information if we are in the same mood.

interactive angles

Go back to the section on evaluating studies in Chapter 1 (p 6). Use these key questions to evaluate the Godden & Baddeley study. In addition, go to www. youramazingbrain. org/yourmemory. Try the task of naming the capital cities. Using what you know about cue-dependency explain your results.

Figure 3.13
Divers recall information learned underwater better when underwater again

Discussion of cue-dependency

The effects of state and context have been demonstrated in many studies. Duka *et al.* (2001) had 48 participants perform a range of memory tasks with or without alcohol at learning and retrieval. Overall the alcohol had no effect on the accuracy of retrieval, however those who had drunk alcohol in the encoding tasks remembered better when they had drunk alcohol again at retrieval stage, whilst those who had learned having drunk a placebo remembered better without alcohol. Another study by Baker *et al.* (2004) looked at whether chewing gum when learning and recalling material produces a similar context effect. Eighty-three students (57 male, 26 female) aged 18–46 (mean average 24) took part in the experiment. They were randomly assigned to one of four conditions. In all conditions they were given two minutes to learn 15 words. They were asked to recall the words immediately and 24 hours later. In one condition they chewed gum during learning and when recalling (gum-gum). In the second they chewed gum when learning but not when recalling (gum-no gum). In the third condition they chewed gum when recalling but not when learning (no gum-gum) and in the final condition they did not chew gum at either point (no gum-no-gum). In immediate recall there were only very small differences in the mean number of words remembered. However 24 hours later the differences were significant, with an average of 11 words recalled in the gum-gum condition and only seven in the gum-no gum condition. In both conditions where the gum was present or absent at both learning and recall, more words were recalled than when the gum was present at only learning or recall. This suggests that chewing gum when learning and recalling information significantly aids memory due to context-dependency effects.

Figure 3.14
Chewing gum can be an effective memory cue

Field, lab and natural experiments

Most of the experiments we have looked at in this chapter have been based in the laboratory. In this case a laboratory is simply a controlled environment where the experimenter can regulate precisely what happens. The room may or may not have specialised equipment depending on the nature of the experiment. This has the advantage of experimental control. Consider the study by Baker *et al.* on chewing gum and context dependent memory. Because the study was carried out in a laboratory it was possible to ensure that participants were not distracted by outside factors such as phone calls, friends walking past and so on. It was also easy in the lab to ensure that they had precisely two minutes to learn the words. The potential disadvantage of conducting experiments in the lab is that in unnatural conditions people may not act naturally.

An alternative to carrying out experiments in the lab is to carry them out in participants' natural environment. The environment needs to be not just outside the lab but entirely natural to the particular participants involved. For example in their study of context-dependency (p. 66) Godden & Baddeley used divers as participants and their two environments were a beach and underwater. In one sense this is a better approach to locating experiments because we can be sure that the divers used their memory as they would normally. On the other hand it is harder to achieve good experimental control once we leave the laboratory. Ideally we carry out lab and field experiments on a topic. If the results agree then we have very convincing evidence for a phenomenon. For example, following the Baker *et al.* and Godden & Baddeley studies we can say there is convincing evidence for cue-dependency.

True and natural experiments

Sometimes we want to compare two naturally occurring conditions rather than two conditions we have set up ourselves. This is an experiment of sorts because we are attempting to look at the effect of an independent variable on a dependent variable. However it is not a true experiment because there is little or no experimental control, and the two situations we are comparing may differ in any number of ways. Most importantly participants are not randomly allocated to conditions, meaning that they are less likely to be similar groups. This sort of study is called a natural experiment or quasi-experiment. An example of a natural experiment in memory is Pezdek's study of memory of the 9/11 terrorist attack. She compared the recall of students from New York, California and Hawaii. As we might expect given the greater relevance of the events to New Yorkers, the New York students remembered events better. However, we cannot be sure that the three groups were comparable. All sorts of factors for example might have influenced where they were studying. Sometimes natural experiments are the only practical way of investigating something, however this lack of experimental control is a serious weakness.

How to randomise your own experimental groups

If you are carrying out an experiment in class, and this has an independent measures design you should really randomly allocate your participants to each condition. If it is a repeated measures design you can still randomise the order in which participants encounter the conditions. The easiest way to do your randomisation is online. Go to http://www.assumption.edu/users/avadum/applets/applets.html and follow the link to *random assignment*. Here, once each participant has a number you can randomly allocate them to the conditions.

interactive angles

Test your understanding of the experimental method so far, using the Baker *et al.* (2004) study (p. 67).

1. Identify the IV and DV.

2. Write an appropriate experimental hypothesis.

3. This was a laboratory experiment. What is the difference between a lab and field experiment?

4. Was this a repeated or independent measures design?

5. What variables were controlled?

6. Draw a bar chart to show the results.

The phenomenon of cue-dependency has important practical applications. Jerabek & Standing (1992) found that students taking exams in a different room from the one they studied in could enhance their recall in the exams by imagining their classroom. This is called *context reinstatement*. In similar vein Cassaday *et al.* (2002) tested the effect of arousal and relaxation on students' (40 undergraduates and 40 nine- to ten-year-olds) recall of learned material. They found that students' recall of the material was better when they were in the same state of arousal as at the point of learning. This was particularly true when the students were relaxed.

State dependency also has clinical applications. In a fascinating recent study, Mystkowski *et al.* (2003) gave participants caffeine or a placebo while being treated for a phobia of spiders. A week later they were shown spiders, either with or without receiving caffeine. Those who had the caffeine during the treatment were much more likely to be afraid if they had no caffeine in their system when later shown the spider. It appears that they only remembered that they weren't afraid of spiders any more if they had the state cue of caffeine!

Although cue-dependency is probably the single most common reason for forgetting, there are instances that it cannot easily explain. For example, we retain a vivid memory for distinctive and emotionally charged events (called flashbulb memories), even though we may encounter relatively few cues after the event (Brown & Kulik, 1977). Neither does cue-dependency easily explain why we tend in general to recall happy memories better than unhappy ones.

Figure 3.15
Students who take exams in their classrooms have more memory cues

media watch

Shock tactics

Kevin Toolis
The Guardian 13 November 1999

Gary Meadows does not like the smell of roasting meat. It gives him bad thoughts. He says it gives him flashbacks to his days as a paramedic ambulanceman attending car crashes, seeing smashed skulls, mangled limbs and burning flesh.

Truth in the broken mirror

Gunter Grass
The Guardian 27 January 2001

Suddenly I was standing outside the closed bathing station, beside the entrance next to the kiosk, likewise chained and padlocked. And all in a moment I could feel once more the thrill of one of the modest pleasures of my childhood: lemonade crystals tasting of strawberry, lemon and lily of the valley. But the minute this refreshing drink began to sparkle in my memory it began to stir up stories, deceitful stories, which had been waiting, needing only a single word of recognition to bring them to the surface.

1. Explain how each of the cases described above might be a result of cue-dependent memory.
2. Think of an example from your experience of remembering details of something after you have the correct cues.

For & Against
cue-dependency

FOR
there is a wealth of experimental evidence to support the importance of cue-dependency in remembering and forgetting. For example Baker *et al.* (2004) showed that chewing gum, when both learning and recalling words, significantly improved recall. Tulving & Pearlstone (1996) showed that people recall words better if they are given category titles when recalling (semantic cues).

FOR
cue-dependency explains some common everyday experiences of memory. For example it explains the very common 'tip of the tongue' experience and the experience of returning to an old haunt and suddenly recalling events that took place there (because of the presence of sensory cues such as smells). It is thus very relevant to understanding our everyday experiences of forgetting.

FOR
cue-dependency has important practical applications, as we can enhance people's recall by introducing context or state cues. For example, Jerabek & Standing (1992) showed that students can enhance their recall of work in an exam by imagining their classroom.

AGAINST
cue-dependency is probably only an explanation of forgetting from long-term memory. Baker *et al.* (2004) found that chewing gum when learning and recalling words affected recall the next day but not immediately. This suggests that cues of this sort do not have a role in short-term memory.

AGAINST
cue-dependency is probably not a complete explanation of forgetting. It does not explain for example why some emotionally charged memories remain vivid in the absence of context cues or why we generally tend to recall happy material better than unhappy material.

Repression

Repression is one of the older explanations for forgetting, but it remains the subject of considerable research and sometimes-angry debate. Sigmund Freud (1894) proposed the idea that we forcibly forget facts or events that provoke anxiety or unhappiness, thus protecting ourselves from having to experience these negative emotions (see also p. 90). Freud believed that repressed memories remain active in the mind, although the individual is not aware of them, and that they can trigger symptoms. The tendency to use repression as a defence against negative emotions is acquired in childhood, a response to poor quality relationships with parents.

Repression can take a range of forms. At its most dramatic, repression involves the complete blanking out of highly traumatic memories. There are for example numerous recorded cases of people who suffered sexual abuse in childhood, then forgot their abuse throughout adolescence only to have the memory recur in early adulthood. More common is the general tendency to recall happy memories more easily than unhappy ones. On occasion we may recall events but repress the emotion attached to them.

"" Discussion of repression

Repression is debated in two different areas of psychology. The psychodynamic approach, which has continued to develop and apply Freud's ideas, most importantly in psychotherapy, is dealt with in detail later in this book (see p. 90). Here we are concerned with the cognitive view of repression.

Cognitive psychologists generally find repression a source of some frustration because it is so difficult to investigate using the sort of research methods most cognitive psychologists prefer. For ethical reasons we cannot experimentally traumatise participants to see if they repress the experience.

Or can we? Clearly we cannot deliberately induce real trauma, however there are now some ingenious experimental procedures designed to test memory for stimuli that make participants a little uncomfortable. In one such study Koehler et al. (2002) showed German students 50 words and recorded their galvanic skin response (GSR) as a measure of stress induced by each word. If repression occurred we would expect that the words producing the largest GSR responses were the worst remembered, and this was in fact what happened. An alternative approach to investigating repression involves the use of diaries. Walker et al. (1997) had participants keep a diary of pleasant and unpleasant events for a few weeks. When tested later they showed good recall of pleasant events but poor recall of unpleasant events, suggesting that these may have been repressed.

We can see then that there is some solid evidence for the existence of repression. However, there are also equally convincing studies that point against repression. When Berntsen (2002) asked students to recall highly positive and highly negative personal memories she found that they recalled central details of shocking events *better* than those of other events. This is the exact opposite of what we would expect if we used repression. More recently, Hadley & MacKay (2007) presented 16 students with taboo words such as *snatch*, *whore* and *prick*, and non-taboo words matched for length and frequency of use (e.g. *snack*, *wheat* and *plate*). The repression hypothesis would predict that taboo words would be recalled more poorly, however the opposite was found. Taboo words turned out to be more memorable! Studies like these do not demonstrate conclusively that repression does not occur. They do however show that under some circumstances the opposite takes place and the sort of memory we might expect to be repressed is in fact enhanced.

repression

FOR there is evidence from Koehler *et al.* (2002) that words that appear to be stressful to participants are poorly recalled compared to neutral words. This suggests that the stressful words were repressed, supporting the existence of repression.

AGAINST on the other hand Hadley & MacKay (2007) found that taboo words, which we would expect to be repressed, are in fact better remembered than matched neutral words. This calls into question the findings of Koehler *et al.* (2002) and the existence of repression.

FOR diary studies, like that of Walker *et al.* (1997), tend to show better recall of happy memories and poorer recall of unhappy memories. This suggests that the unhappy memories are being repressed, and thus that repression exists.

AGAINST on the other hand some studies such as that of Berntsen (2002) show that when participants are asked to recall shocking memories they recall more detail than for more emotionally neutral memories. This points against repression taking place.

REALlives

You have now explored a selection of ideas, theories, studies and research methods from the cognitive approach to psychology. We have also come across a number of real life issues that can be examined using a cognitive perspective. The aim of this section is to show in some detail how we can take an issue of real world importance and apply cognitive psychology to understand it. We will do this for you with one issue then challenge you to do the same with a real-life situation.

The reliability of eyewitness memory

Background

One of the ways in which cognitive psychology has been put to use in the real world is in understanding the accuracy of eyewitness testimony. The outcome of many criminal trials hinges upon the accounts of crimes provided by witnesses. However, In the 1970s a series of experiments by American cognitive psychologist Elizabeth Loftus called the accuracy of eyewitness testimony into question. Loftus applied Bartlett's idea of reconstructive memory to show how memory for events can be distorted, in particular by the sort of questions asked of witnesses. Remember that according to the reconstructive memory model, when we remember something we access not only memory itself, but also all the relevant information we have access to. Following questioning, the information contained in the questions forms part of the information we can access when we try to reconstruct a memory. This is an example of post-event information.

Loftus (1975) tested whether misleading questions could lead participants to remember false details of a film. A piece of film showing a car that was involved in a crash was shown to 150 students. They were then presented with ten questions about the film. Nine of the questions were given to all participants but one differed. In one condition, the participants received the question 'How fast was the white car going when it passed the barn?' There was in fact no barn. In a control condition in which the equivalent question contained no misleading information, participants instead were asked 'How fast was the car going while travelling along the country road?' One week later the participants were given a further ten questions about the film, one of which was 'Did you see a barn?' Participants in the misleading condition, who had seen the question 'How fast was the white car going when it passed the barn?' were more likely to respond a week later by saying that they had seen the barn; 17% reported seeing a barn as opposed to less than 3% of the control group. This shows that witness memory can be seriously altered by post-event information in the form of misleading questions.

Figure 3.16
Loftus' research suggests that our memory for events like car crashes can be distorted by questioning

what's new?

The effect of co-witness accounts

Another important source of post-event information, which we use when reconstructing our memory for an event, is what other witnesses say happened. This means that as witnesses hear each other's stories, their accounts become more similar. This co-witness effect was an important aspect of the investigation into the Oklahoma bombing of 1995, in which 168 people were killed when right-wing anti-government terrorists bombed a Federal Building in Oklahoma City, USA. Memon & Wright (1999) studied what took place following the bombing. In one case a witness reported seeing McVeigh with a second man renting the truck that was used in the bombing. Although other witnesses had not reported this second man, following the publicity over John Doe 2, as he became known, they later came to believe that they had in fact seen him.

A recent study by Paterson & Kemp (2006) compared the power of leading questions and co-witness information as sources of post-event information. Participants saw a video of a crime and were questioned under one of four conditions. In a control condition they were not exposed to any inaccurate post-event information. In an experimental condition they were interviewed using misleading questions. In another experimental condition they discussed the video with stooges who fed them inaccurate information. In the final variation they read a report in which other witnesses were quoted giving misleading information. As we would expect the participants gave their most accurate accounts when exposed to no misleading information. Interestingly, both the conditions in which they were exposed to false accounts by co-witnesses led to greater distortion of recall than did the use of misleading interview questions.

Experimental reliability and validity

If you have read Chapter 2 on social psychology you will already know something about the terms reliability and validity in relation to the survey method. Surveys can be evaluated on the basis of their reliability – how consistently they measure something, and their validity – the extent to which they measure what they set out to measure. Experimental procedures can be evaluated on the same sort of criteria.

Reliability

An experimental procedure is reliable if it can easily be repeated and the same results are consistently obtained. Take the experiment by Elizabeth Loftus in which she gave students misleading post-event information to see if it distorted their memory. This procedure is highly reliable because it can be repeated easily with other groups of participants. Replications of the procedure have reliably produced similar findings. Field studies like that of Memon & Wright (1999) do not have the same reliability because they cannot be replicated – they require unique sets of circumstances that cannot be set up artificially.

Validity

Experimental validity can be divided into internal and external validity. The internal validity of an experiment is the extent to which we can be sure that changes to our dependent variable or variables are purely a product of our independent variable. This is why we control all variables other than the independent variable we are interested in (thus the environment, timings etc. will be the same in different conditions). Experimenter bias and demand characteristics also threaten internal validity but can be controlled by standard instructions and blind conditions. In an independent measures design internal reliability is threatened by differences between participants in the different groups. This can be controlled by randomly allocating participants to conditions or using matched pairs. In a repeated measures design order effects can be a problem but counterbalancing can control these.

External or ecological validity is the extent to which we can be sure that our results generalise from the experiment to real life. Field experiments are likely to have better ecological validity than lab experiments because they are carried out in a real-life setting. However to have really good ecological validity the tasks participants have to carry out also need to be similar to those we encounter in real life. The Loftus procedure falls down rather on both these criteria. Not only were the surroundings in which her experiment was carried out artificial, but the situation presented to participants with slides and misleading questions differed from the task faced by real witnesses. We could not therefore say that it had good external validity. Field studies like that of Memon & Wright (1999) have good ecological validity although their reliability is poor.

Applying cognitive psychology to understanding eyewitness memory

To the layperson, remembering something we've seen is a straightforward process, rather like playing a DVD. From that common sense point of view we might expect eyewitness memory to be accurate. However, having studied memory, you might begin to get a handle on why witnesses might not always remember accurately what took place. Levels of processing, reconstructive memory, cue dependency and repression theories can all explain to some extent why eyewitness testimony can sometimes be so inaccurate.

Levels of processing

Recall the levels of processing approach to explaining memory (p. 47). This approach suggests that we remember things well when they have been deeply processed, that is analysed for meaning rather than for structural or phonetic information. Clearly much of the detail witnesses are asked to remember is concerned with how people or objects looked. For example when Loftus asked participants to recall information about the appearance of a country road this information would only have been structurally processed. The same is true when asked about the appearance of people in real crimes. We would therefore not expect it to be well remembered.

Reconstructive memory

The reconstructive memory approach emphasises the active process of reconstruction that takes place as we retrieve memories. Reconstruction leads to inaccuracies in memory because we use all the information we have available to us when we reconstruct memories. This includes our existing schemas, sometimes leading to stereotyped recollections. If for example we believe that armed robberies generally involve sawn-off shotguns then, if we were to witness a few moments of a robbery we might afterwards remember seeing a sawn-off when none existed. We also tend to include post-event information when we reconstruct memories. This explains why our memories can be distorted by misleading questions and why memory-conformity occurs.

Cue-dependency

Research has shown that both our internal state and our surroundings when we store a new memory serve as memory cues, and that unless these cues are present when we recall the memory we often find ourselves unable to recall accurately. A problem witnesses have in recalling critical events at the Police Station or in Court is that both the surroundings and physiological state are likely to be quite different from those at the time of the events they witnessed. A technique called the cognitive interview or CI (Fisher & Geiselman, 1988) has been developed to try to maximise the memory cues available to witnesses. The CI is an interview procedure designed by cognitive psychologists in order to maximise the accuracy of witness recall. Its aim is to maximise the range of retrieval cues available to the interviewee without introducing post-event information that might distort the memory. Questions like 'how did you feel then?' are designed to act as state cues, reinstating the same mood as at the time of the witnessed event. Witnesses are asked to imagine as many details as possible of the setting in which the witnessed event took place in order to make use of context cues. They may also be asked to recall events from the beginning, the end and the middle in order to maximise the number of semantic cues available.

BBC News

Wednesday 24 August 2005
http://news.bbc.co.uk/1/hi/uk/4177082.stm

The aftermath of the shooting of Jean Charles de Menezes at Stockwell Tube station has shown that eyewitness testimony may not always be as reliable as it seems. On the day Mr Menezes was killed, a picture was quickly painted by eyewitnesses of a suspect who had vaulted over a ticket barrier, ran away from police, and had worn a bulky jacket that could have concealed a device.

Identification errors

According to the documents, Mr Menezes was wearing a light denim shirt or jacket, walked through the barriers having picked up a free newspaper, and only ran when he saw his train arriving. It has left many scratching their heads as to how the witnesses could have got it so wrong.

The reliability of eyewitness accounts of crime has proved a rich seam for psychologists and criminologists to mine over the years. Andrew Roberts, a lecturer in law at Leeds University specialising in evidence, said courts have recognised for a long time that eyewitness identification evidence is "inherently unreliable".

News reports

Witnesses' recollection of every aspect of an incident can be contaminated by what they hear from other people. Forensic psychologist Dr Fiona Gabbert has been working at Aberdeen University with Professor Amina Memon on the distortions in eyewitness recollection. "Memories are very vulnerable to error. If you witness a crime and then read a local news report everything can be combined in your memory at a later date," she said.

1. Use your understanding of reconstructive memory to suggest how pre-existing schemas and post-event information could have led to the differing witness accounts in this case.
2. How might we explain the poor witness memory using a levels of processing approach?
3. Why is it hard to recreate state and context cues for witnesses after an event like this?

Figure 3.17
Eyewitnesses recalled a range of different events when de Menezes was shot

Thinking critically

We should perhaps be a little cautious about applying the results of laboratory studies like those of Elizabeth Loftus and colleagues to real life. Often, studies of eyewitness memory for real events have found that witnesses do rather better than is the case in laboratory studies. Yuille & Cutshall (1986) followed up 13 of the 21 witnesses to a shoot-out between an armed robber and a gun shop owner in Vancouver, Canada. Five months later they were re-interviewed, the interviews including two misleading questions. They were unfazed by the misleading questions and produced highly detailed and accurate accounts. More recently, Riniolo et al. (2003) studied the eyewitness accounts of 20 survivors of the sinking of the *Titanic*, and found that in general they recalled events accurately. The stereotypical scene of a ship sinking is that it slides intact beneath the surface. In fact the *Titanic* broke apart and sank in bits, and 15 of the 20 witnesses clearly recalled this.

Figure 3.18
Survivors of the *Titanic* disaster generally did recall the fact that the ship broke up before sinking, in spite of stereotypical images of ships sinking in one piece

interactive angles

Go to the homepage of Gary Wells, currently located at www.psychology.iastate.edu/faculty/gwells/homepage.htm. You can download a range of academic and newspaper articles related to eyewitness testimony, in particular concerned with identifying suspects from line-ups.

exercise

Key ~~issue~~

Look at the following extract, which is concerned with the phenomenon of recovered memory. Sometimes adults appear to recover memories of childhood trauma, often though not always in therapy. There is plenty of literature around expressing extreme views about whether recovered memories are of real events or are in fact false memories. The British Psychological Society (1999) has advised that both real and false recovered memories probably exist.

'Remembering Dangerously'

Skeptical Inquirer March 1995

Like the witch-hunt trials of old, people today are being accused and even imprisoned on 'evidence' provided by memories from dreams and flashbacks, memories that didn't exist before therapy. What is going on here?

A woman in her mid-seventies and her recently deceased husband were accused by their two adult daughters of rape, sodomy, forced oral sex, torture by electric shock, and the ritualistic murder of babies. The older daughter, 48 years old at the time of the lawsuit, testified that she was abused from infancy until age 25. The younger daughter alleged abuse from infancy to age 15. A granddaughter also claimed that she was abused by her grandmother from infancy to age eight.

The memories were recovered when the adult daughters went into therapy in 1987 and 1988. After the break-up of her third marriage, the older daughter started psychotherapy, eventually diagnosing herself as a victim of multiple-personality disorder and satanic ritual abuse. She convinced her sister and her niece to begin therapy and joined in their therapy sessions for the first year.

The two sisters also attended group therapy with other multiple-personality-disorder patients who claimed to be victims of satanic ritual abuse.

In therapy the older sister recalled a horrifying incident that occurred when she was four or five years old. Her mother caught a rabbit, chopped off one of its ears, smeared the blood over her body, and then handed the knife to her, expecting her to kill the animal. When she refused, her mother poured scalding water over her arms. When she was 13 and her sister was still in diapers, a group of Satanists demanded that the sisters disembowel a dog with a knife. She remembered being forced to watch as a man who threatened to divulge the secrets of the cult was burned with a torch. Other members of the cult were subjected to electric shocks in rituals that took place in a cave. The cult even made her murder her own newborn baby. When asked for more details about these horrific events, she testified in court that her memory was impaired because she was frequently drugged by the cult members.

Explain using ideas, theories and studies from cognitive psychology why these memories might have appeared in adulthood. Bear in mind that recovered memories can probably be genuine or false. Why might genuine memories not have been available to the sisters for so long? Why also might such memories be false? You may wish to draw particularly on the ideas of repression, cue-dependency and reconstructive memory.

over to you

Your practical exercise for this approach is to design and carry out a memory experiment of your own. If you have read this chapter thoroughly you will by now know quite a lot about experiments. You can carry out this task individually or in small groups. The experiment should be related to a topic you have studied as part of the cognitive approach. For ethical reasons, steer clear of anything involving repression or recovered memories. Suitable examples of studies include the following:

- A levels-of-processing experiment in which you compare how well words are remembered after having been processed in different ways (see Craik & Tulving, 1975; p. 47).
- An experiment to see whether exposure to an active mobile phone affects students' ability to learn word lists (see Smythe & Costall, 2003; p. 54).
- An experiment to test whether words are lost from short-term memory on a first-in-first-out basis (see Gelkopf & Zakai, 1991; p. 59).
- A context-dependency experiment in which people learn words in a room and their recall is compared in the same room and in a different environment (see Godden & Baddeley, 1975; p. 66).
- An eyewitness testimony experiment in which you see how accurate people's memory is for a videoclip of a crime under two conditions.

You can be asked questions about this task in your exam, so make sure you clearly understand the following as you design your experiment:

1. What are you aiming to find out?
2. What are your independent and dependent variables? How are they operationalised?
3. What conditions are you comparing? What factors will be kept constant between the conditions?
4. What is your experimental hypothesis?
5. Will this experiment be carried out in a laboratory or in the field? What are the advantages and disadvantages of this method?
6. Will you use a repeated or independent measures design?
7. Will you randomly allocate participants to conditions (or if repeated measures the order of conditions)? See p. 68 for instructions.
8. What ethical considerations will you have to consider particularly carefully in this study? See p. 16 for a run-down of the BPS ethical principles.
9. When you have run your study, show your results by means of a table of central tendency and range, and box and whiskers and frequency distribution graphs.
10. Comment on the reliability and validity of your design.

Make sure that when you have carried out your experiment you keep a record of your answers to all these questions and a record of your findings as part of your cognitive approach notes.

interactive angles

If you haven't already done so, visit the *Your amazing brain* website at http://www.youramazingbrain.org/. You can find experiments here involving memory cues and eyewitness testimony that you can run online.

Conclusions

Cognitive psychology regards the human mind as an information-processing system, rather like a computer. Here we have looked at memory as an example of a cognitive function. There are a number of different ways of thinking about memory. Some think in terms of separate systems of short- and long-term memory. By contrast others explain memory in terms of levels of information processing. A third approach is to focus on the reconstructive nature of memory. How we forget information is of crucial importance to understanding memory. Repression is a defence mechanism in which memories associated with strong negative emotions are pushed out of consciousness to prevent the unpleasant experience of recalling them. Psychologists fiercely debate the existence of repression and evidence is mixed. The most common reason for forgetting is probably cue-dependency. We experience this when we require a cue that was present when the fact or event was stored before we can recall it.

There are many practical applications of memory research. One such application is in eyewitness testimony. There is some debate as to how accurate witnesses' memories of crime are. Most laboratory experiments have found considerable distortion to memory, in particular as a result of post-event information. However, the smaller number of studies conducted in real-life settings have sometimes painted a more positive picture. A related debate concerns recovered memories of traumatic childhood events.

what do I know?

1. Outline the central ideas of the cognitive approach to psychology. [6]

2. (a) Describe the levels of processing model of memory. [4]

    (b) Evaluate the levels of processing model. [4]

    (c) Compare and contrast the levels of processing approach with one other theory of memory. [6]

3. (a) Describe **one** study from the cognitive approach. [5]

    (b) Evaluate the study you described in (a). [5]

4. Evaluate **one** explanation for forgetting other than cue-dependency. [4]

5. (a) Describe **one** study into the accuracy of eyewitness testimony. [4]

    (b) Using psychological theory, explain how eyewitness memory can become inaccurate. [6]

what's ahead

By the end of this chapter I should know about:

- the psychodynamic approach to psychology
- Freud's view of the unconscious mind
- psychological defence mechanisms, in particular repression and *either* denial *or* reaction
- Freud's structure of personality
- psychosexuality and Freud's stages of psychosexual development
- two studies from the psychodynamic approach including the case of Little Hans (Freud, 1909) and *either* Axline (1964), Bachrach *et al.* (1991) *or* Cramer (1997)
- Freud's explanation of gender development
- applying Freudian theory to real-life situations

In addition I should understand:

- the distinction between qualitative and quantitative data
- the case study method
- issues of generalisability, credibility and ethics in the use of clinical case studies
- subjectivity and objectivity in research
- the use of longitudinal and cross-sectional research designs

Where does the psychodynamic approach take us?

↖ Slips of the tongue: what do they reveal?

← Toilet humour: what does it say about you?

↘ Shopping: what makes us choose melons?

↑ Adult baby syndrome: why do some adults like to wear nappies and drink milk?

↙ Homophobia: are homophobes secretly gay?

what's that ?

- **Unconscious:** mental processes of which we are not aware. In Freudian theory these include instincts and repressed memories

- **Conscious:** mental processes we are aware of

- **Preconscious:** mental processes we are not normally aware of but which can show themselves through dreams and slips of the tongue

The psychodynamic angle

The psychodynamic approach is one of the older approaches to psychology, having been developed as far back as the 1890s. It is concerned with the influence of the **unconscious** mind – that is the mental processes of which we are not consciously aware – on the feelings, thinking and behaviour of the individual. Different psychodynamic theories have different views of how the unconscious mind operates. In this chapter we are mostly concerned with the work of Sigmund Freud and his view of the unconscious.

The psychodynamic approach is also very much tied up with child development and our relationships with other people. Our reactions to people and events as adults (both normal and in the case of psychological problems) are seen in this approach as rooted in our early childhood experiences. Our early experiences of relationships with significant people such as our parents are of particular importance. Our early experiences affect us because memories of our past relationships and experiences remain in the unconscious and affect the ways we perceive situations and interact with people as adults. We can look at how early experience affects our unconscious responses to adult circumstances using a case study of executive coaching (Kilberg, 2004).

REALpeople

The case of Ron

Ron, a religious man in his mid-forties, sought executive coaching during a period as a temporary regional president in an American company. His boss had been removed some months before and Ron was covering his job but had not been permanently appointed to it. Ron expressed to his coach that he felt that his employers were treating him like 'a big jerk' (2004: p. 247). When asked if his situation reminded him of anything he had faced before, Ron recalled his grandfather's death. Ron's mother had regularly visited him whilst ill, however the grandfather was more concerned about his son, Ron's uncle, who had not visited. After the grandfather's death it turned out that the uncle had been stealing the grandfather's money for some time, leaving him with debts that Ron's parents took on, leaving them in poverty through Ron's childhood. The coach asked Ron how this memory might relate to his current position. Ron replied, 'that's easy now that I've remembered' (2004: p. 248). Following his childhood experience of having his uncle take advantage of his grandfather and parents he resented intensely any situation in which he saw himself as being taken advantage of. Following this revelation Ron was able to see his present situation more calmly and plan how to resolve the situation.

Prior to his coaching Ron did not know why his situation was making him so angry. However, it became clear that his memories of being taken advantage of as a child were having an unconscious influence on his reaction to his current situation. Once he was aware of this, i.e. it wasn't unconscious any more, he was able to respond more rationally to his circumstances.

Freudian theory

Sigmund Freud, who wrote from the 1890s to the 1930s, remains the best known and the most argued-about psychologist of all time. He developed a collection of ideas, which have together formed the basis of the psychodynamic approach to psychology. Freud was a therapist and his ideas are based largely on what his patients told him during therapy, together with reflections on his own life. Freud wrote on a wide variety of topics and developed his ideas throughout the period of his writing. It is not possible to look at all or even most of Freud's ideas in this chapter, but we can examine some of his more important ideas:

- The unconscious mind
- Dreaming
- Psychological defence mechanisms
- The structure of personality
- Psychosexual development
- Gender

Figure 4.1
Sigmund Freud

The unconscious mind

Freud was not the first person to propose that there is an unconscious dimension to the human mind, but he was the first to develop a detailed theory of how it operated. Freud distinguished between three levels of consciousness. These levels of consciousness are sometimes shown as the iceberg model. This is shown in Figure 4.2:

- The **conscious** mind consists of the mental processes of which we are fully aware, including memories that can easily be recalled and the more obvious motives underlying behaviour.
- The **preconscious** mind comprises memories that can be recalled to consciousness under particular circumstances.
- The true **unconscious** involves material that can never be recalled to consciousness, in particular instincts and deeply buried memories. There are two instincts of particular importance. *Libido* is the life instinct that manifests itself as sexuality. *Thanatos* is the death instinct, manifesting itself in aggression and destructiveness.

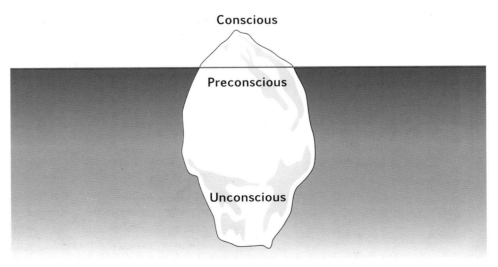

Figure 4.2
The iceberg model of consciousness

what's that?

- **Psychic energy:** a metaphor. Freud saw instinct and emotion as functioning like physical energy

- **Conversion disorder:** a condition in which patients under stress develop physical symptoms such as paralysis and sensory impairment in the absence of a physical cause

Freud (1915) suggested a number of ways in which the unconscious mind behaves differently from the conscious. There is no logic, hence opposite feelings such as love and hate can coexist without conflict. The unconscious mind makes no distinction between real events and dreams and fantasies. One object can serve as a symbol for another. Although we are not directly aware of our unconscious mind it exerts a constant influence on us, expressing itself in slips of the tongue, feelings for which we cannot logically account, dreams, irrational behaviour and psychological symptoms. Freud observed that many of our irrational impulses, dreams and symptoms take an aggressive or sexual form, and he explained this in terms of the influence of libido and Thanatos.

The hydraulic model

Freud saw emotion and instincts such as libido and Thanatos as having **psychic energy**, which functioned like physical energy – it could be stored, converted or discharged but not destroyed. This is sometimes called Freud's hydraulic model because it sees the mind as operating like a hydraulic machine. If our instincts are not satisfied or our emotions not expressed, psychic energy builds up and causes problems until it is discharged. This process of discharging psychic energy is called catharsis. A common psychological problem in Freud's time – rather less so today – was hysteria (now known as **conversion disorder**), in which patients lose the use of senses or motor abilities in response to extreme stress. This is illustrated by Breuer & Freud's (1895) case of Anna O.

REALpeople

The case of Anna O

Anna O was a 21-year-old woman. She was extremely intellectual in her interests. Her symptoms developed when nursing her father through a long illness. For the first five months of his illness Anna O devoted herself to caring for him, however her own health then deteriorated and she suffered weakness, anaemia and lack of interest in food. She became bed-ridden, and was thus unable to continue to nurse her father. It was at this point that her hysterical symptoms began. She had a range of symptoms, including headaches, a narrowing of the visual field, deafness, paralysis of the neck, and loss of sensation in the limbs. Just before her father died she also suffered speech-related symptoms, forgetting words, then becoming mute for two weeks.

Following the death of her father Anna's symptoms got worse. She suffered new symptoms including prosopagnosia (inability to recognise faces). During this period Anna also had symptoms of dissociation, displaying two personalities. One was anxious and depressed but aware of what was happening. The second was irrational and aggressive. At this point Anna was removed from the family home to a country sanatorium. Here she began what she called her 'talking cure'. This is the first recorded reference to the term and marks the birth of psychodynamic therapy. Breuer noted that when allowed to speak unchecked Anna tended to speak of events prior to the development of her symptoms, and that she would frequently link events to her symptoms. For example, she made an association between her deafness and an embarrassing childhood incident where Anna's brother had caught her listening at her parents' door one night as they had sex.

Figure 4.3
Anna O

During this process the symptoms would often worsen, however following the focus on each symptom it would disappear. Anna's deafness for example disappeared as soon as she had recalled the incident with her brother.

Breuer & Freud explained Anna's symptoms and treatment in terms of Freud's hydraulic model. Her frustrated intellectual abilities had led to a build-up of psychic energy. The trauma of her father's illness had triggered a process where this energy was converted into physical symptoms. When she talked to Breuer she underwent catharsis and so her symptoms were relieved.

Based on the Breuer & Freud article, the Anna O case appears to be a good illustration of the Freudian unconscious, clearly showing the hydraulic nature of psychic energy. However, there have since been various alternative interpretations of the case, in particular based on recent translations of Breuer's original case notes (Ramos, 2003). For example, Anna O's family had a history of schizophrenia. In addition, Anna O was prescribed high doses of morphine and a sedative called chloral hydrate. These factors could well have contributed to her symptoms. It is also worth noting that Anna had several later admissions to psychiatric hospitals, so Breuer's cure was rather less effective than he and Freud described in their book. The credibility of the Anna O case is thus poor. However, there is modern evidence for a link between conversion disorder and unconscious factors (see for example the study by Kanaan *et al.*, 2007, discussed on p. 90).

how **science** works

Research Methods

The case study method

The major research method used in the psychodynamic approach is the clinical case study. This stands apart from the other major research methods used in psychology in a couple of ways. One important difference is that the research aspect of the case is secondary to the more pressing aim of helping a patient or client in difficulty. Another key difference is that clinical cases tend to be written up after the event in order to *demonstrate a point*. This is quite different to experimental and survey studies, which are deliberately conducted in order to *find something out*.

Psychodynamic practitioners, who include some therapists (such as Freud) and some coaches (such as Kilberg), often write up their more interesting cases to share with colleagues. Typical case studies involve a background to the history and symptoms of the patient or client followed by a detailed description of the therapeutic work and the outcome. There will normally be some discussion of psychodynamic theory, and the practitioner-researcher will generally make interpretations of what took place in the light of theory. For example the Kilberg (2004) case illustrates the link between childhood experience and reactions to adult events.

Case studies are also used in other areas of psychology, usually for slightly different purposes than in the psychodynamic approach. For example in Chapter 3 we looked at case studies of brain damaged patients. These studies were carried out to test ideas that cannot easily be tested in other ways. For example if we want to know about the effects of damage to a particular area of brain we cannot deliberately harm people to find out. We must look at people who already have the type of brain damage.

Similarly in social psychology (Chapter 2) we are interested in real cases of destructive obedience. Although we can simulate these conditions in the lab (like Milgram did) we cannot directly test our ideas with real killings, so we look at cases where such killings have taken place.

Freudian slips

Freud (1914) suggested that one way in which we can observe the unconscious mind in action is during slips of the tongue. The influence of the unconscious mind leads us to substitute an unintended action (such as a word) for an intended one. This phenomenon is known as parapraxis or the 'Freudian slip'. Two of Freud's examples are shown in Table 4.1.

Table 4.1 Examples of Freudian slips (from Freud, 1914)

Situation	Intended phrase	Substituted phrase
A poor patient who had difficulty swallowing large pills made a request of Freud.	'Please don't give me big pills'	'Please don't give me big *bills*'
A patient was complaining how much harder it was for women to find a suitable partner than men.	'Men just need four straight limbs'	Men just need *five* straight limbs'

This type of *action slip* is now studied by cognitive psychologists. Reason (2000) has concluded that although there are many causes for action slips, a minority probably are true Freudian slips, reflecting the influence of the unconscious mind. He suggests that where the substituted word is more commonly used than the intended one it is most likely that the error is a simple cognitive one. However, whenever an uncommon word is substituted for a more common one then it becomes much more likely that it represents a true Freudian slip.

Dreaming

Another way in which the unconscious mind shows itself is in dreaming. Freud (1900) famously called dreams 'the royal road to a knowledge of the activities of the unconscious mind' (1900:769). He believed that dreaming performs important functions for the unconscious mind and that dreams give us valuable clues to how the unconscious mind operates. Freud suggested that the major function of dreams was the fulfilment of wishes. Freud distinguished between the *manifest content* of a dream – the scenes and 'story-line' that the dreamer is aware of, and the *latent content* – the underlying wish. The manifest content is often based upon the events of the day. The process whereby the underlying wish is translated into the manifest content is called *dream-work*. The purpose of dream-work is to transform the forbidden wish into a non-threatening form, so reducing anxiety and allowing us to sleep in peace.

Some dreams, particularly those of children, express innocent wishes and therefore no dream-work is required. For example Freud recorded the time when his 19-month-old daughter, after being sick and so not having had dinner, cried out in her sleep 'Anna F'eud, st'awberry, wild st'awberry, omelette Pap!' Presumably there was no need to disguise the child's wish for food. However adult dreams that express sexual and aggressive impulses

interactive angles

Looking back at the two examples in Table 4.1, apply Reason's rule. In the context of that situation which word is more common, the substituted or the intended? Are these likely to be real Freudian slips?

do require disguise for their latent content. Otherwise they would be too arousing and prevent us getting a good sleep. Memory of vivid, arousing dreams would also prove disturbing once we are awake, so Freud proposed that such dreams are *repressed* upon waking. Repression is discussed later in this chapter (p. 90).

media watch

Melons feel the squeeze at Tesco

Libby Brooks
The Guardian March 1999

The supermarket psychologists who brought us the theories of trolley daze and aisle alignment, who calculated the relative spend increase induced by the smell of freshly baked bread, have surpassed themselves: they have entered the realm of the psychosexual.

As a consequence, Tesco, Britain's biggest supermarket chain, has asked its suppliers to grow smaller melons after focus groups of shoppers revealed that shoppers subconsciously selected fruit according to the trend in breast size.

After investigating a marked drop in melon sales, a retail psychologist's report for Tesco suggested that the modern preference for smaller breasts, as modelled by superwaif Kate Moss, is informing customers' decisions to reject larger melons.

The possibility of a subconscious relationship between breast and melon size was first raised by a member of an all-female focus group, set up when Tesco buyers sought to find out why customers consistently picked the smallest fruit from store displays.

The theory was then tested by the retail psychologist, who found that seven out of ten women questioned agreed that 'breast size was the most likely subconscious factor when selecting size of melon'. Half the women went further, attesting that breast size was a conscious thought when choosing melons.

A Tesco spokesman yesterday said that the findings surprised him, but that the sales spoke for themselves.

'Since we introduced the smaller melons two months ago we have sold more than a million.'

Figure 4.4
Every little melon helps!

1. Explain using Freud's ideas about the unconscious mind why the retail psychologist might have found these results.
2. How convincing do you find this study?

how **science** works

Research Methods

Issues in the use of qualitative case study data

Subjectivity

Put simply, objectivity involves seeing what is really there. To get a bit more philosophical, to see something objectively is to see it as it would be if there were no one perceiving it. To be subjective means to look at something from the perspective of an individual, with the inevitable biases and distortions that go with that. We looked at subjectivity in relation to the survey method in Chapter 2. Recall that we said that as long as we are looking at peoples' feelings, opinions and so on it is right and proper that we gather subjective information. However, surveys are a special case and most of the time we are more interested in being as objective as possible. Indeed, one of the primary aims of science is to be objective. The clinical case study, the dominant research method within the psychodynamic approach, is one of the most subjective research methods in psychology. This is one of the reasons that many psychologists do not consider this approach to be good science. Researchers recording clinical case studies are inevitably subjective for several reasons:

- They know their participants extremely well. No one can study a person they know objectively.
- Psychodynamically trained practitioners interpret what they see in the light of particular theories. This sort of interpretation is the opposite of objectivity.
- Psychodynamic practitioners probably selectively record cases and aspects of cases that fit neatly with psychodynamic theory.
- Psychodynamic practitioners have a vested interest in recording and publishing cases that support their own perspective. This makes it hard to be objective.

However, although clinical cases are limited because of the degree of subjectivity involved, some researchers have brought more objective data to bear on psychodynamic theory. Take for example the studies of repression we referred to in Chapter 3. Experiments like this are therefore very important in giving the psychodynamic approach some credibility with other psychologists.

Generalisability

Clinical case studies are useful in illustrating how aspects of psychodynamic theory hold true in particular instances. They are therefore extremely useful for training purposes. Detailed information is gathered and recorded, and can be re-examined later by other researchers. A single, accurately recorded case *is* evidence that a phenomenon can occur. There are however some limitations to the method, and many psychologists consider clinical case studies to be poor science. Although a single well-recorded case demonstrates that a phenomenon can occur it does not tell us how common it is. This is a particular problem when we try to generalise from studying individuals with serious psychological problems to how everyone's mind works – as Freud did. When it comes to Freud's cases there is also some question about how well recorded they were. For example, Ramos (2003) has shown some serious shortcomings of Breuer & Freud's (1896) account of the Anna O case (p. 85).

Reliability and validity

Reliability means consistency. The issue here is that the sort of data we look at in psychodynamic case studies is very open to interpretation. Different psychologists are likely to make different interpretations of the same case material and so its inter-rater reliability will be poor. Validity is the extent to which we are really assessing what we set out to. Again, this is a tricky issue for psychodynamic researchers because we never really know to what extent an interpretation is correct. A therapist may interpret a dream or slip of the tongue as meaning one thing in particular, but there is no way to validate this interpretation. Interpretations that patients accept as true during therapy are more likely to help them get better, but this does not mean they are literally true.

Psychological defence mechanisms

Freud (1894) proposed that we use mental strategies called *defence mechanisms* to protect ourselves from painful, frightening or guilty feelings. Some of the major defences are shown in Table 4.2.

Table 4.2 Defence mechanisms

Defence	Description	Example
Repression	Forgetting an unpleasant memory or the strong emotion associated with it.	Childhood sexual abuse is frequently forgotten and rediscovered in adulthood.
Denial	Refusal to admit an unpleasant fact.	Patients who learn that they are seriously ill often refuse to accept their diagnosis.
Reaction	Adopting an attitude directly opposed to one's real feelings.	People who are afraid that they might be gay often adopt a homophobic attitude.
Projection	Shifting an undesirable emotion or motive from ourselves on to someone else.	People who envy someone else often claim that in fact that person envies them.
Displacement	Shifting an emotion directed at one person towards another person or other object.	Coming home angry at the boss and snapping at one's partner.
Intellectualisation	Using flawed logic to convince oneself there isn't in fact a problem.	Smokers often argue that there is no proof that smoking is bad for them.
Regression	Using the comforting behaviours typical of an earlier age.	People often cry, eat comfort food and become helpless in response to stress.
Sublimation	Using the energy of negative emotion to achieve something positive.	Artists and musicians often create their best work when desperately unhappy.

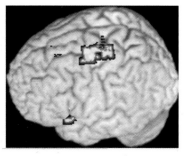

what's that?

- **Repression:** a defence mechanism in which we partially or completely forget

- **Depression:** a condition characterised by low mood and energy levels, often accompanied by disruption to eating and sleep

Repression

Repression is also discussed in Chapter 3, which deals with cognitive psychology, including the study of memory and forgetting. In Chapter 3, in keeping with the spirit of cognitive psychology we approached the issue from the experimental perspective. In this chapter we are more concerned with repression from the psychodynamic perspective, studied predominantly by means of clinical case studies. The term 'repression' applies to a range of related phenomena in which memory processes are used to protect us from unpleasant emotions. We can partially or completely repress entire events. We may thus have no conscious recollection of them, although more commonly we can recall the events with some effort. According to psychodynamic practitioners repressed memories can still exert a powerful influence on us. Bateman & Holmes (1995) give an example of repression in a man who came for therapy for **depression**. When talking about the death of his mother many years earlier, he suddenly remembered – for the first time as an adult – that his mother had committed suicide. Once he retrieved this memory his symptoms lessened. From a Freudian perspective his depression could be explained by the effort required to keep the memory repressed.

Repression is controversial for a number of reasons. One reason is the difficulty of researching repression using anything other than the case study method. Although there are a huge number of case studies in which people recovered memories during therapy that they had no access to for some years, you should by now be aware of some the limitations of case study evidence. A related reason is the inconsistency in the small volume of research findings using other methods. In Chapter 3 we looked at experimental studies and found conflicting findings. Some studies support the existence of repression while other equally credible designs do not (see p. 71). With our increasingly sophisticated understanding of the brain, a way forward is to examine the possible neural mechanisms underlying repression. A study attempting this comes from Kanaan *et al.* (2007). They made use of a case of conversion disorder, the same problem with which Anna O was diagnosed.

what's new

Studying repression in the brain

Until recently, certainly in Freud's time, there was no way to see the sort of unconscious processes the psychodynamic approach is interested in taking place in the brain. With modern technology however this is starting to change. This is illustrated by a study by Kanaan *et al.* (2007). A single participant took part in the study, a 37-year-old woman suffering numbness and weakness down her right side. Scans showed no evidence of a stroke, so it is likely that her symptoms were psychological in origin, perhaps like those of Anna O (p. 84). She was assessed for the severity of life events in the previous three months, and two events emerged with very high scores; a suicide attempt by her daughter and her partner announcing his intention to leave her. Interestingly, although the symptoms had followed immediately after her partner told her he was leaving, she insisted this was not significant to her. This suggested the possibility that she was repressing the trauma of the event. The patient then underwent brain scanning whilst answering questions about the two traumatic events and a non-traumatic control event (a visit to her sister).

Figure 4.5
A scan of the patient studied by Kanaan *et al.* (2007). Activity in the left motor cortex declined when the repressed event was recalled.

The traumatic event to which she attributed no significance was associated with a distinctive pattern of brain activity as compared to the other two events. Several areas of the brain including the amygdala (associated with memory) and the right frontal lobe (associated with thinking) were more highly active in response to the break-up memory. However at the same time there was a reduction in activity in the left motor cortex, which controls movement in the right side of the body. These results suggest that some distinctive neurological process took place in response to the trauma of the patient's partner announcing his intention to leave. This involved memory centres and the motor cortex, and appeared to show repression of the emotion associated with the event linked to loss of right-side movement.

Denial

Denial takes place when we refuse to admit the existence of a fact in the face of what would normally be sufficient evidence. This is often how people respond to bad news. Willick (1995) has provided a case of denial. A woman was brought into hospital two days after her husband died following a heart attack. She was convinced that he was in fact alive, and for some reason being kept from her by medical staff.

Freud believed that denial is often used to defend against anxiety about our sexual and aggressive instincts. In other words we deny these impulses because they are likely to be socially unacceptable. There is some evidence to suggest that we use denial in this way. Griffith (1999) analysed the case records of adolescent criminals for evidence of denial and found that this was more frequent among sex offenders, whose impulses are particularly socially unacceptable, than in other categories of offender.

Reaction

Reaction is an extreme form of denial. It takes place when we go a stage beyond not admitting something to ourselves and adopt an attitude that is directly opposed to our real feelings. The classic example of reaction is homophobia, in which people who worry that they might be gay deal with the resulting anxiety by adopting a harsh anti-homosexual attitude – this helps convince them of their heterosexuality. There are other examples of reaction: a religious person who suffers a bereavement might adopt a harsh atheist attitude to help deal with the conflict of belief in a benevolent deity and the loss of a loved one.

Like many Freudian ideas, defence mechanisms such as reaction have proved fairly tricky to test empirically, but there have been some imaginative attempts. Adams et al. (1996) demonstrated the role of reaction in homophobia by showing homophobic and non-homophobic men heterosexual, lesbian and gay pornography and measuring their sexual arousal using a penile plethysmograph, a pressure sensitive penis ring connected to a dial. As the penis enlarges, the pressure on the ring increases, and this can be seen on the dial. Over 80% of homophobic men were aroused by the gay scenes, as opposed to around 30% of non-homophobic participants. There was no difference in the rates of arousal in response to lesbian and heterosexual scenes. This suggests that homophobic attitudes may indeed be a defence against a fear of being gay.

Figure 4.6
A plethysmograph

Projection

We can project wishes and emotions, both positive and negative, onto other people. This allows us, as Freud put it, to get rid of them. Projection takes place when we behave unreasonably, for example shouting in an argument, then accusing the person we are arguing with of shouting. We can also project our unfulfilled needs on others. Anna Freud (1936) (Sigmund's daughter) gave the example of a woman who served as a 'matchmaker' in other people's relationships. Freud interpreted this as meaning she had projected her need for love on to others. Our conscience allows us to express emotions and needs in this way because they are not associated with the self.

Defences and adolescent identity formation

Although we all use psychological defences to some extent, Freud believed that over-use of particular defences was associated with poor psychological adjustment, self-esteem and mental health. There is some research to support this. One line of research has involved looking at the use of defences in adolescence. Psychologists studying adolescence from a psychodynamic perspective are particularly interested in the period as a time when we form our adult identity. Marcia (1980) suggested that adolescents surrender their childhood identity but have to acquire an adult identity. Marcia identified four identity states into which adolescents can be classified at any point:

- **Identity diffusion:** (usually early) adolescents who have not experienced an identity crisis or committed themselves to an adult identity.
- **Identity foreclosed:** adolescents who have committed themselves to an adult identity but through unquestioning acceptance of other people's values rather than following an identity crisis.
- **Identity moratorium:** adolescents currently experiencing an identity crisis and without any commitment to an adult identity.
- **Identity achieved:** adolescents who have experienced a crisis of identity but who have committed themselves to an adult identity.

Most of us begin our adolescence in a state of identity diffusion. Those who successfully manage adolescence reach the identity-achieved state. Emotional stability, self-esteem and mental health should be best in adolescents in the identity-achieved state. Phebe Cramer has looked at the relationship between adolescent identity status and the use of psychological defences. We can look at one of her studies in detail – see Classic Research.

Classic research
Optional

Cramer, P. (1997)

'Identity, personality and defence mechanisms: an observer-based study'

Journal of Research in Personality 31, 58–77.

Aim: To look for relationships between adolescent identity states and the use of projection and denial. Specifically, to test the hypothesis that individuals in foreclosed and achieved states make less use of defences than those in diffused and moratorium states.

Procedure: Forty-six female and 45 male young adults took part in the study. They were of mixed education and socio-economic status. Their

identity state was classified using a procedure in which observers attributed key terms associated with each identity state to each person. For example, the identity-achieved group were those given key terms such as 'dependable', 'ethically consistent' and 'productive'. Participants were also assessed for their use of denial and projection by means of a Thematic Apperception Test (TAT). This involves the participants looking at picture cards and making up stories based on them. Each participant was rated for denial according to leaving out obvious characters from stories, misperceiving what the cards showed, interpreting negative images in positive ways and seeing unexpected goodness or gentleness in pictures. Projection was rated according to how often participants saw hostility in the people pictured on the cards and adding scary people or objects not in the pictures into stories. Correlations between use of denial and projection and measures of each identity state were calculated.

Findings: Moratorium scores correlated positively with both denial (+0.3) and projection (+0.27). Diffusion correlated with denial (+0.2). There was no relationship between achieved score and defences. Foreclosure scores correlated negatively with denial (–0.34) and projection (–0.29).

Conclusion: Adolescents with a stable identity state (achieved or foreclosed) made less use of defence mechanisms than those whose identity state was less stable.

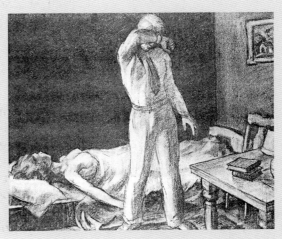

Figure 4.7
An image from the TAT

Studies like this are potentially very valuable in understanding adolescent behaviour. If an adolescent is visibly relying on denial and projection they may be difficult to get along with. Understanding their behaviour as part of adolescent identity formation might make this easier. The sample size and representativeness are strengths in Cramer's study. Potential weaknesses centre around her measures of defences. There is considerable debate amongst psychologists about the reliability and validity of tests like the TAT.

The structure of personality

One of Freud's most important ideas was that the human personality has more than one aspect. We reveal this when we say things like 'part of me wants to do it, but part of me is afraid to …' Freud (1923) tried to explain this type of experience by 'dissecting' (as he put it) the personality into three parts: 'I', 'it' and 'above-I'. Each of these parts represents a different aspect of the person and plays a different role in deciding on a course of action.

- **It** represents the instinctive aspect of the personality, present from birth. *It* operates on the pleasure principle – *it* wants to be satisfied, and *it* does not willingly tolerate delay or denial of its wishes.

- **I** is the aspect of the person that is aware of both the demands of *it* and the outside world, and which makes decisions. *I* can thus be said to operate on the reality principle. *I* develops through experience of dealing with the world, and has the capacity to think logically.

- **Above-I** is the aspect of the personality formed from experience with authority figures such as the parent, which poses restrictions on what actions are allowed. These restrictions represent the rules of society. Your *Above-I* can reward you with pride and punish you with guilt according to whether you go along with its restrictions. It can thus be said to operate according to a morality principle.

These three aspects of the personality are commonly called the **id** (it), the **ego** (I) and the **superego** (above-I). Figure 4.8 shows how the three aspects of the personality interact.

Freud's term	it	I	above-I
Common name	id	ego	superego
Aspect of personality	instinct	logic	society's rules
Operating principle	pleasure principle	reality principle	morality principle

Figure 4.8
Freud's three aspects of the mind

Freud (1933) saw this *structural* model of the mind as largely replacing his earlier *topographical* model of the conscious, preconscious and unconscious. In terms of the topographical model, the ego is largely conscious whilst the id is entirely unconscious. The superego exists in the conscious, preconscious and unconscious. We are fully conscious of the pride, shame, guilt we experience when the superego approves or disapproves of our actions. We are not conscious however of our memories of childhood when our superego develops.

Discussion of personality theory

Freud (1933) suggested that his model of personality had two major strengths. First, it provided an explanation for the experience of being pulled in different directions by different aspects of the self when making decisions, especially decisions with moral implications. *Phenomenology* is the study of human experience. From a phenomenological perspective, whether or not we can literally divide the mind into id, ego and superego, it is still valid to think of the mind in this way if it helps us understand human experience. Secondly, the idea of the *above-I* aspect of personality is useful in showing how relationships with others affect our personality. Someone with a harsh and punitive upbringing is thus likely to feel guilty a lot of the time – because the *above-I* aspect of their personality is powerful and punitive.

Jarvis (2004) has commented that the structural model is perhaps the most *complete* theory of personality achieved to date. This is because it shows the three major influences on human nature and on individual differences in our behaviour: instinct, logic and society. Modern evolutionary psychology tells us about the possible influence of instinct, cognitive psychology tells us about logic, and social and developmental psychology tell us about the influence of other people. No approach other than Freud's, however, suggests so neatly how instinct, logic and society all affect us. Of course psychology has come a long way since Freud's time in terms of how we see the influence of instinct, logic and society. Thus the Freudian views of instinct, logic and social influence all seem rather oversimple to modern psychologists.

For & Against

the structure of personality

FOR Freud has successfully described the experience of being pulled in different directions when making decisions. The structural model can thus be said to be helpful as a phenomenological model.

FOR Freud produced a very complete model of human experience. The concepts of id, ego and superego take account of the three influences of instinct, logic and society on both human behaviour in general and individual differences.

AGAINST ideas such as id and ego – and even instinct – are rather abstract and very difficult to study. Many psychologists are uncomfortable with concepts like this. If a concept cannot be studied scientifically its scientific status is poor.

Psychosexual development

Freud (1905) proposed that psychological development in childhood takes place in a series of fixed stages. These are called *psychosexual stages* because each stage represents the fixation of libido on a different area of the body. If this sounds slightly odd, it is important to realise that Freud's use of the word 'sexual' was quite broad in meaning, and he did not mean that the child experiences these instincts as 'sexual' in the adult sense. Libido is manifested in childhood as *organ-pleasure*, centred on a different organ in each of the first three stages of development.

The oral stage (0–1 year)

In the oral stage (the first year of life), while the child is breast-feeding and being weaned, the focus of organ-pleasure is the mouth. As well as taking nourishment through the mouth, children in the oral stage are taking comfort and their knowledge of the world via the mouth. We take away from the oral stage a number of 'oral characteristics', collectively known as *orality*. Oral characteristics can include an enjoyment of food and drink and attitudes of dependence, helplessness and acceptance. These attitudes represent on an unconscious level the relationship a baby has with the world. Oral characteristics also include aggression, representing the child's wish to bite. Oral aggression can manifest itself verbally (hence the term biting sarcasm) or physically.

We all take away a degree of dependent orality from our first year – without this we would not take an adult enjoyment in food and drink or in being dependent on the people we have relationships with. However, if the person experiences a trauma in the first year, for example a prolonged separation from the primary carer or a feeding difficulty, they can become fixated in the oral stage and their adult personality can become dominated by orality.

The personality characteristics of orality can be assessed by various tests. One of the most commonly used is the Rorschach inkblots (shown in Figure 4.9). The idea of tests such as the Rorschach is that we see different things in the images according to our own personality. The Rorschach can be used

Figure 4.9
A figure similar to a Rorschach inkblot

to assess various characteristics and scored in different ways, which vary in their reliability and validity.

The Rorschach Oral Dependency (ROD) scale measures the extent to which people see food, aggressive and dependency images in the inkblots. This is one of the more reliable scales that make use of the Rorschach inkblots (Bornstein *et al.*, 2000). A recent study by Huprich *et al.* (2004) attempted to test the validity of the orality concept by seeing whether it distinguished between offenders committing different crimes. As predicted, when sex murderers, non-sexual **psychopaths** and **non-violent paedophiles** were assessed for orality sexual psychopaths emerged as significantly higher than the others in oral aggression whilst the non-violent paedophiles were significantly higher in oral dependence.

The anal stage (2–3 years)

In the anal stage (years 2–3), the focus of organ-pleasure now shifts to the anus. The child is now fully aware that they are a person in their own right and that their wishes can bring them into conflict with the demands of the outside world. Freud believed that this type of conflict tends to come to a head in potty training, in which adults impose restrictions – for the first time in the child's experience – on when and where the child can defecate. Successful negotiation of the anal stage is what gives us the qualities of assertiveness and order. However, early or harsh potty training can lead to fixation in the anal stage, leading to an adult personality dominated by the three anal personality characteristics of stubbornness, orderliness and lack of generosity.

Studying age-related change

If we wished to study nowadays whether children actually shift focus from oral to anal at around one year there are two possible approaches. First, we could observe a group of children aged 0–1 and another group aged 1–3 and compare the extent of oral-related and anal-related behaviour in the two groups. This is known as a cross-sectional design. Alternatively, we could follow the same children from birth to three and track changes in oral-related and anal-related behaviour in each child. This is known as a longitudinal design. To summarise, a cross-sectional design involves comparing different groups of people of different ages whilst a longitudinal design involves following one group of people, seeing how they change with age. Longitudinal designs have the advantage that, as the same people are being studied at each age, results are not spoiled by differences between the people in different age groups. The advantage of cross-sectional designs is that they are considerably quicker.

Consider the following case study from Pate & Gabbard (2003) and answer the following questions, using your knowledge of Freudian theory.

Mr A was a white male aged 35 years. He lived alone in a flat. He worked in law enforcement, keeping his unusual behaviour a secret. He described himself as heterosexual but had not dated women for some years and had never had sex. He had previously sought a psychiatric evaluation but never followed up for treatment because 'the lady was mean' (2003: 1932). Mr A described himself as a baby. He had wanted to be a baby since the age of 12. Since the age of 17 he had worn nappies, in which he would urinate, defecate and masturbate. He frequently ate baby food and slept in a crib. He described wanting to 'be taken care of by a mommy who can hold me and rock me and give me a bottle' (2003: 1932). Mr A was the older of two children who had been adopted. He reported a good relationship with his adoptive parents, being generally closer to his adoptive father than his mother. He had never sought contact with his biological parents. In therapy Mr A frequently missed or refused to schedule appointments. He was also very conflicted between wanting to grow up and remain a baby. Although he reported seeking treatment in order to stop wanting to be a baby he demanded nappies on prescription and to be admitted by the psychiatrist to a nursery. Treatment failed in that Mr A decided in the end that he liked being a baby and did not wish to change.

Questions

1. What defence mechanism might Mr A be employing?

2. What evidence of orality can you see in the case?

3. What evidence of anality can you see?

4. Freud described the oral and anal stages as sexual in nature. What aspect of Mr A's behaviour supports this?

5. What childhood trauma do we know about that might be linked to his symptoms?

6. What evidence do we have that Mr A's adult behaviour might be compensating for a poor maternal relationship?

what's that ?

● **Oedipus complex:** the 3-way rivalry dynamic in 2-parent heterosexual families in which children attach strongly to the opposite sex parent and see the same sex parent as a rival for their love

The phallic stage (3–6 years)

By the start of the *phallic stage* (years 3–6), the focus of organ-pleasure has shifted to the genitals, as the child becomes fully aware of its gender. This coincides with a growing awareness of the child's exclusion from some aspects of its parents' lives, such as sleeping in the same room. The resulting three-way relationship is known as the **Oedipus complex**, named after Oedipus, who, in a Greek legend killed his father and married his mother (not realising who they were). In the Oedipus complex, a rivalry relationship develops between the child and the same-sex parent for the affection of the opposite-sex parent. Freud believed that on an unconscious level, a boy is expressing instinctive wishes to have sex with his mother and kill his father. This is not to suggest that children possess a conscious awareness of sexual intercourse or death in the adult sense. Freud was mainly concerned with writing about boys' development during the phallic stage. We return to his account of different development in boys and girls later in this chapter in the section on gender (p. 104). One of Freud's case studies, Little Hans (Freud, 1909) illustrates Freud's ideas about the Oedipus complex.

Classic research

Compulsory

Freud, S. (1909)

'Analysis of a phobia in a five-year old boy'

Collected papers vol. III, 149–295.

Background: Little Hans, a five-year-old boy was taken to Freud suffering from a phobia of horses. Freud's therapeutic input in this case was extremely minimal. Accounts vary as to how many times Freud saw Hans but it was probably only once or twice. Most of his information came from weekly reports by Hans' father.

Case history: From the age of three, Hans had developed such an interest in his own penis or 'widdler' that at age five his mother had threatened to cut it off if he didn't stop playing with it. At about the same time Hans developed a morbid fear that a white horse would bite him. Hans' father reported that his fear seemed to be related to the horse's large penis. At the time Hans' phobia developed his father began to object to Hans' habit of getting into bed with his parents in the morning. Over a period of weeks Hans' phobia got worse and he feared going out of the house in case he encountered a horse. He also suffered attacks of more generalised anxiety.

Over the next few weeks Hans' phobia gradually began to improve. His fear became limited to horses with black harnesses over their noses. Hans' father interpreted this as related to his own black moustache. The end of Hans' phobia of horses was accompanied by two significant fantasies, which he told to his father. In the first, Hans had several imaginary children. When asked who their mother was, Hans replied "Why, mummy, and you're their Grandaddy" (1909: 238). In the second fantasy, which occurred the next day, Hans imagined that a plumber had come and fitted him with a bigger widdler. These fantasies marked the end of Hans' phobia.

Interpretation: Freud saw Hans' phobia as an expression of the Oedipus complex. Horses, particularly horses with black harnesses symbolised his father. Horses were particularly appropriate father-symbols because of their large penises. The fear began as an Oedipal conflict was developing around Hans being allowed in the parents' bed. Freud saw the Oedipus complex happily resolved as Hans fantasised himself with a big penis like his father's and married to his mother with his father present in the role of grandfather.

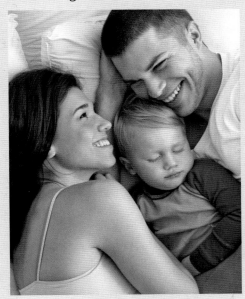

Figure 4.10
Freud saw the three-way relationship between parents and children as particularly important in child development

The case of Little Hans does provide limited support for the Oedipus complex. However, there are serious limitations with the case, above and beyond those always associated with clinical case studies. Hans' father, who provided Freud with most of his evidence, was already familiar with the Oedipus complex and interpreted the case in the light of this. It is also possible therefore that he supplied Hans with clues that led to his fantasies of marriage to his mother and his new large widdler. A further problem is that Freud ignored a more obvious explanation for Hans' fear of horses – he had recently witnessed the distressing sight of a white horse collapsing and dying in the street. In the light of this Freud's link between the fear of horses and the Oedipus complex seems less credible.

Later stages

Although Freud believed the adult personality to be largely formed by the end of the phallic stage he did propose two later stages of development. *Latency* runs from the end of the phallic stage until puberty. No psychosexual development takes place at this point as the child is focused on practical aspects of their development such as education. The difficulties of the Oedipus complex are repressed, allowing the child to have a happier relationship with parents. At puberty the child enters the *genital stage*. This is Freud's final stage, and represents the transition to psychosexual adulthood. The genital stage is a chance to revisit the early stages and resolve any remaining issues before moving into adulthood. Adolescence is often a difficult time for parents and children to get on with one another. According to Freud this is because anything not dealt with in early development comes back to haunt the parent–child relationship at adolescence. An unresolved Oedipus complex for example will cause child–same sex parent conflict. Discipline problems not sorted out in the anal stage are likely to resurface in adolescence as the child faces the same issues of increasing independence. Table 4.3 summarises the five stages.

Table 4.3 Summary of Freud's psychosexual stages

Age	Stage	Features of stage	Consequences of fixation
0–1	Oral	Libido attached to mouth Stage of nurturance	Smoking, eating problems, dependency, gullibility
1–3	Anal	Libido attached to anus Stage of conflict with authority	Anal personality characteristics of stubbornness, orderliness and stinginess
3–6	Phallic	Libido attached to genitals Oedipus complex	Sexual under- or overconfidence
6–puberty	Latency	No psychosexual development	
Adolescence	Genital	Earlier stages are revisited	

how science works

Research Methods

Ethical issues in published case studies

The publication of clinical cases can raise ethical issues, for example identifiability, confidentiality and potential embarrassment. Take the case of Anna O. Breuer & Freud's account of her condition and in particular its possible origins in childhood events could have been highly embarrassing to her should her identity have become public. Freud, like modern therapists, took steps to keep his patients anonymous, for example changing their name. Anna O's real name, Bertha von Pappenheim, was not released into the public domain until after her death in 1954, so it did not cause her personal distress, although it may have done so to her family. Whilst Kilberg's client, Ron, would be seen by most people to have no cause for embarrassment, the biographical details published might be sufficient for someone to recognise him. We can of course change some biographical details to make patients or clients harder to recognise but when we do this we take away from the realism of the case and make it less useful. Little Hans raises slightly different issues, being a child. Unlike adult patients, Hans was not really capable of giving real consent to have the details of his unconscious mind in the public domain, even if anonymously.

" " Discussion of psychosexual development

Setting aside for a moment the details of Freud's stages, his essential idea was that early family relationships and traumatic events affect our development. There is ample support for both the role of relationships and trauma in shaping our development. Massie & Szeinberg (2002) followed the development of 76 people from birth to 30 years. Quality of parental relationships was assessed in infancy and traumatic events were recorded throughout the 30 years. At 30, mental health was assessed using standard psychiatric measures. Mental health problems were moderately associated with poor parental relationships and strongly associated with traumatic events during childhood.

Because it operates unconsciously, psychosexuality is extremely difficult to study scientifically. However (bizarrely, you might think!) there is considerable support for the idea of anality. Numerous studies have found that the three anal personality characteristics cluster together in the same people (Jarvis, 2004). O'Neill *et al.* (1992) have gone a stage further and investigated whether the 'anal' personality type would respond differently to 'anal issues'. Forty women were assessed for the three anal characteristics and their responses to 'lavatorial' jokes. A positive correlation between anality and enjoyment of toilet humour emerged, suggesting that there is indeed something truly 'anal' about the anal personality! Anality is associated with other characteristics, for example right-wing politics. Maltby & Price (1999) assessed anality and political conservatism in 238 university students. There was a strong tendency for highly anal students to be politically conservative, suggesting that conservative politics may be the result of dodgy parenting in toddlerhood. It may be that the orderliness of conservative politics appeals to the anal personality.

Figure 4.11
The fact that children are unaffected by having same-sex parents suggests the Oedipus complex is not an important part of development

One idea that has been firmly rejected by modern psychology is the over-riding importance of the Oedipus complex. Remember that Freud believed that this is the most important aspect of psychological development. One way of assessing the Oedipus complex is to compare the development of children from single and same-sex parent families, who have no opportunity for Oedipal conflict, with that of children from two-parent heterosexual families. In a major review Golombok (2000) has concluded that there is no evidence of any deficit in the development of children who have not had the chance for Oedipal conflict because of their family structure. This clearly shows that it does not occupy the central place in psychological development proposed by Freud.

Brown & Pedder (1991) have suggested a useful way of thinking about Freud's stages of development. They suggest that Freud's labels of oral, anal and phallic were too narrow to describe what occurs in these stages. They suggested that we should think of the oral stage as a stage of complete dependency on the caregiver(s), the anal stage as a period of separation from the caregiver and the phallic stage as a time of passionate emotions in which a rivalry may form between the child and the same-sex parent for the affection of the opposite-sex parent. The concepts of dependency, separation and rivalry are extremely useful in understanding the developing relationship between a child and its parents.

For & Against
Freud's stages of child development

FOR   Freud was correct to say that our early years and our early relationships with our families are extremely important in affecting our development. He is also probably correct that the themes of dependency, separation and rivalry can be important aspects of the child's development.

AGAINST   Freud probably overemphasised the importance of body-parts, libido and the 'sexual' nature of children's development. Thus although his general ideas have validity some of the specifics of his theory probably do not.

FOR   there is fairly strong support for the existence of the oral and anal personalities. For example measures of orality reliably distinguish between different sorts of criminal. The three anal characteristics do tend to cluster in the same people and are associated with attitudes to body elimination and political views.

AGAINST   Freud appears to have over-emphasised the importance of the Oedipus complex. Modern research suggests that, even though three-way family dynamics of this sort do occur, they are not strongly associated with later psychological development. Evidence for this comes from studies of single and gay parent families in which the absence of an Oedipus complex appears to have no impact on development.

The correlational method

Two variables are said to be correlated when there is a measurable relationship between them. There are various types of correlation representing the different sorts of relationship two variables can have. A positive correlation exists when, as one variable increases, so does the other. When, on the other hand, as one variable increases the other decreases the correlation is said to be negative. The easiest way to show correlations is using a scatterplot. Figure 4.12 shows two scatterplots, one representing a positive correlation and one a negative correlation. On a scatterplot each dot, cross or star represents one participant. The stars are located level with the participant's score on each variable. The line of best fit is drawn at the angle where it comes closest to most dots. The closer the dots are to the line of best fit the stronger the correlation.

The correlational method lends itself to carrying out research in the psychodynamic method because we can measure psychodynamic characteristics such as orality and anality and look for relationships with other variables. For example, we have seen that anality correlates positively with enjoyment of toilet humour (O'Neill *et al.*, 1992) and with political conservatism (Maltby & Price, 1999).

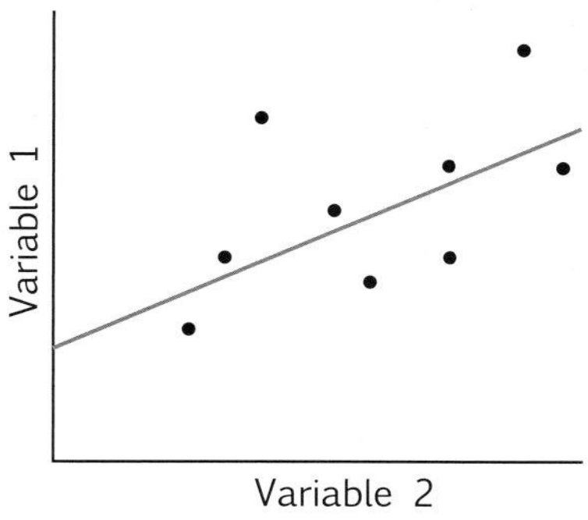

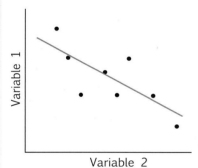

Figure 4.12a
A positive correlation

Figure 4.12b
A negative correlation

Correlational coefficients

Another way of showing the strength of a correlation is to calculate a correlation coefficient. This is a number between 0 and 1, or in the case of a negative correlation –1. The closer to 1 or –1 the stronger the correlation is between these two variables. Visit http://www.ruf.rice.edu/~lane/stat_sim/reg-by-eye/index.html and follow the links to experimental www pages and from there to correlation coefficients. If you play around with these Java applets you will see that the closer to 1 the correlation coefficient the closer points will get to the line of best fit. There are various mathematical formulae that you can use to calculate a correlation coefficient. For the sort of data gathered using tests for psychodynamic variables we recommend using a formula called Spearman's rank order correlation. To run a Spearman's test online, go to http://faculty.vassar.edu/lowry/VassarStats. html. Follow the link to Correlation and Regression on the navigation bar, scroll down to Rank Order Correlation and click on it. The first thing you will have to do is say how many participants you wish to enter data for. Enter 10 and scroll down the page until you come to Data Entry. In the Raw Data columns enter the following data.

Participant	1	2	3	4	5	6	7	8	9	10
Anality	6	9	2	8	5	7	6	4	2	6
Conservatism	23	30	12	30	20	26	26	15	10	25

Click on Calculate from Raw Data and look for the r_s box. The figure here is your correlation coefficient, in this case 0.97. Being almost 1, this is a very strong correlation.

Correlations and causality

Establishing correlations like this can tell us useful things, for example that highly anal people are generally more conservative. However, we need to be a little cautious – what this simple statistic does not tell us is the direction of causality, that is what causes what. It could be that anality causes political conservatism. Less obvious, but possible, it could be that political conservatism leads to anality. Alternatively, a third variable could influence both anality and conservatism and neither might affect the other. Faced with a single correlation coefficient like this we cannot say that anality causes conservatism, although we might believe it privately.

Given sufficient time to conduct our research there are ways around this problem. A simple approach is cross-lagging. To conduct a cross-lagged correlation between anality and conservatism we would measure each variable at least twice, leaving a reasonable interval between the measurements. We then correlate each variable measured early with each measured late. If early anality correlates more strongly with later conservatism than early conservatism does with later anality this suggests that the anality influenced the conservatism and vice versa.

Bringing it together: gender development

In this unit we compare three angles on gender development: the psychodynamic perspective, the learning theory perspective and the biological perspective. But what do we mean exactly by the term **gender**? In common speech 'gender' is often used interchangeably with 'sex' to refer to the male/female distinction. More strictly, 'sex' refers to biological differences between men and women whereas 'gender' refers to the social and psychological differences. Of key importance is the concept of *gender identity*. This is the individual's experience of being male or female.

From a biological perspective male–female differences are due to biology, so sex and gender mean effectively the same thing. The psychodynamic angle is a little more complex. Freud believed that gender differences and gender identity result not so much from biological differences but from the individual's *reaction* to those differences. To Freud the crucial events in gender development take place when children realise they do or don't have a penis.

Freud (1925) pointed out that both boys and girls realise by the phallic stage that they may or may not have a penis. Freud believed that this was threatening because it implied that the penis could be removed. Boys, who are at this point going through a phase of rivalry with their father for the affection of the mother, experience *castration anxiety*, fearing that their father will cut off their penis. To escape castration anxiety and resolve the Oedipus complex, boys identify with their father, taking on his gender role and experiencing a sense of maleness.

Having no penis girls go through a different process. When they realise that they lack a penis girls experience a sense of inferiority known as penis envy. They also blame the mother for having removed their penis. They are thus angry with her and experience an Oedipus complex, seeing the mother as a rival for the affection of the father. In the same way as boys, girls resolve the Oedipus complex by identifying with their same sex parent. They thus take on a female identity. Freud believed that girls' desire for a baby comes about as the substitute for wanting a penis, and that both babies and penises are symbols of social power.

""Discussion of Freud's account of gender

Freud's account of gender development is perhaps the least credible aspect of his work. While it is quite true that children aged 3–7 are particularly interested in genitals, they are generally aware of their own gender at a rather earlier age (Fagot & Leinbach, 1993). The concepts of castration anxiety and penis envy are extremely difficult to investigate scientifically and there is little credible scientific evidence for their existence. Feminists have also taken issue with Freud's view that girls feel inferior because of their lack of a penis and the idea that babies are penis-substitutes. By modern standards (though not by the standards of his time) Freud's theory is sexist. In fairness to Freud he did admit that his theory focused on male development because he did not understand women!

The credibility of the psychodynamic approach

The term 'credibility' refers to how believable and trustworthy a source of ideas and information is. We can separate out two questions from this definition of credibility; how believable are Freud's ideas and how trustworthy are his sources of evidence. Nobody doubts the historical importance of Freud's work, but there is enormous disagreement about how credible his ideas are. In fact it is fair to say that responses to Freud range from complete acceptance to complete rejection! Even by the standards of psychologists, who take part in fierce debates over many issues, responses for and against Freud are extreme.

The believability question

Some of Freud's ideas are rather more believable than others. The idea of the unconscious mind is believable because it fits with our everyday experiences, for example of dreams and slips of the tongue. The idea that we are influenced by our relationships with our parents is also highly believable. We can look at Kilberg's (2004) case study of executive coaching (p. 82) and see both these fundamental psychodynamic principles playing out in real life. Basic psychodynamic principles are thus quite believable.

The question becomes trickier however when we start to deal with the fine detail of Freud's ideas. There are some aspects of Freudian theory that very few psychologists dismiss entirely. Examples of more credible details of Freud's theory are seen in the defence mechanisms. Ask any doctor or police officer who has regularly given people bad news and they will tell you they have seen denial many times. Most of us will at some point have the experience of an argument with someone who projects by shouting at us that we are shouting! On the other hand some aspects of Freud's theory are distinctly unbelievable. The emphasis on unconscious sexuality, especially in child development, is perhaps the most dramatic example of this. The Oedipus and castration complexes in particular appear ridiculous nowadays. On the other hand, think back to the section on adult baby syndrome. This would be extremely difficult to explain without using Freud's ideas about psychosexual development.

Freud's ideas have won more favour amongst therapists than in academic psychology. Although there are a number of 'schools' of therapy (and some of these reject Freud's ideas utterly), many therapists have found an understanding of unconscious desires, defences, actions slips and dreams invaluable to understanding what is going on in the minds of their patients – see What's new?.

what's new?

Freud has more credibility with psychiatric patients

A recent study suggests that psychodynamic ideas have more credibility with psychiatric patients than the general public. This is interesting as it suggests that those with particular first-hand knowledge of what their unconscious can do to them see something in Freudian theory that many of us miss. Frovenhalt *et al.* (2007) compared perceptions of different theoretical approaches to psychology that underlie psychological therapies in the layperson and in psychiatric patients. A total of 119 participants were chosen from the population at large (a minority had had some contact with the mental health system); 115 psychiatric outpatients and 48 long-term inpatients also took part. A survey method was used. Participants were given descriptions of the theoretical basis of a range of psychological therapies including psychoanalytic psychotherapy. They were asked to rate the credibility of each from 1–5 and say which sort of therapy they would prefer to receive.

All three groups rated the theoretical basis of psychoanalytic therapy as less credible than that for the alternative therapies. However the difference was much less marked for the two groups with experience of the mental health systems. Preference for psychoanalytic therapy was much higher amongst the psychiatric patients. As compared with 15% of the general public that gave psychoanalytic treatment as their first choice of therapy, 23% of outpatients and 30% of inpatients ranked it as their first choice. Freud's ideas therefore have more credibility with people who have direct experience of mental health problems.

There are of course different interpretations of findings like this. The obvious interpretation is that people with experience of wrestling with mental health problems recognise the importance of Freud's ideas in a way that most of us cannot. On the other hand it may be that patients had already had some contact with professionals influenced by Freud, so the ideas behind psychoanalytic treatment were more familiar to them. There is of course a really cynical interpretation of these findings that says that that positive attitudes to Freudian ideas are irrational and therefore probably a product of patients' conditions.

The evidence question

One of the most important criticisms made of Freud concerns the sort of evidence on which he based his ideas. Looking back through this chapter we can see that Freud's ideas came from self-analysis and clinical cases studies. His explanation for dreaming came from a dream of his own and the Oedipus complex is based on Freud's own childhood memories. By modern standards

Go back through this
chapter and identify:

1. One idea of Freud's
   with clear supporting
   evidence.

2. One idea of Freud's
   that appears to be
   untrue in the light of
   modern research.

3. One idea that
   remains very hard
   to investigate
   scientifically.

single clinical cases and self-analysis are hopelessly subjective and therefore unscientific. It is important to realise that Freud was a medical researcher and so was familiar with other ways of gathering evidence, for example experiments. He was therefore not an incompetent scientist even though his methods were unusual. It is important as well to realise that Freud himself did indeed worry tremendously that he was not acting like a good scientist. Despite these worries, however, Freud was convinced that the methods of traditional science were too clumsy to investigate the subtleties of the unconscious mind.

Some modern commentators suggest that if Freud's methods were dodgy, then the entire basis of his theory is also dodgy and untrustworthy, and should be abandoned. Logically, if modern evidence for Freudian ideas exists that is scientifically acceptable to psychologists, then the original basis of Freud's ideas is not important. However, we have seen that in fact modern scientific evidence is quite mixed, and that even using the most modern and imaginative methods some of Freud's ideas are still extremely difficult to investigate. Yet another way of looking at this debate is to say that what really matters is whether the applications of Freudian theory – most importantly psychotherapy – work. If psychoanalytic psychotherapy can be demonstrated to help people then whether the theory on which it is based is correct is much less important. Evidence here is conclusive; psychoanalytic psychotherapy is helpful to many people (see p. 109).

REALlives

Key

You have now explored a selection of ideas and studies from the psychodynamic approach to psychology. We have come across some real life issues that can be examined using a psychodynamic perspective. The aim of this section is to show in some detail how we can take an issue of real world importance and apply psychodynamic theory to understand it. We will do this for you with one issue then challenge you to do the same with a different situation.

Should you have therapy?

Background

The major application of the psychodynamic approach to psychology is in providing psychological therapy to help people suffering mental health problems or life difficulties. There are now literally hundreds of 'brand name' psychological therapies available, of which psychodynamic varieties are among the most popular. There are a number of variations on psychodynamic therapy, the most intensive and long-term being *psychoanalysis*, which takes place 4–5 times week for several years. Psychoanalysis involves the patient (or *analysand*) free-associating, that is, saying whatever comes into their mind, including childhood memories, dreams, current life situations and feelings towards the analyst. The analyst responds to this with interpretations of the links between past experience, current problems and symptoms and nature of the patient–analyst relationship. Slightly less intense and long-term is psychoanalytic psychotherapy, which takes place 1–3 times a week, typically for a year or two. There are now also short-term varieties of psychodynamic therapy. What these therapies have in common is an exploration of the unconscious mind, in particular the links between current functioning and early relationships.

Figure 4.13
Traditionally patients in analysis lie on a couch facing away from the analyst

Psychodynamic techniques are also used with children. Long-term psychodynamic treatments for adults are now rarely funded in the NHS because of the cost of keeping someone in therapy over a long period, however child psychotherapy is still largely publicly funded. We can look in detail at a classic case of child psychotherapy, the case of Dibs – see Classic Research.

Classic research

Optional

Axline, V.M. (1947)

Dibs in Search of Self
London, Penguin

Background: Dibs was referred for therapy with a clinical psychologist when he was five years old. He was displaying a range of disturbed behaviour. At school he played alone, attacking any other children that tried to interact with him. He would become particularly violent with adults when anyone tried to take him home. Dibs' father was a scientist and his mother a surgeon. She had given up her practice when Dibs was born. Both parents believed that Dibs' behaviour was the result of some biological problem, either brain damage or retardation. However his teachers believed he was suffering from an emotional-behavioural disorder resulting from his poor relationship with his parents.

The therapy: In the first session Dibs revealed for the first time that he could read. He was painting and he read out the labels of different paints. At the end of the session he showed his usual reluctance to return home. In the next session (a week later) Dibs played with a doll's house. He closed all the shutters and doors and drew a lock on the front door. He spoke of this: 'A lock that locks tight with a key, and high hard walls. And a door. A locked door' (1947: 42). Dibs then played with finger paint, but commented 'Oh come away Dibs. It is a very silly kind of paint. Come away!' (1947: 44). In another session shortly after this Dibs told his therapist that he was glad to come to therapy but sad to leave at the end of each session. When the therapist asked Dibs if he took any of the gladness from his therapy home with him he responded by burying three toy soldiers in sand. He said 'This makes them unhappy. They cannot see. They cannot hear' (p.67). Dibs dug them up but said of

one 'this is papa' and punched it to the ground repeatedly. Dibs' father picked him up that day, and appeared to be embarrassed by Dibs, saying 'can't you stop that senseless jabber?' when Dibs tried to speak to him. When they got home after the therapy Dibs' father had commented that Dibs was 'babbling like an idiot', and Dibs attacked him and was locked in his room.

Dibs' mother came to see the psychologist and told her that Dibs had been an accident and that his birth had ruined her career and annoyed her husband. They both resented Dibs and found it hard to relate to a child. A week after this, in his next session Dibs took down the locked front door to the doll's house. He sang 'I hate the walls and the doors that lock and the people that shove you in. I hate the tears and the angry words and I'll kill them all with my hatchet and hammer their bones and spit on them' (1947: 85). Note the clarity of expression from a five-year-old who had been considered brain-damaged or retarded only a few weeks before.

During Dibs' therapy his behaviour at school gradually got better. He spoke to his teachers and began to show some interest in other children. However he was still angry with his father. Once Dibs asked to play in the therapist's office rather than the playroom. He dictated into her tape recorder: 'Once upon a time there was a boy who lived in a big house with his mother and father and sister. And one day the father came home to his study and the boy went in without knocking. "You are mean man," the boy cried. "I hate you. I hate you. Do you hear me I hate you." And the father began to cry. "Please," he said, "I'm sorry for everything I did. Please don't hate me!'" (1947: 159). Outside the therapy Dibs' relationship with his father improved. A week after therapy finished Dibs' IQ was tested and he scored 168, in the top 1% of the population. By then he had no symptoms of emotional difficulties.

Interpretation: Dibs' behaviour resulted from severe relationship difficulties with his parents, in particular his father. He displaced his anger towards them on to other children, thus becoming violent. During therapy Dibs expressed this anger in his play as well as his dislike of being locked up, one way in which his parents responded to his anger. Once he had expressed this anger and developed a good relationship with his therapist he was able to build a better relationship with his parents and regulate his emotions more effectively.

Applying psychodynamic ideas to understanding the benefits of analysis

From a psychodynamic perspective there are several factors that make psychoanalysis and other psychodynamic therapies helpful. What these all have in common is that they involve bringing unconscious influences to the surface, making the unconscious conscious.

Figure 4.14
Children in therapy explore their problems through play

Early experience and catharsis
From a psychodynamic perspective we are all unconsciously influenced to a greater or lesser extent by the nature of our early experiences, in particular traumatic ones. One of the key aims of psychodynamic therapies such as psychoanalysis is to loosen the hold these experiences have on us. Trauma can be remembered, re-experienced and worked through in the safety of the therapy room. This process is called *catharsis*. Catharsis is undoubtedly one of the factors that make all psychological therapies helpful.

Early relationships and transference
A key factor affecting our mental health and our ability to relate to other people in adulthood is the quality of our early relationships. In therapy, there is a tendency to play out the nature of our relationships with key people such as parents in our behaviour towards the therapist. This is called *transference*, because feelings towards important figures such as parents are being *transferred* onto the therapist. By feeding back to the patient how their current relationships are distorted by the influence of early relationships, the analyst can give the patient insight into what goes wrong in their relationships. Transference interpretation is arguably the most important technique in classical psychoanalysis.

Interpretation of dreams, action slips and defences
Transference is just one thing that can be fed back to patients in analysis to give them insight into the unconscious influences on their feelings and behaviour. Dreams and action slips also give away things that are bothering the patient, and interpretations of these can be fed back to them. Defences are also important because they can profoundly affect the way we interact with other people. The use of defences in therapy sessions gives valuable clues as to the patient's defensive style in everyday life. For example, someone who uses projection a lot is likely to spend a lot of time blaming and arguing with

others. Similarly, someone who uses denial a lot is likely to devote much of their energy to not facing problems head on. An analyst can give the patient feedback on their use of defences and help them modify their defensive style.

Thinking critically

There are two key questions to be asked when evaluating the usefulness of psychodynamic therapies such as psychoanalysis. First, does it work? Second, what are the downsides?

Does it work?

Yes. Although early studies (e.g. Eysenck, 1952) cast doubt on the effectiveness of psychoanalysis and other varieties of psychodynamic therapy in helping alleviate mental health problems, modern research paints a much more optimistic picture. The standard procedure in medicine for reaching conclusions about the effectiveness of a treatment is the systematic review. Systematic reviews work by choosing a set of criteria that studies of effectiveness have to meet, then locating studies that meet the criteria and drawing conclusions from their combined results. We can look at an example of a systematic review in detail in Classic Research.

Classic research

Optional

Bachrach, H.M., Galatzer-Levy, R., Skolnikoff, A. & Waldron, S. (1991)

'On the efficacy of psychoanalysis'.

Journal of the American Psychoanalytic Association 39, 871–913.

Aim: To review the findings of existing studies of the effectiveness of psychoanalysis and reach overall conclusions about its effectiveness.

Procedure: Studies were selected for inclusion in the review according to a set of criteria.

- The therapy studied was psychoanalysis
- The therapists involved were qualified and experienced
- Appropriate conditions were being treated
- Patients were assessed as appropriate for psychoanalysis
- Whatever variables were studied were defined and measured

adequately using quantitative measures

Seven studies met these criteria, making up a combined sample size of 1700 patients and 450 analysts. Conclusions were drawn from the combined findings of the seven studies.

Findings: Depending on how improvement is measured, between 60 and 90% of patients improve significantly during psychoanalysis. However, it is impossible to predict based on initial assessments, which patients will benefit.

Conclusion: Overall, psychoanalysis is of substantial benefit to the majority of patients.

At first sight this review looks impressive. Its combined sample size is large and the studies included were conducted by well-known researchers in institutions with good reputations. However, there were important methodological limitations. Studies were included that did not use control groups. This makes it difficult to say how many patients would have improved without treatment. Also, in some studies the data on the success of the therapy came only from the analyst who had conducted the therapy – they may have been biased in their judgements. These are serious problems that take away from the credibility of the review.

That said, more recent reviews of the effectiveness of psychoanalysis and psychoanalytic therapies have generally reached similar conclusions. Leichsenring & Leibing (2007) conducted a recent systematic review, including only studies that met much stricter criteria including randomly allocated control groups and independent judgements about improvement in patients. Twenty-four studies met the inclusion criteria, nine of long-term therapy and 15 of brief dynamic therapy. Of the 24 studies, 23 showed that psychodynamic therapies are as effective as the other standard therapies.

Are there downsides to being in analysis?

We might all benefit from freeing ourselves from the influence of our more negative early experiences. However, there are also some downsides to being in analysis. This type of therapy is expensive and time-consuming, and can prove very disruptive to patients' lives. Existing relationships can break down as the patient develops insight into the unconscious reasons behind their development. It has also been suggested that, for some of us at least, a more effective way of enhancing our quality of life is to focus on the present and future rather than on the past. This is what other, more recently developed psychological therapies do.

The subversive shrink

Nicci Gerrard
The Observer Review 31 October 1999

What is psychoanalysis? Will it heal you, or damage you further by forcing you to dwell upon those sorrows that are part of the human condition? When we feel unbearably sad should we pull up our socks or let down our defences and peer into that raw strange world we call our mind? Can we ever be cured of ourselves: all our fears of risk, of death and love and loss?

"No" says Adam Phillips. "No we can't." Phillips, the anti-Freudian Freudian, the psychoanalyst who deftly pulls out the rug from under psychoanalysis, is the nearest thing we have to a philosopher of happiness.

He thinks Freud offers us "one way of thinking about the things that trouble or perplex us". He is eloquently alert to the dangers of analysis. "It can be a refuge from life." His task is to turn the people who come to him away from their own interesting unhappiness back to the extraordinary vitality of the outside world.

"It [psychoanalysis] can be useful for some people with some pre-occupations. But it can be a refuge from politics — by which I mean group life. And it can induce you to be too fascinated by yourself."

1. What dangers does Phillips see in psychoanalysis?
2. Is he entirely negative in his assessment?

exercise

Key ~~~~

The psychodynamic approach is useful for explaining our more extreme and irrational behaviour. Many commentators influenced by Freudian theory try to explain the behaviour of influential individuals using psychodynamic ideas. This is called *psychohistory*. Look at the following extracts from an article by psychologist Oliver James, which is concerned with the life story of George Bush.

So George, how do you feel about your mom and dad?

Psychologist Oliver James analyses the behaviour of the American president, Tuesday 2 September 2003.
The Guardian

As the alcoholic George Bush approached his 40th birthday in 1986, he had achieved nothing he could call his own. He was all too aware that none of his educational and professional accomplishments would have occurred without his father. He felt so low that he did not care if he lived or died. Taking a friend out for a flight in a Cessna aeroplane, it only became apparent he had not flown one before when they nearly crashed on take-off. Narrowly avoiding stalling a few times, they crash-landed and the friend breathed a sigh of relief — only for Bush to rev up the engine and take off again.

A direct and loutish challenge to his father's posh sensibility came aged 25, after he had drunkenly crashed a car. "I hear you're looking for me," he sneered at his father, "do you want to go mano a mano, right here?"

As he grew older, the fury towards his father was increasingly directed against himself in depressive drinking. But it was not all his father's fault. There was also his insensitive and domineering mother. Barbara Bush is described by her closest intimates as prone to "withering stares" and "sharply crystalline" retorts. She is also extremely tough.

Not long afterwards, staring at his vomit-spattered face in the mirror, this dangerously self-destructive man fell to his knees and implored God to help him and became a teetotalling, fundamentalist Christian. David Frum, his speechwriter, described the change: "Sigmund Freud imported the Latin pronoun id to describe the impulsive, carnal, unruly elements of the human personality. [In his youth] Bush's id seems to have been every bit as powerful and destructive as Clinton's id. But sometime in

Bush's middle years, his id was captured, shackled and manacled, and locked away."

One of the jailers was his father. His grandfather, uncles and many cousins attended both his secondary school, Andover, and his university, Yale, but the longest shadow was cast by his father's exceptional careers there.

His moralism is all-encompassing and as passionate as can be. He plans to replace state welfare provision with faith-based charitable organisations that would impose Christian family values. The commonest targets of authoritarians have been Jews, blacks and homosexuals. Bush is anti-abortion and his fundamentalist interpretation of the Bible would mean that gay practices are evil. But perhaps the group he reserves his strongest contempt for are those who have adopted the values of the 60s. He says he loathes "people who felt guilty about their lot in life because others were suffering".

Figure 4.15
Oliver James uses psychodynamic ideas to understand George Bush

Explain George Bush's behaviour using ideas from the psychodynamic approach. You might wish to consider general psychodynamic principles such as the importance of early experience and Freud's ideas, for example the structure of personality, orality and the relationship with his mother, and the Oedipus complex.

We have already discussed sampling methods in detail in Chapter 2, which deals with the social approach to psychology. Note however that sampling can also be examined in relation to the psychodynamic approach. With this in mind, consider the following questions:

1. Psychodynamic case studies usually have only a single participant, and no attempt is made to choose a 'typical' person. Why is this a problem when case studies are used as evidence?

2. Look back to the Huprich study of orality in criminals (p. 96). Why would it be very hard to obtain a representative sample of each category of criminal?

3. Make sure you can explain what is meant by random, opportunity, self-selecting (volunteer) and stratified sampling methods.

over to you

Your practical exercise for this approach is to design and carry out a correlational study and write up your findings, showing your results using a scatterplot and correlation coefficient. As this study is potentially sensitive as regards ethics we recommend you carry it out as a whole class, and be absolutely sure your teacher has vetted the design before you carry out the study. You need to correlate self-report data, that is what people say about themselves. To get this you will need to devise two short questionnaires, one or both of which could possibly but not necessarily be related to psychodynamic psychology. Each questionnaire must be a rating scale, so you are using questions to generate a score for a variable. Remember that the sort of variables we might wish to measure related to this approach are usually very sensitive, and that you are ethically obliged to be sure you are not harming or distressing any of your participants. Remember as well that you will have to debrief your participants. Anything you or they would be likely to find embarrassing or stressful at this point is a no-no. With this in mind you should **NOT** attempt to measure any of the following:

✗ orality or anality
✗ signs of an unresolved Oedipus complex
✗ recall of traumatic childhood events or experience of recovered memories
✗ sexual orientation or homophobia
✗ mental health problems or experiences of therapy
✗ number or nature of sexual partners
✗ family history.

There are however some things that you could measure that are relevant to the psychodynamic approach, which don't raise too many ethical issues. These include:

✓ how well dreams are recalled
✓ credibility of Freudian theory
✓ belief that adult behaviour is affected by childhood experience
✓ belief in recovered memories
✓ credibility of psychoanalysis
✓ individual characteristics associated with anality such as orderliness or lack of generosity.

These can be measured by questionnaires of the type described in Chapter 2 (p. 27), or you could present participants with stimulus material and ask them to rate it, for example for credibility. Scores could be correlated with one another or with other variables such as age. It is tempting to formulate a hypothesis based on psychodynamic theory. For example, recalling very few dreams and according little credibility could both be signs of denial. A negative correlation between number of dreams recalled in a given time period and credibility of Freudian theory would support the idea of denial. However, this sort of study treads a delicate ethical boundary, and we would advise you to play safe. Safer correlations might be between age and orderliness or between credibility of Freudian theory and credibility of psychoanalytic therapies.

You can be asked questions about this task in your exam, so make sure you clearly understand the following as you design your study:

1. What is the aim of your study?
2. What are the two (dependent) variables you are measuring?
3. How are you measuring each?
4. What ethical considerations are you taking into account (see p16 for a run-down of the BPS ethical principles)?
5. What hypothesis are you testing?
6. When you have your results for each variable for each participant, plot them on a scatterplot.
7. Looking at the spread of your results on the scatterplot does there appear to be a correlation? Is it positive or negative? Does it appear to be strong or weak?
8. Go to http://faculty.vassar.edu/lowry/VassarStats.html and find the Spearman's rank order correlation. Enter your data here and produce a correlation coefficient. What does the coefficient tell us about your results?
9. Identify strengths and weaknesses of using a correlational design to gather and analyse this data.

Keep a record of your study under the following headings:

- **Procedure** – what you did, including how you communicated with your participants and took ethical issues into account, along with the details of the scales you measured your two variables on.
- **Sample** – details of who participated in your study, including age range and gender balance, and what sampling method you used to choose them.
- **Apparatus** – what tools you used in the study, including your two measures, the VassarStat website, etc.
- **Results** – your correlation coefficient and scatterplot.

Conclusions

The psychodynamic approach to psychology, and in particular the work of Freud, stands apart from the other major approaches in many ways. Freud's reliance on self-analysis and the interpretation of clinical cases is considered poor science by many psychologists. However, psychodynamic ideas have proved extremely valuable for people seeking to understand what is going on in the mind of the individual, hence they remain popular with therapists. As we have seen, some aspects of psychodynamic theory (such as reaction-formation, anality and repression) do have solid empirical support. Psychodynamic theory is at its strongest when applied to understanding irrational behaviour. There are thus behaviours, such as adult baby syndrome, that are probably best-explained using psychodynamic concepts. The major application of psychodynamic ideas is in psychological therapies. There is firm evidence showing that many people benefit greatly from psychotherapy based on psychodynamic ideas, although there are issues in long-term psychoanalytic therapies of cost and disruption to the life of patients.

what do I know?

1. (a) Describe in detail one study from the psychodynamic approach to psychology.

   (b) Outline **one** strength and **one** limitation of case studies.

2. Compare and contrast the psychodynamic and biological approaches to psychology.

3. How did Freud explain gender? How credible do you find his explanation?

4. What aspects of Freud's theory do you consider have good credibility?

5. Explain how we can understand one contemporary issue in psychology using two ideas from the psychodynamic approach.

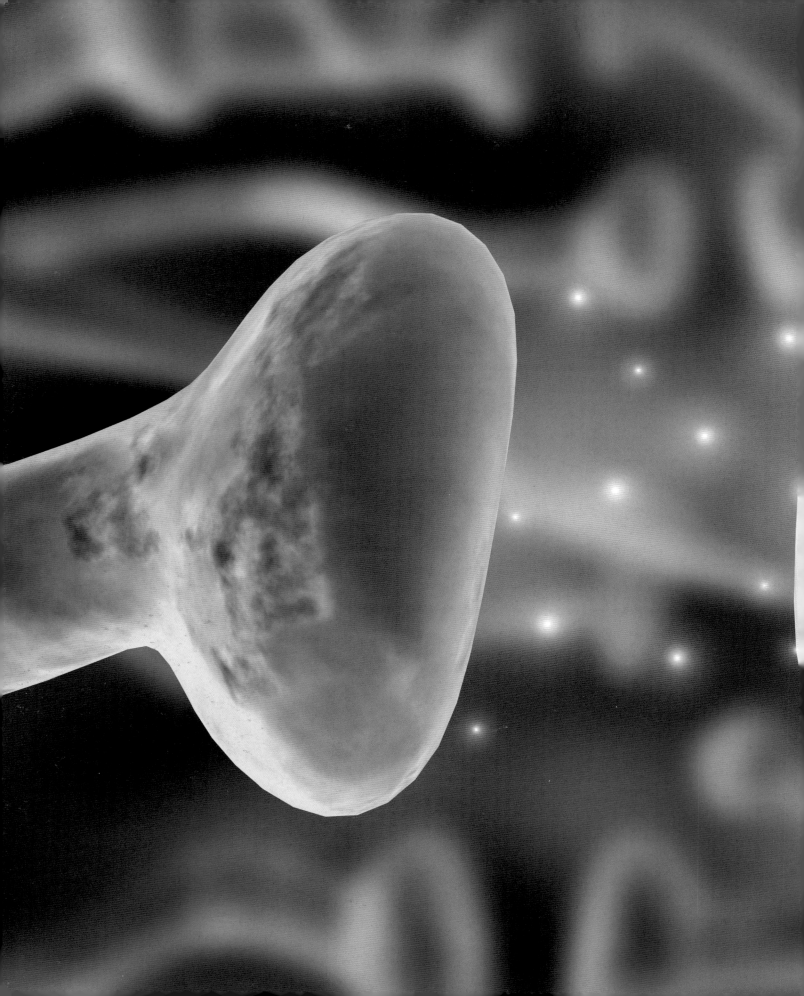

what's ahead?

By the end of this chapter I should know about:

- the biological approach to psychology
- the role of the central nervous system and neurotransmitters in behaviour
- the role played by genes in behaviour
- the importance of biological factors in gender development
- research by Money (1975) into gender development
- one other study from the biological approach: *either* Gottesman & Shields (1966), Raine *et al.* (1997) *or* Bellis *et al.* (2001)
- applying bio-psychological ideas to explain real life situations

In addition I should understand:

- twin and adoption studies
- PET and MRI scanning techniques
- how to use the Mann–Whitney U test
- when to use a control group
- levels of measurement
- why animals are used in psychology

where does the biological approach take us?

→ Sleep: is it dangerous?

↙ Placebos: do sugar pills make people better?

← Lying: can brain scans tell the difference between lies and the truth?

↓ Gender: are boys' and girls' brains the same?

↗ Directions: who should you ask: man or woman, gay or straight?

chapter **5**

The biological approach

- **Neurone:** a nerve cell. They send electrical messages, called nerve impulses, along their length

- **Neurotransmitter:** a chemical released at the end of a neurone to pass a message on to another neurone, a muscle or a gland

- **Localisation:** specific functions of the brain are controlled by particular, ie localised, areas of the brain

- **Genes:** units of information that are inherited from our parents. They control, or influence, characteristics such as risk of mental health disorders, personality and sexual development

The biological angle

The biological approach has its roots in the much older study of biology. Biological psychology therefore tries to explain how we think, feel and behave in terms of physical factors within the body. Two important biological factors involved in the control of human behaviour are the nervous system and genetics.

The nervous system, including the brain, is made up of special nerve cells called **neurones** that convey messages around the body. Within a neurone, the message is an electro-chemical one called a *nerve impulse*. However, there are minute gaps between neurones and purely chemical messages are passed between them. The chemicals that cross the gaps between neurones, called **neurotransmitters**, are an important way in which psychologists can study the function of the nervous system. The brain itself is organised by function, that is, it has regions devoted to different roles; this is called **localisation**. So another way that psychologists study the nervous system is to look at the jobs performed by different parts of the brain.

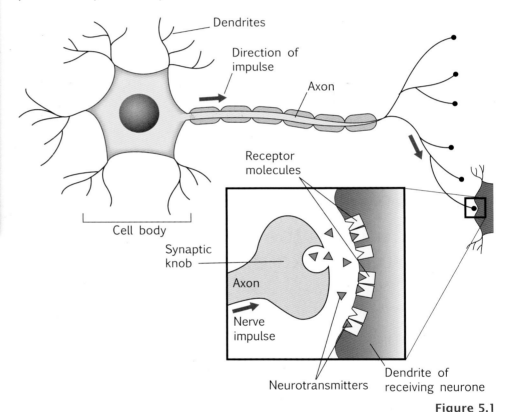

Figure 5.1
Neurones carry electrical messages. The cell body of a neurone is grey and, because there are many cell bodies in the brain, this is sometimes called 'grey matter'.

Our genetic make-up is also important in determining our individual characteristics, abilities and behaviour. **Genes** are the messages that we inherit from our parents that control aspects of our development. They are sections of strands of a chemical called DNA found in our cells. Genes control physical processes in the body. By doing this, some genes control specific behaviours, such as whether we are able to roll our tongue. However, it is vary rare for a single gene to control a particular behaviour that is of interest to psychologists. More typically, genes interact with one another to produce an effect on behaviour. Genes may also interact with environmental factors to determine behavioural outcomes.

The nervous system

Neurotransmitters

The whole of the nervous system is composed of interconnected neurones. These are long, thin cells, ideal for conveying messages from one place to another. The neurotransmitters are responsible for passing messages from one neurone to the next, crossing the gap between them called the synapse. Neurotransmitters are released from the end of one neurone, cross the synapse, and attach to receptors on the next neurone. When there are enough activated receptors, another nerve impulse is created and the message is passed on. The receptors are specific to each type of neurotransmitter and are shaped so that only one particular type of molecule can fit into them. For example there are different receptors for neurotransmitters such as acetylcholine, dopamine, serotonin, endorphins and endocannabinoids.

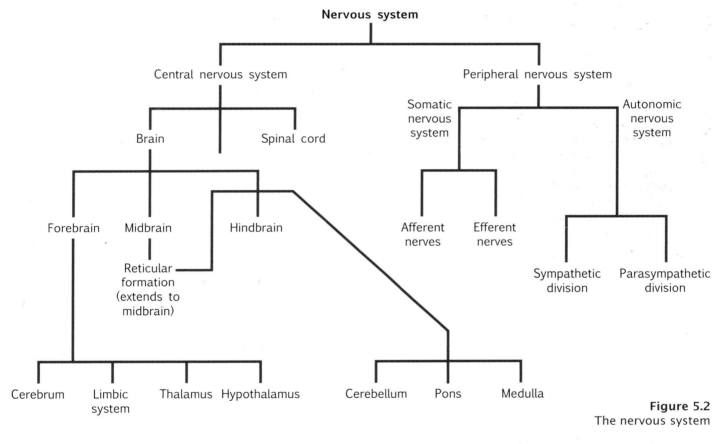

Figure 5.2
The nervous system

By passing messages on from one neurone to the next, neurotransmitters are directly responsible for our behaviour. They are crucial to both the functioning of the brain – which makes decisions about how we will behave – and the transmission of instructions from the brain to the body. Neurotransmitters therefore also have a direct effect on behaviours such as moving or sleeping. This can be most readily understood by looking at examples of situations in which neurotransmitter systems are used or are disrupted. For example, neurotransmitters from the group called *endorphins* are produced by the body in response to physical pain and psychological distress. When endorphin levels are low (due to genetics or habituation) other ways to reduce distress, such as drinking alcohol, become more frequent (Dai *et al.*, 2005; Volpicelli *et al.*, 1999).

The neurotransmitter *acetylcholine* is important in controlling voluntary movements. During dream sleep (also called Rapid Eye Movement or REM sleep) the activity of acetylcholine in specific parts of the body is blocked and we are paralysed. This prevents us from acting out our dreams. Since acetylcholine serves other important functions, this blocking is normally very precise. An area of the brain called the magnocellular nucleus appears to be responsible for sending signals to the spinal cord that prevent motor neurones from being activated. Sometimes, however, this system malfunctions. In the condition 'REM sleep behaviour disorder' the normal blocking of this neurotransmitter fails. As a consequence, the sleeper acts out their dreams. This condition is, for obvious reasons, dangerous for both the dreamer and their bed partner.

what's that?

- **Synapse:** the space between two neurones which is crossed by chemicals called neurotransmitters.

- **Receptors:** special locations on the surface of a neurone to which neurotransmitters attach and cause action potentials.

- **Central nervous system:** the brain and spinal cord which together organise communication within the body.

- **Spinal cord:** a collection of neurones that communicates between the brain and body, transmitting information inwards to the brain and outwards to the body.

- **Reflex:** a simple response to a stimulus. It may pass only through the spinal cord and not the brain.

media watch

A dangerous sleep

Judith Woods
The Daily Telegraph 18 October 2004

Figure 5.3
Cruel blow: Chris Sheldrick's musical career was cut short after an accident while sleepwalking

As a teenager, musician Chris Sheldrick's sleepwalking was a great source of amusement to his friends and family.

A former head musician at Eton, his disturbed sleep patterns were well known; he would often wake his fellow boarders with his blood-curdling howls, or be discovered by staff asleep in a cupboard or the laundry room. At youth hostels, he would clamber into strangers' beds in the middle of the night — to their consternation — or stroll through public areas dressed only in his underpants.

But a year ago, Sheldrick's sleepwalking took a tragic turn. One night, while staying with a friend, former BBC Musician of the Year Guy Johnston, Sheldrick, 23, severed eight tendons, a nerve and an artery in his left arm after punching a window pane. The accident was to spell the end of his promising career as a performer, as he was no longer able to play the clarinet, bassoon or piano properly.

"I couldn't remember what had happened, but by following the trail of blood, it was easy to deduce that I'd smashed the window, then wandered around the house before going outside, where I was stopped by the next-door neighbour," says Sheldrick.

"He'd heard the glass breaking and thought I was a burglar, but the fact that I was in my boxers convinced him otherwise. He took me into his house and saved my life. Because I had lost so much blood, I was losing consciousness."

1. Which neurotransmitter was faulty in Chris Sheldrick's brain when the accident occurred?
2. Would the level of this neurotransmitter be disrupted all the time, or only some of the time?
3. Which part of the brain could be responsible for the problem?

In another disorder, Parkinson's disease, production of the neurotransmitter dopamine is faulty. Because one of the roles of dopamine is the control of deliberate movements, these become difficult to produce and the patient becomes very rigid. One drug used to treat patients with Parkinson's disease is L-DOPA, which is converted into dopamine in the body and helps patients to regain spontaneous movement. As Parkinson's disease progresses, another neurotransmitter, GABA, is affected. This worsens the patient's symptoms.

media watch

Gene breakthrough for Parkinson's disease

Roger Highfield (edited)
The Daily Telegraph 22 July 2007

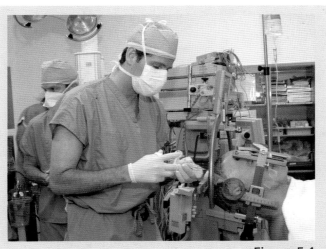

Figure 5.4
Dr Michael Kaplitt injects a virus into the brain of Nathan Klein

A major worldwide breakthrough in gene therapy was signalled last night after injections into the brain were used for the first time to successfully treat a degenerative brain disease.

In a pioneering study, researchers used the treatment to bring about significant improvements in the mobility of Parkinson's sufferers. The 12 patients involved in the study all reported a substantial reduction in their symptoms after having a human gene injected. Within months, their ability to move had improved on average by 30 per cent. Some reported a 65 per cent improvement in their mobility.

Parkinson's affects about 120,000 people in Britain, with 10,000 new cases diagnosed every year. It robs sufferers of the ability to walk and even eat, causes long motionless periods known as "freezing" as well as head and limb tremors. As the disease progresses, higher doses of drugs are required, leading to side-effects that include involuntary movements.

Parkinson's occurs when the brain cells – neurons – that release the messenger chemical known as dopamine die. Protein deposits also form in the brain, and levels of another messenger chemical called GABA – which calms overexcited brain cells – drop.

The study, begun in 2003, was carried out on 11 men and one woman with an average age of 58, who had all had severe Parkinson's for at least five years and for whom current therapies were no longer effective. They were given injections of billions of copies of a genetically altered virus into part of the brain called the subthalamic nucleus. The altered virus carried the human gene for an enzyme, called

GAD, which helps to make GABA. Once implanted, brain cells of the patients started to make the GABA chemical, said Prof During.

To show that the treatment was truly having an effect, the doctors injected the virus into the subthalamic nucleus of each of the 12 Parkinson's patients, but only on one side of their brains. One reason for this was out of concerns for the patients' safety, after deaths caused by gene therapy.

"This ground-breaking study represents not only an encouraging first step in the development of a promising new approach to Parkinson's disease therapy, but also provides a platform to translate a variety of new gene therapy agents into human clinical trials for many devastating brain disorders," said Paul Greengard, the chairman of the Neurologix Scientific Advisory Board.

1. Why was it important that the genes caused the production of GABA?
2. One reason for injecting the genes into only one side of the brain was health-related. Why might this have also been a good control to use in the study?
3. Why does this represent such an important step in developing new therapies?

how **science** works

Research Methods

Control groups

You will recall from Chapter 3 how to design experiments. One important aspect of experimental design is the role of a control group. The control group is a baseline to which an experimental group is compared. Whereas the experimental group(s) encounter the independent variable, this is absent from the experience of the control group. However, it is often important to ensure that the experiences are well matched. For example, if a researcher was looking at the effect of music on recall, they might compare some participants who are exposed to music (the experimental group) to others who are not. This looks like a control group, but it's not really controlling for anything – it's just the absence of the independent variable. A better control group in this case might be exposure to white noise at the same volume as the music that was played. This would control for the possible effect of interference by the volume of the sound rather than, say, the rhythm of the music or meaning of the lyrics.

In studies on the nervous system, such as the effectiveness of drug treatments, the control group is often given a 'placebo'. This is a 'sugar pill' or treatment that appears to be the real thing but which actually has no active ingredient. It is important that the control participants are given placebos and that they are unaware that these are not real drugs. This is because believing that you are going to get better may have an effect on recovery. If the participants were given no treatment at all, this effect would be missing. It is this possibility which the control group is cancelling out. Adams *et al.* (2005) conducted a meta-analysis of studies investigating the effectiveness of the drug chlorpromazine in the treatment of schizophrenia. After combining findings relating to 5276 patients treated with either the drug or a placebo control, they concluded that, although the drug was effective, a considerable placebo effect could also be seen. For example, relapse was prevented in 47% of patients taking chlorpromazine but 17% of those receiving a placebo also remained in remission. A similar pattern in seen in the treatment of obsessive compulsive disorder (Fineberg *et al.*, 2007 – see What's new?).

You will already have encountered hypotheses in earlier chapters. The experimental hypothesis proposes the difference or pattern that is anticipated in the results of experimental research. It is specific to the situation being tested. In contrast, the null hypothesis suggests that no such difference or pattern exists in the population being sampled. There are two important differences here. One is that the experimental hypothesis suggests a difference will be found, whereas the null hypothesis suggests that one won't. A second difference, which we will return to later in this chapter, is that the experimental hypothesis relates to the findings of the research whereas the null hypothesis relates to the population in general. Think about the experimental and null hypotheses that might have been used by Adams *et al.* above and Fineberg *et al.* (2007) (see What's new?). Remember that it is important to mention both the experimental and control group in your hypotheses.

what's new?

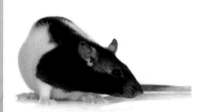

Figure 5.5
The neurotransmitter anandamide, like cannabis – a drug that mimics it – causes rats to move around less

Studies investigating the roles of neurotransmitters, receptors and the drugs that affect them can help us to understand how the nervous system works. For example, de Lago *et al.* (2004) investigated the effect of one neurotransmitter from the endocannabinoid group, that, is neurotransmitters that naturally attach to the same receptors that are affected by the drug cannabis. Anandamide is one of several molecules in this group and de Lago *et al.* showed that is has effects like cannabis – it reduces motor activity. The animals tested moved around less, explored less and spent more time inactive. Importantly, they showed that these effects could be reversed by another compound, called caspazepine. This acts by blocking the receptors so that anandamide could not have any effect. Finally, they checked these findings by looking at the electrical activity in the neurones, which confirmed that anandamide was activating the receptors and caspazepine was preventing this.

Studies of drugs used to treat psychological disorders can also help us to understand how the nervous system works. Fineberg *et al.* (2007) measured the effectiveness of the drug Escitalopram (used to treat symptoms of depression and obsessive compulsive disorder) in comparison to a placebo. A total of 468 patients with obsessive compulsive disorder (OCD) were initially treated with Escitalopram to see if there was any decrease in their symptoms. Of these, 320 responded to the drug and went on to the next stage in the study. These remaining participants were randomly allocated to receive either placebo or Escitalopram treatment. This allocation was double blind: neither the participants, nor the researchers rating their symptoms, were aware which group they were in. Within 24 weeks 52% of the placebo group and 23% of the Escitalopram group had relapsed . This shows that the drug treatment was very effective (2.74 times higher than the placebo). However, it also demonstrates that the placebo itself was effective – since 48% of the placebo group did not relapse either.

The central nervous system

The nervous system is highly organised. The central nervous system (CNS) consists of the brain and spinal cord. Connecting to the central nervous system are the nerves that serve the body. Some of these carry information about movement out from the brain, these are *motor neurones*. Others carry sensory information inward to the CNS, these are *sensory neurones*. One important pathway running between the body and brain carrying messages both inwards and outwards is the spinal cord which runs inside the backbone.

All reactions to stimuli, however simple, must pass through the central nervous system. A *reflex* such as touching a hot pan and moving your hand away involves three stages each with a corresponding type of neurone. The sensory information about the heat is detected and passed to the CNS by sensory neurones. They pass the message on to a relay or interneurone in the spinal cord. This in turn sends a message down a motor neurone to the muscles, which contract, causing you to withdraw your hand. This is the simplest type of behavioural response we can make – it doesn't even involve the brain (see Figure 5.6).

So, the role of the CNS is one of decision making and coordination. Incoming information must be understood and appropriate action initiated. For simple reactions, such as described above, the spinal cord alone can generate a response. When information is more detailed or decision making more complex, however, the brain takes over the processing role.

The brain

The human brain is an amazing organ. It is made up of vast numbers of interconnected neurones. The brain receives inputs through sensory neurones from each of the senses and about other information such as pain, balance and the position of the body. Information passes out of the brain via motor neurones to muscles but also to glands to instruct the release of hormones. In between these sources of input and output lies the brain itself, composed of interneurones. These form many connections, described as networks. These interconnections are essential to the enormous and varied processing capacity of the brain.

The brain is organised into many highly specialised areas. The hippocampus, for example, is important in the transfer of information from short- to long-term memory. As we will see later in the chapter, other brain areas may be important in the development of gender differences. Figure 5.7 shows a scan of the human brain in which you can see the detail of different structures. This view shows a section through the brain from the nose to the back of the head. The central 'core' is made up of the hind- and mid-brain. The larger, top part, on which you can see many folds, is the cortex. This is the outer layer of two halves of the brain called the cerebral hemispheres which lie on the right and left hand sides of the head (see Figure 5.8).

There are now a variety of techniques that produce images of sections of the human body. Such techniques have many medical applications but they have become well known to psychologists for their role in brain scanning. There are two broad categories of brain scan, *structural* and *functional*, which are discussed in How Science Works (p. 125). These methods are much better than earlier methods for investigating what the brain looks like and how this relates to the way it works. The first approach was to cut up dead human brains. This, however, could only tell us about brain structure and only when there was no longer a person to test for the skills or emotions of interest to

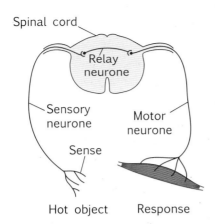

Figure 5.6
A spinal reflex arc

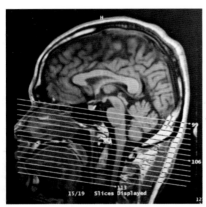

Figure 5.7
An MRI scan of the human brain

what's that?

● **Brain lateralisation:** the differences between the left and right hemispheres

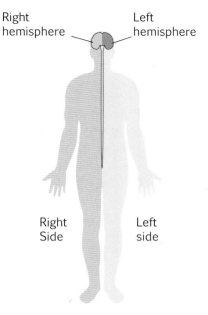

Right hemisphere   Left hemisphere

Right Side   Left side

Figure 5.8
The left hand side of the brain controls the right hand side of the body and vice versa

psychologists. In contrast, structural scanning allows us to look at images of live brains. We can then test the owners of those brains in order to look for relationships between the presence or absence of structures and an individual's behaviour.

Functional scans, however, offer a more informative way to link brain activity to behaviour. This technique measures changes in the level of activity in different brain areas while the behaviour is actually happening.

One of the things brain scans can be used for is to identify structural differences between the left and right sides of the brain. This is called **lateralisation**. In terms of functions, there are some that are replicated evenly on the left and right sides, such as the sensorimotor cortex. Other functional aspects are predominantly found on one side of the brain. A very clear example of this is language. For the vast majority of right-handed people, the language function is found in the left hemisphere. However, the reverse is not true for left-handers. Language is exclusive to the right hemisphere in less than 20% of left-handers and is bilateral (i.e. found in both halves of the cortex) in another 20%. In the majority of left-handers, however, language functions are found on the left as in right-handers.

how **science** works

Research Methods

MRI scanning

Magnetic resonance imaging (MRI) is a structural technique. It provides an image showing the details of structures inside the brain without actually having to cut through any tissue. It produces very high quality images either on film or a TV monitor. The scans look like a photograph taken of a slice through the brain. An example of an MRI scan is shown in Figure 5.7. MRI scanning uses a powerful magnetic field to influence the hydrogen atoms in water molecules. Positively charged particles in hydrogen atoms (called protons) act like compass needles so all 'point' the same way when the magnetic field in the scanner is turned on. Radio waves are then passed through the head by the scanner. As the protons return to their original positions they emit radio waves that are detected by the scanner. Different areas of the brain emit differing amounts of radio waves and this variation appears as different densities (shades of grey) on the image. If there are lots of hydrogen atoms, the area appears white, if there are very few it is dark.

During an MRI scan the participant lies down inside the scanner which is like a narrow tube and must keep very still. The environment is very noisy because of the powerful magnet, although the participant can hear and speak to the researcher through a headset.

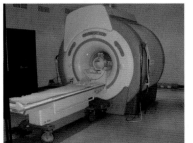

Figure 5.9 participant lies on the bed which moves into the tube of the scanner

MRI is of value to psychologists because it allows us to compare the structure of brains that are functioning normally and abnormally. Looking at these differences helps to establish whether a physical abnormality is responsible for a symptom. For example, damage to the brain resulting from a stroke or the presence of a tumour could be detected using such scans. Another use is to look at physical differences between the brains of younger and older people, or between men and women. Any differences visible on MRI scans could again help to explain behavioural or cognitive differences related to age or gender.

PET scanning

Positron emission tomography (PET) is a functional scanning technique. It records the activity of different parts of a working brain. Functional methods are more useful to psychologists than structural scanning because they allow us to visualise events that are actually happening in the brain. A PET scan involves injecting a molecule, called a tracer, into the blood stream of the participant. Tracers are radioactive versions of chemicals used up during brain activity, such as water or glucose. The tracer reaches the brain about 1 minute after being injected and takes 10–15 minutes to decay. As the tracer decays it releases minute amounts of radioactivity (initially in the form of positrons). The emission of radioactive particles is detected by the scanner (see Figure 5.22) and used to produce a record of the levels of activity in the brain tissue. By measuring the radiation levels in different parts of the brain we can determine where most blood is flowing to and hence which parts are most active. This radioactivity is in the form of gamma rays which are produced when the positrons collide with electrons. They are detected by a doughnut-shaped scanner that surrounds the participant's head. Greater levels of brain activity appear on the scan as different colours (see Figure 5.10).

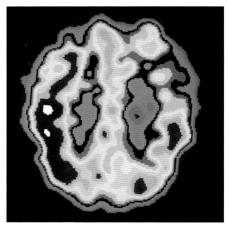

Figure 5.10
A PET scan of a brain

The participant is generally scanned several times in two conditions. One set of recordings is taken when they are inactive, as a baseline. Another set of records is made when they are performing a particular task. The difference between the scans tells us which parts of the brain are involved in that activity. This technique has enabled researchers to investigate active brain areas involved in tasks such as recognising different stimuli. For example, different brain areas are active when viewing famous faces and famous buildings (Gorno Tempini & Price, 2001).

PET scanning has also been used to study the brain areas involved in cognitive tasks such as remembering. Piolino et al. (2005) asked participants to recall relatively recent memories and some from longer ago. Their PET scans revealed that, although there was some overlap in the brain areas activated, the older memories also triggered activity in some different locations in the brain. Looking specifically at memories for smells, Djordjevic et al. (2005) compared PET scans when participants were actually smelling an odour and when they were just imagining it. They also found that there were some similarities and some differences between the brain areas that were active in the two tasks. In What's new? (pp. 128–29) we look at the use of PET scanning to investigate the effects of long-term drug abuse (Galynker et al., 2000) and how our brain responds when we lie (Abe et al., 2006).

Brain scanning can be used to investigate normal and abnormal brain function by looking at differences between responses to different types of information or in different brain areas. For example, normal differences between males and females have been investigated using PET scans. Jaeger *et al.* (1998) found differences in activity on the left and right side of the brain during a language task in men but not in women (see p. 147). Abnormal differences, such as in the brains of murderers (see Raine *et al.* (1997), Classic Research, below) have also been identified.

Classic research

Optional

Raine, A., Buchsbaum, M. & LaCasse, L. (1997)

'Brain abnormalities in murderers indicated by positron emission tomography'

Biological Psychiatry, 42: 495–508.

Natural born killers?

Aim: To investigate patterns of brain activity in murderers compared to a matched sample of non-murderers using Positron Emission Tomography (PET) to see whether there are differences in areas of the prefrontal cortex thought to be involved in violent behaviour.

Procedure: An experimental group consisted of 41 participants charged with murder or manslaughter who had pleaded 'not guilty by reasons of insanity' but had been convicted (referred to as 'murderers'). Their mean age was 34.3 years and there were 39 men and two women. A control group was matched for sex and age. Six of the murderers had a diagnosis of schizophrenia and were matched

to controls who were also diagnosed schizophrenics. No participants took any medication for at least two weeks prior to testing. Following a practice task, participants were injected with a radioactive glucose tracer, then did a 'continuous performance task' – a visual task which increases brain activity in the frontal lobes of normal participants – for 32 minutes. A PET scan was performed immediately after this, taking ten horizontal images through the brain at 10mm intervals. These scans were then used to indicate the level of activity in many different brain areas.

Findings: Significant differences in activity levels in many areas were found between murderers and controls. In areas such as the lateral and medial prefrontal cortex the murderers showed much less activity (see Figures 5.12a and b). Other areas showing

Figure 5.11
Do serial killers – like those depicted in the film *Natural Born Killers* – have different brains?

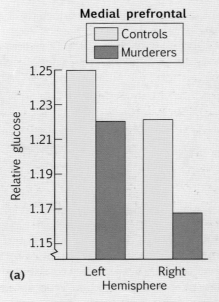

(a)

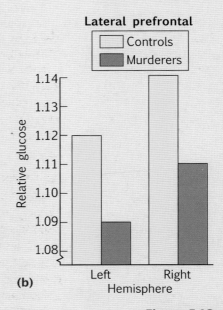

(b)

Figure 5.12
The level of brain activity indicated by the rate of use of glucose in murderers compared to controls

differences included the amygdala, thalamus and hippocampus. In some areas, such as the thalamus and the area surrounding the hippocampus there was a difference in lateralisation. In both cases the murderers' brains were more active on the right than the left. In the control participants' brains there was equal activity in both sides of the thalamus and in the hippocampus the pattern was opposite to that of the murderers, that is there was more activity on the left.

Conclusion: The areas identified as having abnormal activity are associated with a lack of fear, lowered self-control, increased aggression and impulsive behaviours and problems with controlling and expressing emotions. All of these could lead to an increased risk of committing acts of extreme violence. They are also linked to problems with learning conditioned emotional responses and failure to learn from experiences which could account for the type of violent offences committed. Finally, effects on areas associated with learning could lower IQ, which links to lower chances of employment and a higher risk of criminality.

what's new?

PET scans have been used to look at both normal and abnormal brain function. Galynker *et al.* (2000) used brain scanning to compare brain function in people with a history of drug abuse. Drugs like heroin (called opiates) affect the brain by mimicking neurotransmitters called endorphins. It is possible that prolonged use of such drugs may have long-term effects on brain function and this is what Galynker *et al.* were testing. They compared three groups of participants. One group did not have a history of opiate abuse. The other two groups did and had both received methadone therapy (treatment with a drug substitute). One of these groups had not abused opiates for four years. The participants were injected with radioactive glucose and PET scanned. Differences were found between the brain activity of the entirely drug free and non-user groups. The amount of activity in an area of the brain called the anterior cingulate gyrus was greater in the ex-addicts than in the non-user controls. The level of activity in the same area for the participants on methadone therapy was in between these two groups. Galynker *et al.* suggested two possible explanations for these findings. Either opiate use increases activity in this brain area or this pattern of activity reflects a predisposition to take addictive drugs such as opiates.

Abe *et al.* (2006) used brain scanning to identify brain areas associated with lying. Participants performed 20 tasks on a set of stimuli about which they could either lie or tell the truth about activities such as colouring in a tiger face and using two spoons as a musical instrument. They were then PET scanned and asked a series of questions to which they either lied or told the truth. Some of these related to 'old' stimuli, that they had seen before, for example saying 'I know' (meaning I know I have done this) to a coloured in picture of a tiger (as in Figure 5.13). In our example this would be telling the truth. Other questions related to 'new' stimuli for example saying 'I don't know' (meaning I don't know this stimulus) to a picture of a monkey. In each case they were instructed to lie on some trials (e.g. saying 'I don't know' to two spoons). Several brain areas were active during deception. In three parts of the prefrontal cortex this happened whether the item was old or new so these must play a general role in lying. A fourth area (the anterior cingulate cortex) was only active when the lies related to items which had actually been experienced and not when the items were new. This area seems to be specific to pretending *not* to know about something that has in fact been experienced.

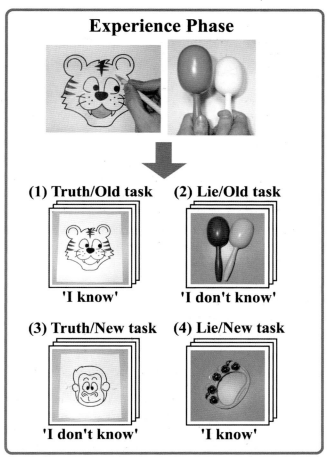

Figure 5.13
The brain responds differently when we lie about things we have done, e.g. 'playing the spoons' (2) and things we have not done, e.g. 'playing the bells' (4)

Figure 5.14
Older adults are less likely to be able to name objects when they are seen from odd angles.

MRI scans can also be used to investigate brain function and malfunction. This uses fMRI, a functional version of an MRI scan. Watanabe *et al.* (2007) used fMRI to investigate the parts of the brain involved in remembering music. They used new compositions to avoid the participants being familiar with the music. They found that the right hippocampus was particularly important in the accurate recognition of music. This is therefore a lateralised ability.

As we get old, we find it harder to remember the names of objects. Gigi *et al.* (2007) found that older adults were even worse at naming objects if they were seen from an unusual perspective. They then used fMRI scanning to investigate the brain areas involved in naming objects seen from usual and unusual viewpoints. They found that, in addition to the typical brain areas involved in vision and memory, two extra areas were used when naming things seen from odd angles (the prefrontal cortex and the cingulate gyrus). These findings suggest that the loss of ability to name things with age may be related to the shrinkage of the grey matter in the brain.

what's that ?

- **Hormone:** a chemical which is released from a gland, travels in the blood and affects target organs (e.g. muscles, sex organs or other glands)

Hormones

The nervous system is not the only communication system that exists within the body. We also have **hormones**: chemicals released from glands that circulate in the bloodstream. Together, these glands and their hormones form the *endocrine system*. Hormones, like neurotransmitters, attach to receptors. In the case of hormones these are on other parts of the body called target organs. Sex hormones, such as oestrogen and testosterone, are released by the gonads (sex organs). Oestrogen is produced by the ovaries in sexually mature females and testosterone is produced by the testes in sexually mature males (although a little of each is produced by both sexes). These hormones are responsible for many of the changes that occur around puberty, such as the deepening of the voice in males and the onset of menstruation in females. These changes are specific to certain parts of the body because these are the target organs, for example the breasts in females or facial hair follicles in males. The changes that hormones induce have psychological as well as physical consequences (see pp. 140–42).

how **science** works

Research Methods

Levels of measurement

As you will have seen in the studies described above, data can be recorded in many different ways. Numerical data can be classified into four different levels of measurement:

- Nominal
- Ordinal
- Interval
- Ratio.

> These initials spell 'noir' – a useful mnemonic

We record nominal data when totals are counted in two or more named, discrete categories. This means that the categories are unrelated – they do not lie on a linear scale. Asking someone to give a yes or no answer to a question produces nominal data as would a closed question about prejudice such as 'would you laugh at a sexist joke?'. When we classify people as left- or right-handed, or describe their personality as anal, oral or phallic, we are putting them into nominal categories. As you can see, it is possible to have more than two categories.

Ordinal data is represented on a linear scale, such as a rating or 'points' system. There is a clear increase in the value of points along the scale but the divisions between those points are not necessarily equal. For example, if we asked participants to rate their night's sleep as very poor, disturbed, somewhat interrupted, fair or very good, we could be sure that someone who answered 'very good' had a better night's sleep than a person who rated their sleep as 'fair'. We could not, however, be sure that the 'gap' between 'very good' and 'fair' was the same as the gap between 'fair' and 'somewhat interrupted'. In an ordinal scale, numbers may be allocated to points on a scale, for example the rating of sleep could be replaced with 'Rate your night's sleep from 1 to 5 (1 is best)'. Even though this is now a numerical scale, we still don't know if the difference between the ratings 1 and 2 is the same as between 2 and 3.

It is important to appreciate the difference between named categories in nominal data (which are separate) and names for points on a scale (which are related) in ordinal data.

In interval data, like ordinal, the points lie on a scale but here the gaps between the points are equal. If we ask participants to remember nonsense trigrams (like XKN) in a recall test, each one is equally memorable. The same may be true for some words, but not all. For example, it is likely that dog, ant, pig, hen, fox and cat are all equally easy to remember – they are all short, familiar animal names that are one syllable long. However, if the list included giraffe, hippopotamus and tyrannosaurus, it is unlikely that each item would be worth the same amount in terms of what it indicates about the participant's memory. This may be because some are longer than others, or more distinctive. In this case we could not say that the level of measurement was interval. Commonly used interval scales include measures of IQ and personality.

Ratio data, like interval data, has equal intervals between the points. The difference between the two is that on a ratio scale there is a true zero. This doesn't mean that it has to be possible for a participant to score zero, simply that the baseline for measurement begins at nought. Imagine a study that is investigating stress. One way to measure the effects of stress would be to measure pulse rate. Even our most relaxed participants at the start of the study would have scores considerably higher than zero, but the scale itself would be measuring from this point. To return to our example of remembering words – if someone could remember no words at all this might not mean they have no memory at all, but if a participant had a pulse rate of zero, it *would* mean they had no pulse at all.

interactive angles

There's a spider running across the floor of your psychology class. There are several different ways that you could measure whether each individual in the room was experiencing stress. Identify which level of measurement each idea represents:

- record the rise in their blood pressure
- ask them to answer the question 'Are you worried about that spider?' yes / no
- ask them to rate how anxious they feel on a scale of 1–5 (1 = most anxious)
- see how distracted they are on a task where they have to cross out every 'e' on a page of text and compare this to a baseline of how many they find when there is no spider.

Genetic influences

Do you know any families with several very tall or redheaded members? If so, this illustrates how physical characteristics run in families. Psychological characteristics can show this pattern too. For example some families have an unusually large number of highly intelligent or particularly bad-tempered individuals. Olson *et al.* (2001) used questionnaires to investigate individuals' attitudes to a range of variables including receiving the death penalty for murder, crossword puzzles, loud music, sweets, taking exercise, and their opinions of their own attractiveness. Olson *et al.* found evidence for genetic effects in 26 of the 30 variables they measured, with identical twins being the most similar. One possible cause of such patterns is heredity, and biological techniques are enabling psychologists to find out more about this influence on behaviour.

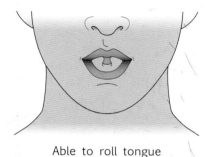

Able to roll tongue

Unable to roll tongue

Figure 5.15
Tongue-rolling – a genetically
controlled ability

Genes are units of DNA, passed from one generation to the next, which contain the information required to build biological structures such as neurones and the brain. It is relatively simple to understand how a characteristic such as eye-colour can be under the control of genes because it is obviously physical in nature. The question of how genes might affect psychological characteristics is a more complex one. It appears that genetic differences between people produce biological differences – that may be very subtle – which, in combination with their environment, lead them to develop into unique individuals.

Tongue rolling is an example of a simple behaviour that appears to be controlled in a very precise way by a single gene. This gene exists in two forms or alleles. One allele, T, is dominant. The other, t, is recessive. If a person inherits two recessive alleles they are unable to roll their tongue (Figure 5.15). It is possible for two parents who can roll their tongues to have a child who cannot (see Figure 5.16).

Tongue rolling is an unusual behaviour as there is little environmental influence. Generally, someone who isn't able to roll their tongue cannot learn. This physical control of behaviour is not typical of most psychological characteristics. Psychologists are interested in the importance of both genetics and the environment on our development. These influences can help to explain differences between people. This is sometimes referred to as the nature–nurture debate. The biological influence on our development is the 'nature' side of the argument – our development may be controlled by aspects of 'nature' through the genes we inherit. The influence of the environment on our development is the 'nurture' side of the debate. This reflects the extent to which our experiences determine our development. These include our food, physical activity and, importantly for psychologists, social factors such as our family environment and relationships and opportunities to learn. In real life it can be quite difficult to study genes and environment separately because people in the same family tend to share a similar environment as well as a similar set of genes. There are, however, various circumstances under which we can investigate the relative importance of genes and environment, including cases of twins and adoption.

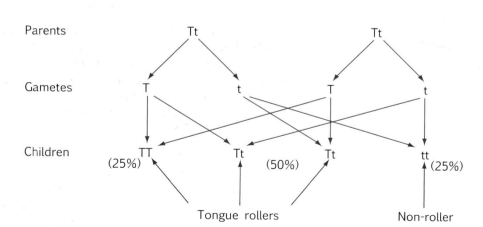

Figure 5.16
The genetic control of tongue rolling

Twin studies

Identical or monozygotic twins (MZs) share 100% of their genes. Fraternal twins or dizygotic twins (DZs) only share 50% of their genetic material. These facts give us the basis for two types of twin study.

Figure 5.17
Identical twins don't just look alike, they share exactly the same genes

Comparing MZ and DZ twins

One design of twin study involves comparing the similarity of MZs and of DZs who have been reared together so have experienced a similar environment. If genes control the characteristic being studied then MZs, who share all their genes, should be more similar than DZs. Gottesman & Shields (1966) conducted a study of this type (see Classic Research, p. 134).

Of course, if a characteristic were entirely a product of our genes, we would expect that both members of any pair of identical twins would always share that characteristic. This is not the case. However, the degree of similarity can be assessed by looking at the average of a large group of twins. To do this we use a correlation (which you will have learned about in Chapter 4). The characteristic (such as a personality factor) is measured and the scores of each pair of twins is compared.

If genetic factors are important in determining a characteristic then the score for one twin will be close to that of the other. So, if one twin has a low score, the other one will have a low score too – similarly with high scores. This would give a positive correlation (see p. 103). This pattern is represented by a single value, between 0 and 1, called the correlation coefficient. The closer it is to 1, the more similar the twins would be (see Table 5.4 for an example). This expresses the probability that both twins will share a characteristic and is referred to as the concordance rate. It can also be expressed as a percentage (see Table 5.3 for an example).

Separated twins

Another way to investigate the effects of genes is to compare the similarity of identical twins who have grown up in the same family or in different environments. If those who have grown up together are more alike than those who grew up apart this would support the role of the environment. Conversely, if the twins are alike despite being reared apart, this supports the importance of genes. Loehlin (1992) investigated the similarity in personality between MZs reared together and apart (see p. 136).

Schizophrenia is a serious mental disorder characterised by hallucinations, delusions and difficulty in thinking coherently. Evidence suggests that it is in part inherited (see Classic research – Gottesman & Shields, 1966).

Classic research

Optional

Gottesman II & Shields J (1966)

'Schizophrenia in twins: 16 years' consecutive admissions to a psychiatric clinic'

British Journal of Psychiatry, 112: 809–18.

Is there a genetic component to schizophrenia?

Aim: To investigate the relative importance of genetic and environmental influences on schizophrenia by comparing MZ and DZ twins.

Table 5.1 Twin type and sex of sample

	MZ	same-sex DZ	Total
Female	11	16	27
Male	13	17	30
Total	24	33	57

Procedure: Records of twins from the Maudsley and Bethlem Royal Joint Hospital provided a sample of 392 patients with twins of the same sex, born between 1893 and 1945 who had survived to age 15 (from a total of about 45,000 psychiatric patients). Of these, 47 had been diagnosed with schizophrenia by the hospital and a further 21 were subsequently diagnosed (giving a sample of 68). Of these, six were omitted leaving 62 individuals whose medical history was of interest (probands), 31 males and 31 females. In five twin pairs, both individuals were on the register so the total number of twin pairs used was 57. Each twin pair was assessed for zygosity (i.e. as MZs or DZs). This was done using blood group, finger prints and similarity in appearance. When last assessed the twins' ages ranged from 19–64, with a median age of 37 years. In addition to records of hospital diagnosis, the following information was obtained:

- case histories based on a self-report questionnaire and interviews with the twins and their parents
- tape-recorded semi-structured interviews to provide a record of verbal behaviour
- a personality test
- a test used to measure disordered thinking conducted on twins and parents.

Findings: Analysis of the data has looked for similarities between each proband and their twin. Concordance was assessed in three different ways:

Grade 1: both proband and co-twin have been hospitalised and diagnosed with schizophrenia.

Grade 2: both proband and co-twin have had psychiatric hospitalisation but the co-twin has a different diagnosis.

Grade 3: The co-twin has some psychiatric abnormality (e.g. out-patient care, GP care, neurotic or psychotic personality profile or being abnormal on interview).

The similarity, or concordance, is expressed as a percentage. There is a significant difference between MZs and DZs on all of these measures (see Table 5.2). On each of the three measures of abnormality, MZs are more similar than DZs. When these results were separated into males and females, the similarity between female twins was greater than male twins (e.g. concordance for Grades 1, 2 and 3 MZs was 91% for females and 69% for males. For DZs the concordance rates were 62% for females and 29% for males).

Table 5.2 Concordance for schizophrenia in twins of schizophrenics

	MZ		DZ	
Grade	N	%	N	%
1	10	42	3	9
1 and 2	13	54	6	18
1, 2 and 3	19	79	15	45
Normal	5	21	18	55
Total	24	100	33	100

Similarity was also analysed in terms of severity of schizophrenia. Severe schizophrenia was defined as having longer than two years hospitalisation and mild as less than two years. A total of 77% of co-twins of severe schizophrenics were themselves schizophrenic compared to only 27% MZ co-twins of mild schizophrenics. For DZs the figures were 15% and 10% respectively. The sample also included 14 pairs of MZ twins and 30 pairs of DZ twins where only one twin was diagnosed with schizophrenia. In several of these cases important environmental factors could be identified. In one pair the schizophrenic twin had suffered nutritional brain damage as a prisoner of war and had symptoms of brain damage. In another pair the non-schizophrenic twin had a much more stable adulthood. In this instance the schizophrenic twin had had two operations and divorced her abusive, bullying husband. The non-schizophrenic twin in contrast had had neither operation and had a kind, understanding husband.

Conclusion: Genes appear to play an important role in schizophrenia because the percentage of schizophrenic co-twins of schizophrenic probands is higher for MZs than DZs. The variation in severity of schizophrenia and the link to heritability suggests that the disorder is polygenic, that is, it is controlled by many genes. Since some MZs did not share a diagnosis, genes alone cannot be a sufficient explanation for the cause of schizophrenia. Other, environmental, factors must also be important such as physical and psychological sources of stress.

Following the research by Gottesman & Shields (1966), Gottesman (1991) investigated the influence of genes on schizophrenia by combining the results of 40 investigations spanning over 60 years. The results of this analysis are shown in Table 5.3.

Table 5.3 Concordance rates of identical and fraternal twins, Gottesman (1991)

Twin type	Concordance for schizophrenia (%)
MZs	48
DZs	17

You can see from the data of Gottesman & Shields (1966) and Gottesman (1991) that MZs have a much higher probability of sharing schizophrenia

interactive angles

Fink *et al.* (2003) found that the risk of smoking in 21- to 40-year-olds was higher for MZ twins with a smoking co-twin than for DZ twins with a smoking co-twin. The same was not the case for younger twins (aged 12–20 years). What could explain the difference between MZ and DZ twins and why might this only appear in adulthood?

than DZs. This tells us that schizophrenia is at least partially a result of genetic factors. Of course, if schizophrenia were entirely a product of our genes, we would expect that all the identical twins of sufferers would also have the condition. This means that there must be other factors at work. Several environmental risk factors have been suggested, such as having a dysfunctional family (Tienari, 1992) or a difficult birth (Torrey *et al.*, 1994).

Even though environmental factors appear to be important, genes clearly play a role in many psychological characteristics. For example, in terms of personality, even separated identical twins tend to be much more alike than two unrelated people (Loehlin, 1992). This demonstrates the importance of genes. The term extraversion refers to how impulsive and sociable we are. Neuroticism refers to being anxious and moody. Looking at Table 5.4, you can see that, although the personality of twins reared apart is less similar than those reared together, they are still more alike than we would expect if their genetic similarity were not a factor. Of course, this assumes that personality can be measured with sufficient accuracy to show up differences between different pairs of twins.

Table 5.4 Similarity in personality between identical twins reared together and apart. From Loehlin (1992)

Twin type and rearing condition	Correlation coefficient	
	Extraversion	Neuroticisim
MZs reared together	0.51	0.46
MZs reared apart	0.38	0.38

Later in this chapter we will look in detail at the biological factors affecting gender development. Here we will consider the idea that one causal factor in homosexuality may be genetics. This idea has generated considerable controversy. One research approach has been to look for specific genes that are linked to homosexuality. Genetic research makes use of identifiable pieces of DNA that are associated with particular genes known as genetic markers. The X chromosome (which both males and females have) sometimes has a genetic marker called Xq28 that is associated with homosexuality. Early research (e.g. Hamer *et al.*, 1993) was disputed but since then the research team has produced further evidence to support their initial results. For example, Hu *et al.* (1995) found that Xq28 was detected in families containing two gay brothers but not in ones containing two lesbian sisters. This suggests the gene is linked to homosexuality in males but not females. Note that it does not suggest that homosexuality in women has no genetic component, merely that this particular genetic factor only plays a role in determining sexuality in males. Another approach to investigating the role of genetics in sexual orientation is to conduct twin studies.

Bailey *et al.* (2000) studied 4901 Australian twins and found that concordance for homosexuality was 20% in male MZ twins and 24% in female MZ twins. The figures for DZ twins were much lower, suggesting a genetic component. However, the concordance rates reported for MZs in this study were considerably lower than in earlier studies (e.g. Bailey & Pillard 1991, 1995) which had found figures around 50%. Other recent research has also produced more conservative estimates (see What's new?).

what's new?

Kendler *et al.* (2000) investigated factors affecting patterns of sexual orientation in families. A total of 1588 twins were asked to identify themselves as heterosexual, homosexual or bisexual. The last two categories were then combined into 'non-heterosexual' for analysis. Non-twin siblings were also assessed. The concordance for non-heterosexual MZ twins was 31.6%. For same-sex DZ twins this figure was 13.3% and for all non-twin sibling pairs and DZ twins it was 15.1%. As MZ twins were much more similar than DZ twins or siblings, this shows that there is likely to be a genetic influence on sexual orientation.

For & Against
twin study methods

FOR   even though twins are quite unusual, twin studies have generated a very large volume of data. This makes the findings, which point towards important roles for both genetic and environmental factors, reliable. For example, Kendler *et al.* (2000) used a sample of 1588 twins.

FOR   twin studies suggest that genetic components may be involved in a wide range of psychological phenomena. For example, in addition to classic studies of the heritability of intelligence, personality or aspects of mental health, other behaviours may have genetic components. For example, Hettema *et al.* (2003) found that MZ twins were more similar than DZs in their tendency to become classically conditioned to fearful stimuli such as snakes and spiders, Fink *et al.* (2003) showed that older MZ twins have a similar more risk of smoking than younger MZs or DZs and several twin studies suggest a genetic component in sexual orientation and in schizophrenia.

AGAINST   the usefulness of data from twin studies depends on the instruments used to gather data, such as personality or IQ tests, being valid and reliable. Such psychological variables are, however, notoriously difficult to measure.

AGAINST   separated twins may have been separated at different ages, in a variety of circumstances and often not assessed for similarity until they are reunited. They may also have experienced a similar environment during the period of separation. These variations mean that it is difficult to know if similarities between separated twins are a result of genes or the environment.

AGAINST   studies showing that MZs reared together are more similar than DZs reared together have this problem too. Adults tend to treat MZs more similarly than DZs as they look more alike. It may be that sharing a more similar environment, as well as having identical genes, leads to the similarity between MZs.

interactive angles

Look up media articles about Xq28, dubbed the 'gay gene', and decide the extent to which they are representing the role of genetics in psychological characteristics.

how science works

Research Methods

Adoption studies

The most direct way to isolate the influence of genes and the environment involves adoption. If children are adopted into a different environment from that of their birth family we have a situation in which the children have the genes of the biological parents but an environment created by the adoptive parents. Similarities between the child and their biological parents would therefore suggest a role for genes. Similarities between the child and their adoptive parents in contrast suggest a role for the environment. To assess this, measures are taken of the behaviour or characteristic being studied, such as personality or mental health disorder. The child and their adoptive parents are compared. The children are often followed up in adulthood to see whether similarities between them and the adoptive parents persist once they have left the adoptive home. Alternatively, the same measures from the child can be compared to those for the biological parents. This was the method used in a classic adoption study conducted by Heston (1966) which demonstrated the importance of genes (see below) and also cast light on the role of genes in individual intelligence and personality.

Both twin studies and investigations using genetic markers have methodological problems. Another way to study the role of genes in determining psychological characteristics is to use the adoption study technique. Heston (1966) investigated genetic influences in schizophrenia by comparing children who had been adopted at birth because their natural mothers had schizophrenia with similar children who had mentally healthy mothers. The participants were interviewed as adults to see whether any had developed schizophrenia themselves. Ten per cent of the adults with a schizophrenic mother had been hospitalised with schizophrenia themselves. None of the adults with non-schizophrenic mothers developed schizophrenia. Like the results of twin studies, this suggests that genes play a role in schizophrenia. These findings are, however, more valid because none of the adults with mentally healthy mothers developed schizophrenia so the experience of adoption could be eliminated as a causal factor.

Since Heston's research, more sophisticated adoption studies (e.g. Tienari, 1992) have confirmed the importance of genetic factors in the development of schizophrenia, but, unlike Heston, they have also discovered possible environmental variables that influence the probability of an individual adopted child going on to develop schizophrenia.

Which conclusions go with the design and findings pairs?

Look back at the section on twin studies and add examples to the diagram

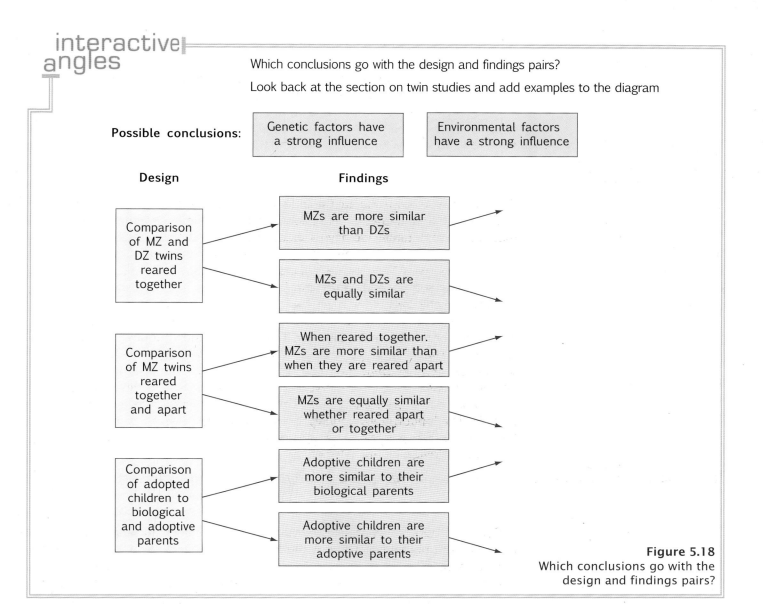

Figure 5.18
Which conclusions go with the
design and findings pairs?

For & Against
adoption studies

FOR   adoption studies provide us with the most direct comparison of the influences of nature versus nurture because they isolate the influences of the environment (due to the effects of the adoptive parents during the adopted individual's childhood) from those of genetics (due to the effect of inherited factors from the biological parents on the development of the adopted child).

FOR   adoption studies can investigate a range of variables and use varied samples and methods. These include trans-racial adoptions and meta-analyses. The similarity of findings across different approaches suggests that the technique is valid.

what's that?

- **Genotype:** the genes an individual has for a particular characteristic
- **Phenotype:** the characteristics an individual displays, this may be physical, behavioural or psychological
- **Sex chromosome:** the X and Y chromosomes that are responsible for determining biological sex in humans and other mammals

AGAINST there is an issue of representativeness of samples. Obviously, most people are not adopted hence, by definition, people who are adopted are not representative of the whole population. For example, in Heston's study there may have been something different about these particular mothers or their babies that led to the adoptions. Any such factor could also have contributed to the development of schizophrenia.

AGAINST adopted children are often selectively placed into families that are very similar to their biological families. This makes untangling the influences of genes and environment difficult.

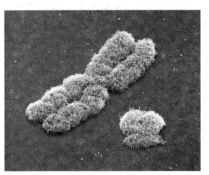

Figure 5.19
The X and Y chromosomes

Gender development

Men and women look and sound different. At least some of these differences are purely biological, that is, they arise because of inherited differences. This section looks at how these differences in development are controlled.

Gender and genetics

A person's genetic sex is determined at conception. It is decided by the combination of **sex chromosomes** (called X and Y) that the individual inherits from their parents (see Figure 5.18). Each egg cell (from the mother) contains an X chromosome. Each sperm (from the father) can contain either an X chromosome or a Y chromosome. If the combination is XX, the child will be female. If there is one X and one Y chromosome (making XY) the child will be male (see Table 5.5). This combination of chromosomes, XX or XY, is called the **genotype**. The resulting characteristic, in this case the genetic sex, is called the **phenotype** – it is the physical expression of the genes that have been inherited.

Chromosomes contain the genetic material that controls the biology of development. The X and Y chromosomes are responsible for guiding the development of an embryo into a male or female baby. This biological influence is very complex and is controlled by many factors. However, some aspects of it are quite clear. One of the key effects of the sex chromosomes is to trigger the development of glands which produce sex hormones. This is the major factor that controls whether a foetus grows into a male or a female.

Table 5.5 Genetic sex determination

		sex chromosomes from the father	
		X	Y
sex chromosomes from the mother	X	XX	XY
	X	XX	XY
Children inheriting XX will be female, those inheriting XY will be male			

Gender and hormones

Early in the development of the embryo, gonads begin to develop. These are sex organs which produce both sex cells (gametes) and hormones. Until about

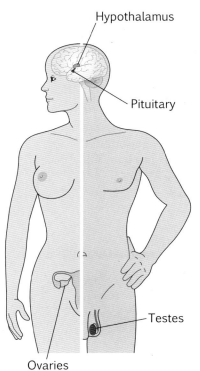

Hypothalamus

Pituitary

Testes

Ovaries

Figure 5.20
Several different glands release hormones that control sexual development

Hormones in puberty

HYPOTHALAMUS: gonadotropin-releasing hormone

ANTERIOR PITUITARY GLAND: gonadotropic hormones

MALE:	**FEMALE:**
TESTES:	OVARIES:
testosterone	oestrogen

eight weeks, all foetuses are the same in terms of their physical sex – their sex organs are identical. It is the presence of a single gene on the Y chromosome, called *SRY*, that dictates whether these organs change into ovaries (to become female) or testes (to become male). If this gene is present, it produces an enzyme called testes-determining factor and the undeveloped glands develop into testes. If the *SRY* gene is absent the foetus will remain female. If a genetically female mouse embryo, which lacks the *SRY* gene, has it implanted, it will develop into a male mouse (Koopman *et al.*, 1991).

In the absence of the *SRY* gene, the 'default mode' of a foetus is to be a female so female sex organs such as the uterus and vagina develop. In males, the newly developed testes produce hormones that change this developmental sequence. Two sorts of effects are important. One effect is to prevent the progression of foetal development as a female. The second is to trigger development into a male – a role performed by hormones called androgens. One important androgen is testosterone. This has the effect of making the foetus into a male, for example triggering the development of the external male sex organs such as the penis.

The process of development of an embryo into a male or female can be disrupted in several different ways. Some naturally occurring problems with sexual development illustrate the roles hormones play in early sexual development. In *Turner's syndrome*, the individual inherits only one sex chromosome, an X. No *SRY* gene is present as there is no Y chromosome, so the foetus cannot develop into a male. Such individuals, however, also lack the second X chromosome needed to change the embryonic gonads into ovaries. Nevertheless, in the absence of androgens, the foetus develops into a female in terms of internal and external genitalia. They are, of course, sterile as they cannot produce eggs.

In normal sexual development, the testes and ovaries are also important after birth. After approximately a decade of quiescence, the gonads become active again during puberty. At this time they control the development of secondary sexual characteristics. These are the physical features that distinguish women from girls and men from boys (see Table 5.6). These changes, although caused by hormones from the gonads, are triggered by another gland, the hypothalamus. The hypothalamus releases a hormone which affects the anterior pituitary gland and it is this which causes the gonads to become active again. In males, androgens are again important. Both males and females are capable of producing testosterone and oestrogen but produce the alternative hormone in only very small quantities. However, there are some important effects, for example testosterone in girls is responsible for the development of underarm and pubic hair at puberty.

Table 5.6 Secondary sexual characteristics

Males (triggered by testosterone)	Females (triggered by oestrogen)
Production of sperm	Growth of breasts
Growth of facial hair (and hair in arm pits and pubic hair)	Development of fatty tissues, e.g. on hips
Enlargement of the larynx (so deepening the voice)	Development of the lining of the uterus (part of the control system of the cycle that releases eggs and causes menstruation)
Increased muscle growth	

Androgen insensitivity syndrome is another disorder of sexual development. In this disorder, as the name implies, the individual's body does not respond to the masculinising effects of androgen. As we know, the 'default' development of a foetus is as a female, and this is what happens. A foetus which is genetically male (XY) but which is insensitive to androgens develops testes under the influence of the SRY gene but no further masculine development occurs. The foetus develops the external genitalia of a female, retaining the testes within the body cavity. The internal female genitalia do not form, but at puberty, the secondary sexual characteristics of female adulthood appear, such as breast and widening of the hips. This shows that both genes and hormones are important.

Classic
research

Compulsory

Money. J, (1975)

'Ablatio penis: normal male infant sex-reassignment as a girl'

Archives of Sexual Behavior 4(1): 65–71.

Boys will be boys?

Aim: To use a surgical accident to investigate whether gender could be reassigned or whether it is biologically determined at birth.

Procedure: Forty-five males were followed up after gender reassignment. One in particular was of interest. This was because he had an identical twin, a natural control. Bruce and Brian were normal twin boys. At age seven months it was decided that the twins would be circumcised for health reasons. The operation on Bruce went wrong and, instead of simply severing the foreskin, burned across the penis. It was impossible to repair the damage surgically. Dr Money, a specialist in sex research, believed the best course of action was to surgically change Brian's external genitalia to appear female and to raise the child as a girl. This decision was based on previous successes with sex-assignment of children born with ambiguous genitalia which suggested that children were 'gender neutral' at

birth. Aged just under two years, Bruce was castrated, received oestrogen treatment and was renamed Brenda. Her family treated her like a little girl, for example letting her hair grow long and buying her dolls. She was seen at regular intervals by Dr Money. She also received further reconstructive surgery and hormone treatment to achieve the transition into a female appearance.

Findings: Money reported that at nine years old, Brenda had a female gender identity and predicted that in adulthood she would have a female sexual life. Although some tomboyish behaviours were seen, these were explained as the result of imitating her brother.

Conclusion: The evidence reported suggested that it was possible to reassign physical appearance through surgery and hormone therapy and gender identity through rearing experiences. This implies that gender identity is undifferentiated at birth i.e. that, in psychological terms, we are born 'gender neutral'.

David Reimer's perspective

John Money continued to report the success of Brenda's gender reassignment and vigorously opposed conflicting opinions. However, the reality of 'Brenda's' experience was very different from that which was implied in his reports. From the outset, she rejected her treatment as a girl and found both her childhood feelings and expectations of others increasingly difficult to cope with. She was ultimately told about her early experiences and chose, with relief but many painful operations, to revert to a male identity and assumed the name 'David'. The evidence of the failure of the gender reassignment conducted by Money was reported by Diamond & Sigmundson (1997). The subsequent reports suggest that Money's conclusion was incorrect and that, in the case of sexually unambiguous individuals, gender identity is biologically determined.

Use the internet to search for information about David Reimer (NB This case is also referred to as 'John/Joan'). Some interesting reports include:

http://www.guardian.co.uk/print/0,,4921671-103680,00.html

http://infocirc.org/rollston.htm

http://slate.com/toolbar.aspx?action=printandid=2101678

http://www.cbc.ca/news/background/reimer/

http://www.ukia.co.uk/diamond/ped_eth.htm

Remember, however, to think critically – not everything that you will read can be substantiated.

Figure 5.21
Bruce as David during his adulthood

Gender differences in brain development and volume

During normal brain development, several changes occur. These include a decrease in grey matter (see page 129) due to 'pruning'. This is a process in which the number of connections between neurones are reduced through the loss of dendrites. There is also an increase in white matter due to the process of myelination. This is the development of a fatty insulating layer around the axons of some neurones that helps them to conduct messages more quickly. Differences in the rate at which these processes occur in the brains of boys and girls lead to differences in the way that their brains develop. De Bellis *et al.* (2001) investigated various physical changes in children's brains and compared the rate of these changes in males and females.

Classic research

Optional

De Bellis, MD, Keshavan, M.S., Beers, S.R., Hall, J., Frustaci, K., Masalehdan, A., Noll, J. & Boring, A.M. (2001) Sex differences in brain maturation during childhood and adolescence. *Cerebral Cortex*, 11(6): 552–7.

Boys' brains, girls' brains

Aim: To investigate sex differences in brain development, looking at the volumes of grey matter (cell bodies and synapses), white matter (axons) and an area called the corpus callosum that links the left and right sides of the brain.

Procedure: A sample of 61 male and 57 female children aged 6.9 to 17 years was obtained by advertising within the local community (of Pittsburgh, USA). They were assessed for cognitive abilities, mental health, handedness, intelligence (IQ) and social variables such as socio-economic status (SES) and ethnicity. There were no differences between males and females in terms of age, ethnic group, SES, handedness or IQ. The males were taller than the females and the majority of participants had a higher than average IQ (median 116). Participants were excluded for a number of reasons e.g. if they had a history of mental illness, prenatal drug exposure, significant head injury or an IQ lower than 80. A full written description of the study was given to potential participants and their parents and written consent was obtained.

Brain volumes were measured using magnetic resonance imaging (MRI). Prior to MRI scanning, participants were desensitised to the sights and sounds of the procedure using a scanning simulator. This, combined with watching their favourite film and the reward of seeing a clear image of their own brain, motivated participants to keep their head still to allow good images to be taken. The head was also held still using foam pads and soft towels. The volumes were assessed from the scans by raters who were blind to the condition (male or female) of the participant. Inter-rater reliability and the reliability of each rater's own judgment was 0.98 or 0.99 in every condition.

Findings: The volume of grey matter significantly fell with age, more so in males than females (see Figure 5.21b) and this difference was significant. The volumes of white matter and the corpus callosum both increased with age, more so in males than females (Figure 5.21c and d). However, the increase was only significant for changes in white matter volume. The difference between males and females was significant for both changes in white matter and corpus callosum volume. Although the whole cerebral volume did not change significantly with age (Figure 5.21a), this was consistently larger in males than females and this difference was taken into account when comparing other measures.

structure	mean volume (cm³)	
	males	females
cerebral volume	1344.53	1188.50
grey matter	850.75	767.96
white matter	493.79	420.34
corpus callosum	8.04	7.69

Conclusion: As boys show faster changes (loss of grey matter and increase in white matter and corpus callosum volume) this shows that boys' brains mature faster. One reason for these differences may be linked to sex hormones. Oestrogen (predominantly in females) delays pruning whereas testosterone (predominantly in males) promotes myelination. The differences in these changes could help to explain differences in cognitive abilities between males and females and the differences in the patterns of development as boys and girls mature. It may also help to explain gender-related differences in early-onset developmental disorders such as autism and attention deficit hyperactivity disorder (ADHD).

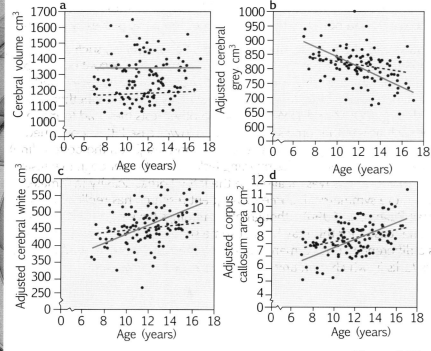

Figure 5.22
Changes in volume of different brain areas for males (blue solid line) and females (red dotted line) with age

Gender differences in brain lateralisation

At the beginning of this chapter we discussed brain lateralisation – the idea that there are some systematic differences between the left and right sides of the brain. We are now going to consider whether any of these patterns are specific to, or more apparent in, one sex than the other.

Language is typically lateralised, with most comprehension and speech functions being controlled by the left hemisphere. Visuo-spatial skills in contrast, are typically lateralised to the right. However, this pattern is more noticeable in men than in women. A man who suffers a stroke (a blood clot that damages part of the brain) on the left is likely to lose considerable powers of speech. Women with similar damage tend to experience less severe symptoms (McGlone, 1978). This is because their language functions are less lateralised – the jobs of interpreting and producing speech are more evenly spread between the left and right sides in women. McGlone observed a similar pattern for spatial tasks. Damage to the right side of the brain in men but not women, caused a decline in non-verbal ability. Again this suggests that there is greater lateralisation in male than in female brains. This pattern of brain asymmetry might even be measurable in terms of brain size.

Wada et al. (1975) used post-mortem measurement of the ratio of the same part of the brain (the 'temporal plane') on the left and right sides. Generally, the left temporal plane was slightly longer. Some of the brains showed a reversal of this pattern, suggesting less lateralisation. The majority of these brains were female. Investigations using more modern techniques have confirmed this difference. Kulynych et al. (1992) used MRI scanning and found that in males, the left temporal plane was 38% longer than the right, but no difference was found between the left and right temporal planes in women.

Lateralisation can also be seen in brain activity. Some studies, such as Shaywitz et al. (1995) have used a functional scanning technique to record blood flow to different brain areas during various cognitive tasks. In language-related tasks, participants have to make judgements such as deciding whether two non-words (e.g. ROOZ and TEWS) rhyme. In other tests they had to make decisions such as whether arrays of upper and lower case letters contained the same sequence (e.g. gDgD on the top line and GdgD on the bottom line). Shaywitz et al. found that for the rhyming task, but not other cognitive tests, activity in males' brains was localised to the left whereas activity in females' brain was more symmetrical. Some subsequent research has replicated this finding (eg Pugh et al. 1996) although other findings have not (e.g. Frost et al., 1999). One reason for this may be that some studies compare tasks in which there is a difference in performance between men and women, whilst others compare tasks in which men and women are equally competent.

how
science
works

Research
Methods

The experiment in cognitive and biological psychology

In cognitive psychology, experiments are mainly laboratory based and explore people's abilities in test situations such as using different kinds of cues to aid memory. In order to overcome individual differences, it is often possible to test each participant under different conditions, that is to use a repeated measures design. This is less often possible in biological psychology, for example if we are studying fundamental differences that cannot be changed, such as sex or handedness. In these instances an independent groups design is essential. Although these studies are laboratory experiments they are also natural experiments as the researcher cannot randomly allocate participants to levels of the IV.

Many studies in biological psychology are conducted on animals. These include experiments on the brain, the influence of hormones on sexual development and the effects of drugs. Fewer studies in cognitive psychology are conducted on animals although there are some, such as those looking for links between particular brain structures and memory. Using animals to understand human behaviour and thinking is useful because animals are simpler, so easier to manipulate and to understand. However, because they are simpler in both their nervous systems and behaviour, generalising from animals to humans may not always be valid. For example, in terms of gender development, although the biological processes governing development are very similar between humans and other mammals it is unlikely that animals have a sense of being male or female in the way that people do.

A recent study, Rossell *et al.* (2002), found both behavioural and brain differences in a language task. The task required participants to judge whether a real word or a pseudoword had appeared on one side of a screen. A pseudoword is one that is legally spelled and pronounceable, such as 'cloom', but is not in fact a real word. The behavioural difference indicated that men were faster if the stimulus was seen to the right, whereas women were faster if the stimulus appeared in the left-hand side of their visual field. Brain scans showed that in men the response mainly generated activity in the left hemisphere, whereas in women both sides of the brain were activated. However, it is not always necessary for there to be behavioural differences in order to identify gender differences in brain lateralisation.

Jaeger *et al.* (1998) found that, even when behavioural differences are not apparent, there are still differences in lateralisation of activity between men and women. They used a PET scanner (see Figure 5.22) to look for active brain areas during language processing. Men and women were scanned while reading verbs and producing past tenses of them. Some of the verbs were real, others were 'nonce' words, that is made up words that could be verbs and that would fit the regular patterns in English, for example making 'blot' into 'blotted' (real) or 'glim' into 'glimmed' (nonce). They found that men and women were very similar in their speed and accuracy on the task. However, when men generated past tenses the brain scans showed that activity was lateralised to the left side. When women performed the same tasks the activity was bilateral, that is, they used both hemispheres.

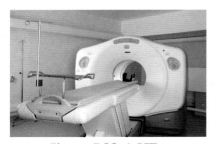

Figure 5.23 A PET scanner

There have been many such studies of lateralisation and there is some controversy over whether the differences are real. One approach to finding a general pattern is to use meta-analysis. Voyer (1996) analysed the findings of 396 comparisons of males and females taken from 266 studies. He concluded that, overall, there was a sex difference, specifically that males show greater lateralisation than females. One very different problem may, however, have inflated this apparent pattern: it is more interesting to report a difference than no difference. It is possible that there are many more unpublished findings demonstrating similarities between the sexes.

Bringing it together: gender development

In the previous chapter on the psychodynamic approach we considered the role that unconscious motives, some of which are innate, have on the development of gender identity. The biological approach shares the idea that there may be inherited factors controlling the development of gender. However, in the case of the psychodynamic approach these influences are unconscious instincts. The biological approach, in contrast, sees genes as being central to the inheritance of biological sex and to related aspects such as sexual orientation and gender-related differences such as in language. Of course, the psychodynamic approach also has explanations for individual differences such as sexual orientation but again they are different from those of the biological approach. Both of these approaches recognise that nature alone does not determine all of our characteristics. In the case of the psychodynamic approach early experiences such as relationships with our parents are also important. In the biological approach the 'nurture' factors can be demonstrated by the dissimilarity of identical twins. Despite having the same genetic blueprint, monozygotic twins differ in many psychological characteristics. These differences must arise as a result of the environment. In the next chapter, on the learning approach, we will look at the ways in which these influences might affect development.

Using inferential statistics

In Chapter 4 we looked at the use of the Spearman test, a statistical test of correlation. We are now going to look in more detail at inferential statistical tests in general and how they are used to assess the findings of studies with experimental designs. One example we will look at in this chapter is the Mann–Whitney test and in Chapter 6 we will look at the chi-squared test. Before we do this we need to learn a little more about statistics.

We have already considered the experimental hypothesis. This is the prediction we test in our research. When we test our findings using inferential statistics, we use two other hypotheses. The experimental hypothesis is replaced by the alternative hypothesis. This makes the same prediction but, rather than referring to the findings of one specific investigation based on a small sample, it makes a more general statement about the whole population. In this respect, the alternative and the null hypothesis are opposites. The null hypothesis refers to the non-existence of a pattern in the general population.

In statistical testing we are aiming to *reject* the null hypothesis. This is what we will do if our results fit the expected pattern. If we can show that it is *unlikely* that the pattern we have found could have arisen by chance, then we can confidently reject the null hypothesis. What do we mean by chance? We simply set a probability, called the significance level, at which we are prepared to say that this 'couldn't have happened by chance alone'. There is, of course, always a risk that we might be wrong! In psychological studies the probability is generally set at 5%. This means that, if the test says our results are significant, we can be 95% sure that the pattern of results could not have arisen by chance. The significance level indicates how confident we are about the pattern in our results and is expressed as a probability. So our 5% level of risk is written as $p \leq 0.05$.

We have said that there is a possibility that we could be wrong in our conclusion. So we could conclude that our IV has an effect when it actually doesn't – sometimes we may want to be more certain. In this case, we make the significance level more stringent, for example accepting only a 1% possibility that the difference between conditions could have arisen by chance. This is expressed as $p \leq 0.01$. Other values can also be used, for example $p \leq 0.025$ or $p \leq 0.001$.

When we conduct a statistical test we are finding out about whether or not a difference in the results could have arisen by chance or is due to the IV. We are interested in whether the pattern within our sample is sufficiently unlikely to have arisen by chance that we can generalise about the effect of the IV in the whole population. This is why the hypotheses we use, the alternative and null hypotheses, are stated in general terms.

So, to use a statistical test we need to know several things:

- our null hypothesis (to accept if the pattern we find is not what we have expected)
- our alternative hypothesis (that we will accept if we reject the null hypothesis)
- whether our alternative hypothesis is directional or non-directional
- the significance level (this is the 'p' value)
- how many participants were in the sample (this is called 'n').

The Mann–Whitney test

The Mann–Whitney test, like the Spearman test that you encountered in Chapter 4, is an inferential test. The Mann–Whitney test is used when we have an independent groups design and ordinal, interval or ratio data. It is therefore suitable for comparing the findings of studies looking for differences such as between males and females. You won't ever have to calculate the Mann–Whitney by hand, but here are some important points about it. The test uses several pieces of information, including the number of participants in each of the two levels of the IV. They may be the same number or different numbers. When the test is calculated, the scores are put in order, that is they are ranked. By doing this the test measures how much overlap there is between the two sets of scores. Basically, if there is a lot of overlap it is more likely that the difference has arisen by chance. When the gap between the groups is bigger, it is unlikely that the difference is due to chance. If this is the case, the final number produced by the Mann–Whitney test, called the observed value, will be quite small.

The observed value produced by the Mann–Whitney, is called 'U'. This is compared to a value from a table called the *critical value*. You need to be careful because there is a different table for each different test. To decide whether there is a significant difference between the levels of the IV, you need to find the appropriate critical value. To do this you need to know:

● the level of significance you have decided to use (e.g. $p \leq 0.05$ or $p \leq 0.01$)
● whether the hypothesis was directional or non-directional (for a directional hypothesis a one-tailed test is used, for a non-directional hypothesis, a two-tailed test is used)
● the number of participants in each level of the IV (n_1 and n_2).

Here is an example:

On page 128 we described the work of Galynker *et al.* (2000) who used PET scans to test the brain activity of people with a history of drug abuse. They used a Mann–Whitney test to see whether there was a significant difference in brain activity between the two groups:

● Group 1: the control group (who did not have a history of opiate abuse)
● Group 2: the experimental group (who had abused opiates but had been drug free for four years).

The amount of activity in the anterior cingulate gyrus was greater in the ex-users than in the controls – but was the difference small enough to have just arisen by chance?

The Mann–Whitney test produced a *U* value of 2.

This is compared to a critical value found from the table. To look up the critical value we need to know:

● the level of significance [$p \leq 0.05$]
● whether the test is comparing a directional or non-directional prediction [directional – so we use a one-tailed test]
● the number of participants (*n*) in each group [$n_1 = 5$, $n_2 = 4$].

Table of critical values for Mann–Whitney U:
one-tailed tests at $p \leq 0.05$ and two-tailed tests at $p \leq 0.1$

$n_1 \rightarrow$ $n_2 \downarrow$	3	4	5	6
3	0	0	1	2
4	0	1	2	3
5	1	2	4	5
6	2	3	5	7

The critical value is 2.

For the Mann–Whitney test to be significant, the observed value must be smaller than or equal to the critical value.

Since the observed value of 2 is the same as the critical value of 2, we can conclude that there is a significant difference between the activity recorded in the brains of the control (non-user) and ex-user participants. This means that Galynker *et al.* could reject their null hypothesis and accept their alternative hypothesis as the rate of glucose use was higher in the ex-users than in the controls. So Galynker *et al.* could conclude that opiate users do, even after prolonged abstinence, show increased activity in one brain area (the anterior cingulated gyrus). Note that, had the hypothesis been non-directional, we would need to look at the actual results to see the direction of the effect.

interactive angles

The Mann–Whitney test at work

A test compared the speed of males and females making plurals from 20 pseudonouns such as 'rog', 'gleep' and 'pouse'. The idea was based on existing evidence that suggests there are gender differences in language, so a $p \leq 0.05$ level of significance was appropriate. A non-directional alternative hypothesis was predicted, saying that 'Males and females differ in the time taken to make plurals from pseudonouns'. The corresponding null hypothesis was 'There is no difference between the time taken by males and females to make plurals from pseudonouns'. The findings were as follows:

Time taken to make 20 plurals of pseudonouns (in seconds)

Participant no. →	Group no. ↓	1	2	3	4	5	6	7	8	9	10	Mean
Males	A	104	121	77	64	98	151	129	196	87	73	
Females	B	51	65	76	56	83	94	53	61	59	72	

First, calculate the means for each group. To calculate the observed value for this Mann–Whitney test online, go to http://faculty.vassar.edu/lowry/VassarStats.html. Follow the link to Ordinal Data on the navigation bar, scroll down to Mann–Whitney test and click on it. You should then see an extra box asking for the number of participants in group A (n_a), type in 10. A second box should then appear asking for the number of participants in group B (n_b), type in 10 again. If this doesn't happen, you need to go back and do a browser check on the home page and allow your computer to accept browser windows. Once you've entered the number of participants in each group you will arrive at the main Mann–Whitney page. Don't be put off by the formulae – just scroll down the page until you come to Data Entry. In the right hand columns labelled 'Raw Data for' enter the data above for 'Sample A' and 'Sample B'. Then click on 'Calculate from Raw Data'. The observed value (U) will appear in the box labelled '$U_a =$'.

Complete the following sentences to draw a conclusion from the test.

Using these figures in the Mann–Whitney test produces a U value of ___ .

This is compared to a critical value found from the table. To look up the critical value we need to know:

● the level of significance [$p \leq 0.05$ or $p \leq 0.025$?]

● whether the test is comparing a directional or non-directional prediction

● the number of participants (n) in each group [$n_a =$ ___, $n_b =$ ___]

Table of critical values for Mann–Whitney U:
one-tailed tests at $p \leq 0.025$ and two-tailed tests at $p \leq 0.05$

$n_1 \longrightarrow$	2	3	4	5	6	7	8	9	10	11	12
$n_2 \downarrow$											
8	0	2	4	6	8	10	13	15	17	19	22
9	0	2	4	7	10	12	15	17	20	23	26
10	0	3	5	8	11	14	17	20	23	26	29
11	0	3	6	9	13	16	19	23	26	30	33

The critical value is ____.

For the Mann–Whitney test to be significant, the observed value must be smaller than or equal to the critical value.

Since ____ (the observed value) is _____ than ____ (the critical value), we can conclude that there is a _____ difference between the time taken to make plurals from a list of pseudonouns by males and females. We can see from the averages that males take longer than females. We can therefore say that we can reject the _____ hypothesis and accept the _____ hypothesis.

REALlives
Key read

You have now explored a selection of ideas, theories, studies and research methods from the biological approach to psychology. We have come across a number of real life issues that can be examined using a bio-psychological perspective. The aim of this section is to show in some detail how we can take an issue of real world importance and apply bio-psychology to understand it. We will do this for you with one issue then challenge you to do the same with a different situation.

Applying biological psychology to mental health issues

The links between biology, brain and behaviour can be clearly seen in many cases of mental illness. You will know already from other areas, such as the psychodynamic approach, that it is unlikely that biological psychology can offer a complete understanding of mental illnesses. However, understandable and useful patterns can be identified between specific mental disorders and brain function. For example, we have already seen how neurotransmitters are important in Parkinson's disease. Similarly, in mental illnesses such as schizophrenia, depression and obsessive compulsive disorder (OCD), changes in specific neurotransmitters are associated with each disorder.

At the beginning of the chapter we discussed the variety and function of neurotransmitters. We have also looked at the role that genetics may play in schizophrenia. We will now consider the role neurotransmitters might have in causing schizophrenia and the ways in which understanding these can assist in treatment.

One explanation of schizophrenia is called the 'dopamine hypothesis'. It suggests that one cause of the symptoms of schizophrenia is an excess of the neurotransmitter dopamine in certain areas of the brain. This is supported by various kinds of evidence:

- Use of the drug amphetamine, which affects dopamine receptors, can produce symptoms that resemble schizophrenia.
- If people with schizophrenia take amphetamine, their symptoms get worse.
- The drug L-DOPA, used to treat Parkinson's disease, increases dopamine levels and can produce side effects that resemble schizophrenia.
- The neurones of people with schizophrenia have more receptors for dopamine so it can attach more readily than in non-schizophrenics.

It is therefore unsurprising that drugs which can combat the symptoms of schizophrenia work by reducing the effectiveness of dopamine. One drug, chlorpromazine, acts by blocking dopamine receptors on the surface of neurones. This reduces access for dopamine molecules so counteracts the effect of high levels this neurotransmitter and reduces symptoms.

A similar pattern is seen in some kinds of depression. One important neurotransmitter here is serotonin. The levels of serotonin in depressed people are relatively low. Drugs called selective serotonin reuptake inhibitors prevent serotonin molecules being re-absorbed. Citalopram is an example of this type of drug. Citalopram causes the neurotransmitters to remain in the synapse and increases the chance of them attaching to receptors. This effectively counters the low serotonin level and reduces the symptoms of depression. Trivedi *et al.* (2006) found that after 14 weeks on Citalopram, 47% of patients had experienced an improvement that had halved their depression score.

In the case of OCD, both serotonin and dopamine are affected. One drug used in the treatment of OCD is Escitalopram. As we saw on p. 123, this is effective in reducing symptoms. It is almost identical to Citalopram and works in a similar way.

Another source of evidence for the role of neurotransmitters in mental disorders comes from studies on animals. By artificially manipulating neurotransmitter levels it is possible to produce models of some of the symptoms of disorders such as schizophrenia. For example, Rung *et al.* (2005 a,b) used rats treated with different drugs and inhibitors to mimic and reverse two symptoms of schizophrenia. By treating them with drugs that affected levels of dopamine and another neurotransmitter, glutamate, they were able to create social withdrawal and changes in levels of motor activity. Because the drug effects could be reversed using inhibitors they could be sure that the neurotransmitters were responsible for causing the symptoms.

It is also possible to genetically manipulate animals to simulate symptoms of mental disorders. Wood *et al.* (1998) used mice in which the gene NCAM-180 had been 'knocked-out'. They exhibited schizophrenia-like symptoms such as being unable to learn that a quiet noise signalled the arrival of a loud noise. The mice, like people with schizophrenia, could not use the quiet noise as a warning to suppress their startle response to the loud noise. Interestingly, these mice showed another similarity to human patients – their brain ventricles (the spaces within the brain) were larger than normal. Recent genetic research suggests that the gene NCAM is also linked to schizophrenia in humans (Sullivan *et al.*, 2007).

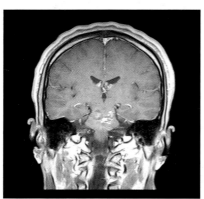

Unaffected

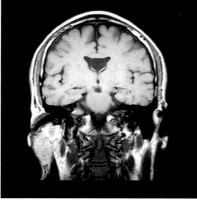

Affected

Figure 5.24
The ventricles of people with schizophrenia are often enlarged as seen in this brain scan

The article you will find at the link below is a discussion of the role of animals in modelling psychiatric symptoms:

http://pn.psychiatryonline.org/cgi/content/full/38/12/20

Read it and identify the relative strengths and weaknesses of this approach to researching mental illness.

exercise

Key

Attack of the munchies

David Concar (edited)
New Scientist, 11 April 2001

Raiding the fridge in the middle of the night is an all too common side effect of smoking cannabis. But you don't have to smoke dope to get the munchies. Certain chemicals you're born with can spark off an attack of hunger as well. Even the most upright citizens have naturally occurring cannabis-like molecules (cannabinoids) circulating in their brains. Now scientists are suggesting that these molecules trigger intense hunger pangs and may even contribute to obesity.

Normally, mice that have been starved eat voraciously. But George Kunos and his colleagues found that the absence of cannabis receptors makes the mice much less hungry. Genetically modified mice lacking the receptors ate far less food than usual after being starved for 18 hours, as did unmodified mice that had been given drugs to block the receptors.

But you can have too much of a good thing. In a finding that could link cannabinoids to human obesity, Kunos and his team found high levels of cannabis-like substances in the brains of excessively fat mice. The mice were born with a genetic defect that prevented them from making leptin, a hormone that is known to have a key role in curbing appetite.

The discovery of leptin's role transformed obesity research in the 1990s. But how the hormone tones down hunger has never been quite clear. Now Kunos believes naturally occurring cannabinoids could be a vital piece of the puzzle. In its latest experiments, his team has found that injecting leptin into rats and mice automatically led to a sharp drop in cannabinoid levels.

The finding backs up earlier work by Raphael Mechoulam and his colleagues who found that injecting newborn mice with drugs that neutralise the effect of cannabis dramatically depressed the mice's appetite. The mice stopped suckling and died.

So could too much natural cannabinoid in the brain make people fat? "It's reasonable to speculate that it contributes to some forms of obesity," says Kunos. "But so far we have no direct evidence."

In France, though, scientists are already giving obese people an experimental drug designed to block cannabinoid receptors. In a trial lasting 16 weeks, patients taking the drug lost more weight than a control group.

Figure 5.25
Cannabinoids stimulate hunger in mice just as cannabis does in humans

Source: http://www.newscientist.com/article.ns?id=dn617

Use the ideas from the biological approach to explain some of the findings described in this article. You might like to comment on the design of one or more of the studies described and the generalisibility of the findings. You might also want to consider the ethical issues raised by the evidence presented.

In need of directions?

Roger Highfield (edited)
Daily Telegraph 27 May 2007

Sexual orientation and gender affects navigation skills, with straight men best at map reading and heterosexual women worst, according to a new study. Researchers at the University of Warwick considered how we perform mental tasks in light of sexual preferences, with straight men performing better at map reading than gay men who in turn perform better than lesbians, who in turn do better than straight women.

But old age withers all men's minds alike, and at a faster rate than women's, according to Prof Elizabeth Maylor of the University of Warwick, who worked with Dr Stian Reimers of University College London on an online survey with the BBC.

"This is a novel finding," she said.

"Only gender has an effect on rate of ageing, not sexual orientation."

Data was taken from over 198,000 people aged 20–65 years (109,612 men and 88,509 women).

As expected they found men outperformed women on tests such as mentally rotating objects, and matching angles, while women outperformed men in verbal dexterity tests, and remembering the locations of objects. So while men may be better at map reading, women are better at finding the car keys. Prof Maylor stressed there is a big overlap when the overall spread of performance of men and women is compared.

"In all the tasks, older people did worse than younger people, whether male or female. In fact, for some of the tasks, people in their thirties were significantly worse than people in their twenties.

"Because of the size of the study, we found reliable effects with ageing. Men showed a greater decline with age than women did, irrespective of whether a task favoured men or women."

But Prof Maylor said that other factors were also important, adding that practice and mental exercise can slow down the rate of decline, whether you're male or female.

source: http://www.telegraph.co.uk/news/main.jhtml?xml=/news/2007/05/24/ndrive124.xml

Use the ideas from the biological approach to explain some of the findings described in this article. You might like to comment on the design of the study and the generalisibility of the findings.

Using animals in psychology

Much of what we know about the structure and function of the nervous system, hormones and the differences between males and females is based on research using animals. There are two issues surrounding this research. On the one hand there is the question about the extent to which can we generalise from animals to humans. On the other hand psychologists must also ask themselves whether such research can be justified on ethical grounds.

Animals in laboratory experiments

We know that hormones affect the development of sex differences from early research on non-human animals. Even now, however, animals are providing us with sources of information that we could not gain through experimentation on humans. For example, studies such as Domínguez-Salazar *et al.* (2002)

manipulated the function of receptors for androgens (male hormones) before birth by treating pregnant female rats in different ways. The offspring born to these females then had their ovaries or testes removed and were treated with hormone replacements or were controls. The findings showed that the different pre-natal treatments affected either male, or female, behaviours in adulthood. They concluded that hormone levels around the time of birth are important in determining later sexual behaviours in rats of both sexes.

The research described above has all the positive characteristics we would expect from a laboratory experiment. It is well controlled, there are appropriate groups for comparison and the sexual behaviours that were recorded were clearly defined. These features help to ensure that the findings are valid and reliable. However, such studies also raise questions about generalisibility. Domínguez-Salazar et al. concluded that the findings related to 'species-specific factors'; to what extent are such studies helpful in understanding human sexual development?

Generalising from animals to humans

One reason to suppose that we can generalise from animals such as rats to humans is that we have a shared evolutionary history. Our hormonal and nervous systems, which are important in the biological determination of sex and many other psychological characteristics, are very similar. We have the same endocrine glands that release similar hormones. We have the same basic brain structure: mammals such as rats and humans all have a hind-, mid- and forebrain. We can reasonably assume therefore that the biological processes determining our development and ongoing functioning are the same. For example, studies such as Rung et al. (2005a,b) and Wood et al. (1998) have successfully used animals to model aspects of mental illness by manipulating brain function and behaviour.

However, there are important ways in which the systems differ. For example, in the case of hormones, women are very unusual among mammals in the way their sexual cycle causes menstruation. Although all female mammals have a biological cycle that affects their breeding capacity, few experience blood loss; most simply reabsorb the lining of the uterus if they do not become pregnant. Another difference is that few other species are sexually active outside the breeding season. Our brains are different too. The most obvious difference is the size of different parts of the brain. In humans, the cortex (outer layer) is very much larger relative to our size than any other animal. So, whilst in some respects generalisation from animals to humans is highly credible in other ways it is not.

Think back to the nature–nurture debate. Not only are human endocrine and nervous systems different from those of animals but we are much more receptive to the effects of our environment. These factors also reduce the credibility of animal studies.

The ethics of animal research

If you look back to the research described at the top of this box, you will see it was highly invasive. This is just one example of the many experiments that are performed on animals to investigate a range of different psychological variables. For example, studies using animals have explored memory, learning, gender and mental health issues. We have to ask ourselves whether the ends

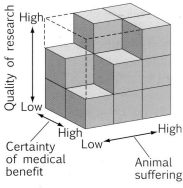

Figure 5.26 Bateson cube

justify the means, in other words, is the animal suffering caused by such experiments outweighed by the benefits to humans? For some, the answer is necessarily 'no' because they hold the view that animals should not be put at the service of mankind. Another perspective looks at whether the overall gain is sufficiently valuable. This was expressed by Bateson (1986) as a three-dimensional graph. When the certainty of benefit is high, the research is good and the suffering is low, the research is worthwhile.

Practical issues in animal research

There are many ways in which experimenting on animals is easier than on humans. For example, they are small, cheap to look after and reproduce quickly so many individuals and whole life cycles can be observed. In addition, greater control can be achieved in animal research, for example, an animal's diet, social companions, sleep and reproduction can all be controlled. Finally, experimental procedures can be conducted on animals that could not be performed with humans, such as organ removal and hormone injections.

In order to minimise animal suffering and to ensure that evidence from animals is not confounded by distress, animals must be well cared for. Ethical guidelines and laws exist to protect animals' welfare. Regulations control their use so that they are well fed and watered, have adequate housing and appropriate care. They cannot be used in stressful or painful experiments without a licence from the Home Office and, even with such a licence, there are limits to what can be done, by whom and where.

over to you

Your practical exercise for the biological approach is to conduct an experiment. To fulfil the requirements you need to undertake an investigation which:

- is a test of difference
- collects ordinal, interval or ratio data
- uses an independent measures design
- you analyse using a Mann–Whitney test
- you write up. This will need to include the following:
  - a hypothesis
  - a table and graph of results
  - interpretation of the findings of the Mann–Whitney test
  - written analysis of results
  - conclusions
  - a consideration of issues of validity, reliability, credibility and generalisibility.

You already know a great deal about experimental design and, from this chapter, have learned about control conditions in experiments. You are not going to be using equipment such as MRI or PET scanners that we have discussed in this chapter, but you may well conduct an experiment that compares males and females. If this seems difficult because you are in a single-sex school, you could still compare results from your class to other people outside school. The samples will of course be different, but that will certainly give you something to write about in your consideration of issues!

Some possible examples might include comparisons between:

- tasks that require differently lateralised functions such as language and spatial relationships
- left- and right-handed people on spatial or verbal tasks
- males and females on spatial or verbal tasks.

Here are some ideas from this chapter that you could use as the basis for your hypothesis:

- *Brain lateralisation, language and handedness*: For most people, language is controlled by the left hemisphere, which also controls the right hand. On a language-related task, right-handers and most left-handed people should therefore be very fractionally quicker to respond to word tasks with their right hand. Two groups could therefore be compared, people using their right hands and people using their left.
- *Left for logic, right for reading*: for reasons that are not yet understood, people seem to look right when answering questions on language but left when answering questions of spatial relations. This probably relates to lateralisation of function within the brain. You could produce one set of questions about words and another about spatial tasks and count how many times participants in each group look left or right.
- *Women and words*: women's brains seem to be less lateralised than men's. In males, language and spatial skills seem strongly lateralised, in women these functions are spread more evenly. This, or other differences, produces sex differences in ability that you could test. On average, women seem to be more verbally competent and men more spatially competent. There are lots of ways to test verbal skills, such as completion of words or changing tenses. This is more challenging when conducted with nonce words (as used by Shaywitz *et al.*, 1995). Spatial skills can also be tested in different ways, such as working out jigsaw puzzles or 'mental rotation'. This is where the outline of a complex shape is shown and the participant has to decide whether several other images could, or could not, be the same shape in a different position.

interactive angles

At http://www.youramazingbrain.org/newresearch/testyourbody.htm you can find out how left- or right-side dominant your body is.

Here are some sites that provide examples of mental rotation tasks. Some illustrate sex differences, the last provides examples other than three-dimensional shape standards:

http://www.sfu.ca/~dkimura/articles/NEL.htm

http://psychexps.olemiss.edu/InstrOnly_Page/mentalrotation.htm

http://www.washingtonpost.com/wp-dyn/content/graphic/2006/08/31/GR2006083100070.html

http://oldwww.cs.umu.se/tdb/kurser/TDBC12/HT-97/LABBAR/6-LABGRP/

You may like to use this information to write a hypothesis and design your experimental materials.

You will not have to submit your experimental write up to the examination board but keep it as in your examination you could be asked questions about what you did. Make sure that you understand and can answer each of the following questions about the experiment you have done:

- What was the difference you were testing?
- What was the experimental design?
- What were your IV and DV, and can you operationalise them both?
- How did you control extraneous variable between conditions?
- What was your experimental hypothesis?
- What was your null hypothesis?
- What was the level of measurement of the DV?
- How did you summarise your data to present it in a table?
- Which graph did you use to present your data and why?
- What was the conclusion from the Mann–Whitney test you conducted? (Remember, you can use http://faculty.vassar.edu/lowry/VassarStats.html to calculate your Mann–Whitney test.
- What was your overall conclusion in relation to your hypothesis?
- What were the key issues relating to reliability, validity and credibility for your experiment?
- Were the findings from your investigation generalisible?

Conclusions

The biological approach to psychology is based on the roles of two key factors: genes and the nervous system. Of course, genes play a large part in determining the function of the nervous system but this is also affected by external factors. One important debate is therefore the nature–nurture debate: the extent to which the development of any characteristic depends on biological factors (nature) or experience (nurture). Twin and adoption studies help us to provide evidence for this, showing that both factors are important in the development of personality characteristics and mental disorders for example. Other research methods such as experiments – including those using animals – are important in the biological approach, and brain scans have helped us to understand how the brain works, for example showing how brain function is lateralised. In addition, we have learned about inferential statistics and the use of the Mann–Whitney test.

The biological approach has also been important in helping us to understand the development of biological sex and of gender identity. Research has shown that biological factors are very important and that manipulating biological appearance and social environment are not necessarily enough to change an individual's gender identity. This is an example of the nature–nurture debate at work. Another major issue that we have considered is the contribution the biological approach has made to treating mental illness. We have seen how drugs can affect brain function by mimicking or altering the action of neurotransmitters.

what do I know?

1. Alongside each of these statements put a tick in **either** the true **or** the false column.

Statement:	True	False
The sex chromosomes in a male are XY	☐	☑
The hormone oestrogen is more important in male sexual development than in female sexual development	☐	☐
Male and female brains differ in the way that language processing is lateralised	☐	☐
All human embryos start life as the same sex	☐	☐

[4]

2. (a) Twin studies are often used as a research method in the biological approach, eg to study the development of intelligence or the role of genes in mental disorders.

   (i) Describe how a twin study is conducted. [4]

   (ii) Evaluate the usefulness of twin studies in biological psychology. Consider at least **one** strength and at least **one** weakness in your answer. [6]

   (b) Animal studies are also used in the biological approach, eg to investigate the causes of sex differences.

   (i) Outline two or more ethical issues raised by studies that use non-human animals. [4]

   (ii) Outline two steps that psychologists must take in their research to limit these ethical issues. [4]

3. (a) Describe the procedure of the study conducted by Money (1975).[5]

   (b) Outline the findings from this study. [3]

   (c) How did the subsequent testimony of David Reimer influence the conclusions that can be drawn from Money (1975)? [4]

4. As part of the course requirements for the biological approach in Unit 2 you will have conducted a short practical testing a difference.

   Answer the following questions using your practical for the biological approach as your example.

   (a) Outline the aim or purpose of your practical. [3]

   (b) Describe how you collected data in your practical. [5]

   (c) Explain how you solved one problem when planning or carrying out your practical. [4]

5. Each of the approaches in Unit 2 (the psychodynamic, biological and learning approaches) have been used to explain gender behaviour. Compare any **two** of these. Include both description and evaluation in your answer. [12]

what's ahead

By the end of this chapter I should know about:

- the learning approach to psychology
- classical conditioning and the effects of extinction and spontaneous recovery
- operant conditioning and the effects of positive and negative reinforcement, punishment and primary and secondary reinforcement
- one treatment or therapy that is based on conditioning
- the importance of learning in gender development including the processes of modelling and shaping
- research by Bandura *et al.* (1961)
- one other study from the learning approach: *either* Watson & Rayner (1920), Pickens & Thompson (1968) *or* Skinner (1948)
- applying ideas from the learning approach to explain real life issues

In addition I should understand:

- observations
- when and how to use different statistical tests

where does the learning approach take us?

↓ Pokemon characters: do you love them or hate them?

↗ Therapy: can you cure drug addicts with a prize draw?

↑ Media violence: are violent videos really bad for kids?

↙ Buffy: do we need more?

← Clip art: is it sexist?

The learning theory angle

This approach is based on the study of learning in non-human animals which, being generally less complex in their behaviour than humans, are easier to study. In this chapter, we look at three particularly important types of learning: classical conditioning, operant conditioning and social learning. The learning approach differs from other approaches such as the psychodynamic and biological approaches in two key ways. First, the learning approach focuses almost exclusively on the influence of the environment on behaviours rather than the role played by internal or innate factors such as instinctive drives or genes. Secondly, research in the learning approach relies on collecting data from observable changes in behaviour unlike other approaches that make inferences about factors which cannot be directly observed, such as the effect of the unconscious or the role played by genes in development.

Theories of learning

Learning can be defined as 'a relatively permanent change in behavioural potential which accompanies experience' (Kimble, 1961). This definition identifies several characteristics of learning, for example:

- the environment provides experiences that govern learning
- learning results in the acquisition of new responses
- learning may have occurred but new behaviours do not, necessarily, have to be demonstrated.

The environment can contribute to learning in a range of different ways. Classical conditioning relies on associations between stimuli (we learn that two things happen together). In operant conditioning, behaviours are determined by their consequences, whilst in social learning one individual learns by imitating another. In each of these routes to learning the environment is central, providing stimuli, consequences (rewards or punishments), or models for behaviour. We can now look at each of these in detail.

Classical conditioning

Research into classical conditioning began with Ivan Pavlov, who was studying digestion. He noticed that his experimental dogs salivated to the sound of his footsteps even when he wasn't carrying food. Pavlov realised that the dogs' responses were anticipatory – because the arrival of their meals was always preceded by the same sound.

Classical conditioning works by building up an association between two stimuli. One, called the *neutral stimulus*, is something in the environment which does not initially cause a response. The other is an existing *unconditioned stimulus* which does produce an effect – called the *unconditioned response*. This response might be a reflex, such as blinking or salivating. The two stimuli are repeatedly presented to the animal at the same time until the previously neutral stimulus acquires the same effect as the unconditioned stimulus; the ability to elicit (cause) a particular response. Note that no new behaviour is learned. All that has changed is that an existing behaviour is elicited in response to a different stimulus. This behaviour is now called a *conditioned response* and the trigger a *conditioned stimulus*. In the case of Pavlov's dogs the sound of footsteps was initially a neutral stimulus, however when the sound was associated with food it became a conditioned stimulus and the salivation a conditioned response.

Pavlov (1927) went on to demonstrate classical conditioning in his dogs in more controlled situations. He used various sounds, such as a bell, as the neutral stimulus (NS) and a bowl of meat powder as the unconditioned stimulus (UCS). Prior to the experiment, the dogs would salivate in response to the meat powder (the unconditioned response, UCR) but not to the sound. During the conditioning phase the meat powder was presented at the same time as the bell. Repeated pairings of meat and bell resulted in conditioning; the animal would subsequently salivate to the sound alone. As a result of the pairings, the NS (the sound) had become a conditioned stimulus (CS) capable of producing the behaviour (salivation) in a new situation. This behaviour, triggered by the CS, is called a conditioned response (CR) (see Figure 6.1).

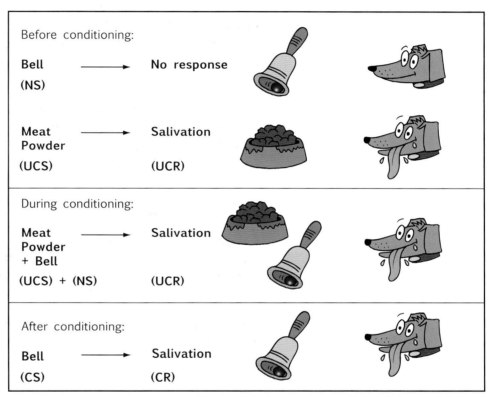

Figure 6.1a The process of classical conditioning

Acquiring a conditioned response may take many, or at least several, pairings of the UCS and CS. For example, Pavlov (1955) describes a conditioning procedure in which a dog learned to salivate when food was associated with an object being rotated – this took five pairings. Once acquired, the CR may be weaker than the UCR (e.g. a dog may salivate less) or it may be slower to start than the UCR.

People can be classically conditioned by the same processes as Pavlov's dogs. For example, you too may have been classically conditioned to salivate. Visual stimuli such as chocolate wrappers (the NS) do not initially cause salivation, although eating chocolate (the UCS) will do so. As we open the wrapper before we eat the chocolate, we tend to have it in sight so it can become a conditioned stimulus. After eating many bars of chocolate the NS and UCS have had multiple pairings so salivation (the CR) becomes conditioned to the wrapper (the CS). Even the noise of someone shaking a box of sweets may make us salivate!

Olson & Fazio (2001) used a laboratory experiment to find out whether attitudes can be classically conditioned. Female participants were told that they were participating in a study about 'video surveillance'. They were shown hundreds

Figure 6.1b
Pavlov's apparatus enabled him to control the exposure of the dog to different stimuli and to measure the response accurately, in this case salivation

of words and images in pairs that included some target images (of Pokemon cartoon characters). In these pairs, the Pokemon character was a neutral stimulus (because it did not elicit emotional responses) and the other word or image was deliberately emotionally positive or negative (so was an unconditioned stimulus). Positive words included 'excellent' and 'awesome' and positive images included puppies and a hot fudge sundae. Negative words included 'terrible' and 'awful' and negative images included a cockroach and a man with a knife. The targets were repeated 20 times during the presentation to produce conditioning. Later, the participants were asked to rate how positively they felt about the targets. Those that had been paired with positive UCSs were rated more positively than those paired with negative items. As gender stereotyped items tend to be presented simultaneously, and same-gender items are evaluated more positively, these findings suggest that classical conditioning could contribute to the development of some aspects of our gender-related attitudes.

Gender-related behaviours may also become associated with new stimuli. For example, Kippin (2000) showed how classical conditioning could explain some sexual responses. Rats were classically conditioned to ejaculate to the smell of lemon or almond. Male rats were allowed to copulate with females smelling of either lemon or almond. The males initially showed no preference for females with a particular smell, but after conditioning they displayed a preference to mate again with those bearing the smell that they had come to associate with ejaculation. It is possible that humans can acquire sexual preferences by classical conditioning in much the same way. This would offer an explanation for how some people acquire bizarre sexual fetishes. An amusing example is shown in the Media Watch below.

media watch

The Barry White experiment

Dr Vernon Coleman's Casebook,
The People 16 January 2000

Q My boyfriend and I tried an experiment that I'd like to tell you about. For two months, we made love every night with Barry White on continuous play on our CD player. Now, whenever either of us hears that music we become sexually aroused.

A A long-dead foreigner called Pavlov did much the same sort of experiment but used dogs, bells and food. Your research project sounds far more interesting and I suggest that you apply for a grant to help you continue with your studies. You might like to see if your boyfriend's enthusiasm can be triggered by constant exposure to the sound of Abergwili Male Voice Choir airing their tonsils.

Alternatively, try Seth Pitt and Eva Legova singing Tonight's the Night. Meanwhile, a warning. You could find yourself in a tricky situation if a Barry White track is played when you're in your local pub.

Figure 6.2 Barry White

1. Explain the couple's experience in terms of classical conditioning.
2. Give an example of how a more serious sexual fetish might be acquired by classical conditioning.

Extinction and spontaneous recovery

What happens if the CS is repeatedly presented in the absence of the UCS? Over time the strength of the CR declines and eventually disappears, an effect called **extinction**. Thus if a dog was conditioned to salivate to a bell, then the bell was rung many times without food appearing, salivation to the bell would eventually stop. However, if the bell is silent for a while, then later rung again, the response may reappear. This is called **spontaneous recovery**.

Classic research
Optional

Watson, J.B. & Rayner, R. (1920) 'Conditioned emotional responses'

Journal of Experimental Psychology, 3(1): 1–14, details from laboratory notes reported in Watson (1924) *Behaviorism*, New York: Norton.

Little Albert

Aim: To explore whether a fear response to an innocuous stimulus could be classically conditioned.

Procedure: A nine-month-old infant was chosen and assessed for emotional stability. He was unafraid of a range of stimuli including a white rat, a rabbit and some wooden blocks although he was afraid of a loud noise (made with a hammer and a steel bar). Two months later he was shown the rat again and, when he reached for it, the loud noise was made, which scared him. This was repeated five times, one week later. After a further 31 days during which Albert was neither presented with the experimental objects (such as the rat or rabbit) nor exposed to the loud noise, he was tested again.

Findings: Whenever the steel bar was struck Albert displayed fear. By the second trial, he was cautious about the rat and leaned away when the rat was presented. A further five days later, Albert cried in response to the rat and various similar objects including a fur coat, cotton wool and a Father Christmas beard and these responses persisted until the final testing, seven weeks after the start of the study. The blocks were not presented at the same time as the noise and he remained unafraid of them. After 31 days, Albert still showed fear towards the conditioned stimuli but he also reached out to touch the rabbit.

Conclusion: Albert was classically conditioned to be afraid of the rat and became afraid of other, similar, white or furry objects such as cotton wool and a Santa Claus mask with a beard. This is a process called generalisation. Albert's initial strong fear of the rabbit and later weaker fear and greater interest in it suggests that extinction had begun to lessen his fear.

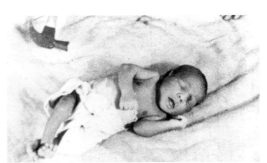

Figure 6.3a One thing he is afraid of

Figure 6.3b After conditioning, Albert is afraid of all furry objects

Watson & Rayner's study of Little Albert is an illustration of how classical conditioning can occur in humans and also shows that extinction affects human behaviour too. This study provides an example of another typical feature of learning – generalisation. This is where a response learned to one stimulus is later produced when other, similar stimuli are presented.

Questions

Films use a classically conditioned association to scare us.

1. How do you feel when you hear the music associated with this film?

2. Explain how classical conditioning could lead to elicit a fear response when we hear the Jaws music.

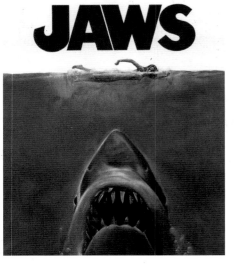

Figure 6.4
Can films classically condition us?

---

what's that?

- **Extinction:** the disappearance of a conditioned response in the absence of repeated associations or reinforcement

- **Spontaneous recovery:** the reappearance of a conditioned response following extinction after a period of absence of the CS or any other triggers

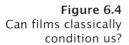
Discussion of classical conditioning

Classical conditioning can explain a range of human and animal behaviours and the existence of this type of learning is not controversial. It is easily demonstrated in the laboratory and is seen in real-life situations. What is up for discussion is how important it is in acquiring complex human behaviours. For example, classical conditioning cannot explain how we learn new behaviours, only how we learn to exhibit existing behaviours in response to different situations. Neither does classical conditioning explain how we learn from the consequences of our actions or from observing others. These are now known to be important learning mechanisms.

Operant conditioning

A pet cat or dog will learn what a tin of food looks like by classical conditioning. However, each time you find a new hiding place for these tins your pet will learn to access them by an entirely different process. Imagine you have hidden the cat food in a cupboard with a very heavy door. Your cat might try some random behaviours to open it – maybe scratching at the gap or lying on the floor and pushing with its feet. Some cats even learn to open cupboard doors by hanging from the top by their paws and swinging!

The cat is not using its sense of smell, nor is it being systematic in its investigation. The behaviours are exploratory attempts that happen to lead to the food. This type of trial and error learning was first investigated by Thorndike (1911). He built puzzle boxes (see Figure 6.6) to study how kittens acquired novel behaviours. A typical experiment involved a kitten confined to a box containing little but a lever, with food outside which it could see and smell. Pushing the lever opened the door of the box via a series of pulleys. A hungry kitten would perform various behaviours, such as biting, clawing, moving around the box or trying to squeeze out between the bars before accidentally operating the mechanism to open the door and thus getting to the food. This process differs from Pavlov's classical conditioning because the kitten only received the food as a result of carrying out the appropriate

Figure 6.5
Some random behaviours lead to rewards, so are reinforced

behaviour, that is the food was a *consequence*. After feeding, the kitten was returned to the box. It would try several behaviours again before stumbling by chance on the one that led to escape. After several repetitions, the kitten opened the door more quickly. The time the kitten took reduced from about five minutes to as little as five seconds over ten trials showing that the kittens were learning the puzzle. They were forming an association between the stimulus of the lever and a response – pushing it – as a result of the consequence, that is food.

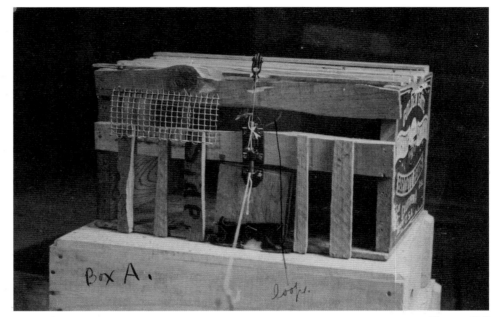

Figure 6.6
Thorndike's puzzle box

The work of B.F. Skinner

The kind of learning studied by Thorndike became known as operant conditioning and was studied in detail by B.F. Skinner. To maximise the objectivity, accuracy and ease of recording behaviour in his experiments, Skinner developed a chamber in which an animal, such as a rat or pigeon, could learn a specific response. The apparatus could present stimuli (e.g. lights or noises) and allowed responses (such as bar presses or pecks) to be measured and recorded. Consequences, for example food or an electric shock, followed the performance of a particular behaviour. These chambers, later known as Skinner boxes, offered precise control over the animal's experience so that the factors affecting learning could be rigorously investigated. They also allowed automated recording, further reducing external influences on the experimental animals.

Like our cat in the kitchen or the kitten in Thorndike's puzzle box, a rat in a Skinner box will perform a range of behaviours (Figure 6.7). The majority of these are irrelevant to the situation. When it chances to strike the bar, perhaps by stretching up against the wall, the mechanism will release a food pellet into the hopper. As this makes a 'click' the rat is likely to find the food quickly. Each time the rat hits the bar another pellet is released and as it discovers food in the hopper it checks more often. Since food is found only after the bar is pressed and not following any other behaviour, the frequency of this behaviour is increased. This is called **reinforcement**. Skinner (1938) summarised this in the statement 'behaviour is shaped and maintained by its consequences'.

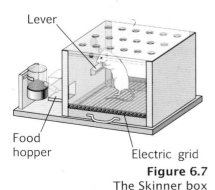

Lever

Food hopper

Electric grid

Figure 6.7
The Skinner box

what's that ?

- **Positive reinforcement**: the effect of increasing the frequency of a behaviour by using consequences that are pleasant when they happen

- **Negative reinforcement**: the effect of increasing the frequency of a behaviour by using consequences that are pleasant when they stop

- **Punishment**: the effect of decreasing the frequency of a behaviour by using consequences that are unpleasant when they happen.

Reinforcement: the effect of rewards

Skinner proposed that the consequences of a behaviour could either strengthen or weaken a response. How can this occur? Reinforcement, the process by which an animal is rewarded for a behaviour, can occur in two ways, each of which acts to increase the frequency of the immediately preceding behaviour.

Positive reinforcement is the arrival of good things, such as receiving food or water, the opportunity to play with a companion or access to a mate. When a behaviour is followed by a positive reinforcer, its frequency increases. An animal is more likely to perform a behaviour which has pleasant consequences. A rat will press a bar to receive food, children will tidy their bedrooms for the opportunity to watch TV.

Negative reinforcement is good because something bad stops happening, such as the reduction of pain when an electric shock is switched off or the relief when drilling outside your house comes to an end. When a behaviour is followed by a negative reinforcer, its frequency increases because the situation is more pleasant than before. This has exactly the same effect as a positive reinforcer. A rat will press a bar to turn an electric current off and I will repeatedly walk across the room to bang the TV to stop it buzzing.

Punishment: learning what not to do

Unlike reinforcement, which always has pleasant effects, **punishment** has unpleasant consequences. The arrival of something nasty (such as a shock) or the removal of something nice (such as pocket money) are punishers. Punishment reduces the frequency of the behaviour which it follows. If I tread in dog mess each time I go to the park, I will stop going there. Similarly, if a student loses their lunchtime to detention each week for being disruptive, they are likely to cease being a nuisance.

interactive angles

Decide whether each of these scenarios is an example of positive reinforcement, negative reinforcement or punishment:

1. A man with toothache visits the dentist and suffers more pain. He does not go back.

2. A girl goes to the dentist with toothache and it is sorted out. She then has regular check-ups.

3. A young man wears deodorant for the first time when going out. He finds that people talk to him and he continues to wear deodorant.

4. A student smokes in bed, setting fire to her room and destroying her Harry Potter DVD collection. She never smokes in bed again.

5. A boy does his homework for the first time and is praised by his teacher. After this he does his homework every week.

6. A student is allowed to drop a boring subject. Her effort in other subjects improves.

Schedules of reinforcement

Do animals learn better when they are reinforced on every performance of the required behaviour or not? The answer to this question depends on what is meant by better. In some respects, frequent, predictable reinforcement is better, in others infrequent, unpredictable reinforcement is more effective.

Skinner investigated the effects of different reinforcement regimes using rats and pigeons in Skinner boxes by varying how many responses they had to perform before receiving reinforcement, or when they had to perform.

An animal which receives a reward for every performance of a behaviour is on a continuous reinforcement schedule. This is like getting a treat every time you go to the dentist. *Continuous reinforcement* results in a low but steady response rate and the behaviour will extinguish very readily if reinforcement is withheld. All other patterns of reinforcement offer rewards for only some instances of the behaviour, this is called *partial reinforcement*.

On a *fixed ratio* schedule (FR), reinforcement is related to the number of behaviours performed. In general, ratio schedules tend to produce high, steady, response rates, although there may be a post-reinforcement pause – PRP – a gap between receiving reinforcement and resuming performance of the behaviour (see Figure 6.8). For example, a person working on a production line might be paid per 100 items they process. Immediately after each batch is completed they may have a break, but work hard again on the next 100. Extinction of behaviours reinforced on FR schedules is quite rapid.

On *variable ratio* schedules animals are reinforced only after several responses have been made, the exact number varying around an average. As with FR, the response rate tends to be high, although in laboratory animals the PRP tends to be absent. A variable ratio of five, for instance, would reward every fifth behaviour *on average*, in reality the first, tenth, thirteenth, seventeenth and twenty-fifth response may be reinforced. This pattern of reinforcement produces the fastest response rate and the greatest resistance to extinction. Gamblers receive payouts after variable numbers of attempts thus their gambling behaviour is persistent even in the face of nil returns.

A *fixed interval* schedule provides reinforcement at regular times, for instance receiving pocket money every Saturday if your room has been tidy. This results in an uneven pattern of response – you suddenly start to clear up on Thursdays and Fridays. The response extinguishes quite quickly; you are unlikely to bother cleaning your room at all if there is no money to be had! In laboratory animals this can be seen as a 'scallop' in response rate – with more responses as the end of the interval approaches (see Figure 6.8). Once the reinforcement has been received, a PRP may follow. The overall response rate tends to be lower than with ratio schedules as the behaviour only needs to be performed once in each interval in order to receive reinforcement.

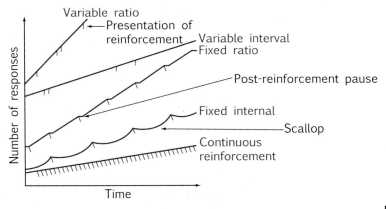

Figure 6.8
The different schedules of reinforcement produce differing response patterns as indicated by records of cumulative reinforcements over time

Finally, a *variable interval* schedule provides reinforcement at timed intervals but the gap between each reinforcement varies around an average. For example, a variable interval schedule of one minute would provide rewards on average every 60 seconds but these may in fact arrive at 20-, 80-, 90-, 40-, 30- and 100-second intervals. The response rate is high and steady and extinction occurs only very gradually. As with variable ratio schedules, there is no PRP. You are most likely to keep working hard if you are unsure when an inspector is going to arrive to judge the quality of your output.

Partial reinforcement clearly affects both response rate and resistance to extinction. Gambling seems to fulfil the criteria of a variable ratio schedule, producing both high response rates and resistance to extinction, in fact gambling shows many properties of addiction. However, Delfabbro & Winefield (1999) have shown that the response rates of gamblers do not exactly replicate the high, steady response rates predicted for a variable ratio schedule of reinforcement. Rather, the response rate of players on poker machines (the Australian equivalent of fruit machines or slot machines) dipped after a pay-out. These post-reinforcement pauses were dependent on the size of the reward and the experience of the players (experienced players taking longer pauses after a big win). These findings suggest that gamblers, unlike rats, are sensitive to machine events. Response rate and extinction using various schedules of reinforcement have also been investigated using cocaine as a reinforcer (see Classic research).

Classic research

Optional

Pickens, R. & Thompson, T. (1968)

'Cocaine-reinforced behaviour in rats: effects of reinforcement magnitude and fixed-ratio size'

The Journal of Pharmacology and Experimental Therapeutics, 161(1): 122–9.

Aim: To compare the effects of food and cocaine as sources of positive reinforcement by varying the size of the reinforcer and the reinforcement schedule.

Procedure: Male albino rats that had not been used in any similar experiments were individually housed in cages containing two levers and a light. They had free access to food (except Experiment 3) and water throughout the experiment. Cocaine could be administered intravenously through a catheter that ran under the skin on the rat's back and into a vein in its neck. This was held in place with a harness and the tubing passed through the roof of the cage to a pump. This could provide different amounts of cocaine directly into the rat's bloodstream or could administer saline (salt solution at the same concentration as the rat's blood).

Experiment 1: Two rats were given 0.5mg/kg of cocaine as a reinforcer (or saline) in four pairs of conditions (A–D) each one changing after 100 minutes.

- A: the drug was administered when the lever was pressed (contingent on behaviour), then at regular intervals regardless of the rat's behaviour (non-contingent).

- B: first the drug was administered when the lever was pressed, then saline.

- C: the drug was administered and a light appeared when the lever was pressed, then the light appeared but saline was injected.

- D: the drug was administered and a light appeared when the correct lever was pressed, then the effective lever was swapped over.

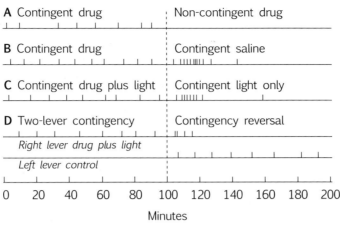

A	Contingent drug	Non-contingent drug
B	Contingent drug	Contingent saline
C	Contingent drug plus light	Contingent light only
D	Two-lever contingency	Contingency reversal
	Right lever drug plus light	
	Left lever control	

0   20   40   60   80   100   120   140   160   180   200

Minutes

Figure 6.9a
Results of Experiment 1 for one animal

Experiment 2: Three rats were treated as per the drug tests in 1C. They were each tested using a wide range of drug doses to find the lower and upper limits for effective reinforcement. Then, varying the doses between 0.25 and 3.0 mg/kg, the rats were tested on a range of fixed ratio schedules from FR5 to FR80 (that is receiving a drug infusion for every five lever presses, every six and so on up to 80). For each dose, the schedule ratio was increased until responding stopped. Each condition was repeated twice and maintained for at least six hours.

Experiment 3: One rat was used in a procedure similar to Experiment 2 but using food rather than cocaine as a reinforcer. Food was dispensed in different 'doses' of 1, 5, 10 or 20 45mg pellets available 24 hours a day. Four days for responding to each dose size were recorded and replicated three times, each time in a different order.

Experiment 4: A single rat kept at 80% of its normal body weight was taught to respond to an FR10 schedule for food over 45 days. The next day it received 1mg/kg of cocaine every hour for five hours before the experiment began that day and for the next two days. The rat then received infusions of 0.5, 1.0 or 1.5mg/kg of cocaine to determine its effect on food-reinforced responding.

Findings:

Experiment 1: All animals responded in a similar way (see Figure 6.9a). A shows that contingent reinforcement (i.e. when it is dependent on the lever pressing) is necessary for steady and frequent responses. Without contingency, responding stops. B shows that cocaine has reinforcing properties as the response rate during saline infusion was initially fast, then the response extinguished in the absence of the reinforcer. C shows that even though the light had been paired with cocaine it did not acquire the strongly reinforcing properties of cocaine. D again shows that cocaine is an effective reinforcer because, in the absence of reinforcement for the 'old' response, it stopped and the response of pressing the other (contingent) lever was rapidly acquired.

Experiment 2: Above a minimum dose, bigger reinforcers, i.e. higher doses of cocaine, produced lower response rates. However, at high doses (more than 1.5mg/kg for two rats, more than 3.0mg/kg for the other) the animals rapidly stopped responding altogether. This pattern was not typical of extinction. Replications produced similar results for each animal so were combined. When the fixed ratio was increased the rats pressed the lever more frequently. The effect was that they received approximately the same amount of the drug per hour regardless of the reinforcement schedule (approximately 6 to 7mg/kg/hr – see Figure 6.9b). As the fixed ratio increased the post-reinforcement pauses (the time gap between receiving reinforcement and starting to respond again) became longer (see Figure 6.9c).

Experiment 3: The same pattern as in Experiment 2 was found with increasing the fixed ratio of food reinforcement. As the number or lever presses required for a food pellet increased the response rate increased. The rate at which pellets were received therefore stayed steady at about 20 per hour.

Experiment 4: When saline was given to rats responding on an FR10 schedule for food, their responses continued, but when this was replaced with cocaine, the rats stopped pressing the lever for food.

Conclusion: The ability of cocaine to reinforce lever pressing and to transfer learning between two levers shows that it is an effective form of positive reinforcement. The pattern of response to cocaine was similar to food reinforcement. Increasing the fixed ratio produced faster responding so that in either case the total reinforcement per hour remained the same. The post reinforcement pause also increased in both cases. Bigger reinforcements of food or cocaine both caused slower responding, again producing the same reinforcement total per hour. However, unlike food, cocaine produced an abrupt loss of responding when reinforcement size exceeded a certain amount. This was not an extinction pattern but showed that the drug prevented the rats from responding.

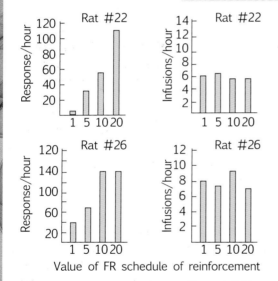

Figure 6.9b
Results of experiment 2: the response rate changes with FR schedule, keeping drug intake the same

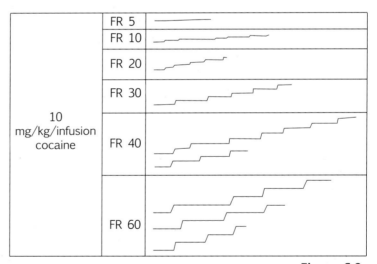

Figure 6.9c
As the fixed ratio increases, the post-reinforcement pause lengthens

Figure 6.10
Squirrels can be taught tricks by offering accessible rewards then making them successively more difficult to reach thus shaping their behaviour

Partial reinforcement schedules in real life

1. Sarah is trying to get hold of Kate on the phone but Kate's number is busy. Sarah keeps pressing redial over and over again.

2. Netball is Sally's favourite sport. She really wants to be a credit to her team and hurtles about trying to shoot as often as she can. Just occasionally she succeeds in scoring and basks in the cheers of the crowd.

3. Pete's cooking a lasagne for some friends. After he's put it in the oven he leaves it alone but, once it's been in for a while, he keeps going to check if it's done – he really wants it to be perfect.

4. Jim works in the post room which is downstairs in his two-storey office block so he has to carry packages up one flight of stairs of 32 steps. The packages are heavy and he feels relieved (a positive reinforcer) each time he reaches the top of the stairs. He tends not to stop on the way up, though often has a rest at the top of the stairs.

Each of the examples above represents one of the partial reinforcement schedules. Which is which?

Shaping: reinforcing successive approximations

Skinner proposed that specific and entirely new actions could be produced through conditioning. He suggested that this could be achieved by selectively reinforcing behaviours which more closely resembled the desired response. This rewarding of successive approximations is called **shaping**. To make children keep their rooms tidy, parents might initially reward them for picking up their dirty clothes, later for putting their books away as well and subsequently only when the entire floor is visible. On each occasion the child is only reinforced if its attempts at tidying are better than the last. Animals can be taught to perform tricks in the same way.

Primary and secondary reinforcers

There are some sources of reinforcement which animals and humans consistently find pleasant. These include food when we are hungry (and even when we are not), water when we are thirsty, feeling good about ourselves, reduction of fear, social company and sexual pleasure. All of these are called **primary reinforcers** because they satisfy our basic needs. We like to eat chocolate because it tastes nice. People have sex because it feels good. When we jump into a cool swimming pool we gain relief from the heat on a summer's day. All of these experiences are sources of reinforcement (either positive or negative) and they meet our basic biological requirements, such as physical comfort, nutrition or reproduction.

Some sources of reinforcement, however, are not reinforcing because they meet basic biological needs but through association. This is called **secondary reinforcement**. Such reinforcers acquire their power to reward us through classical conditioning. For example, a child is pleased to see a high mark in his or her exercise book because it is associated with praise, and praise makes us feel good. We like the sight of Christmas lights because that time of year is linked to pleasant experiences such as receiving presents or seeing friends.

how science works

Research Methods

The experiment in studies on learning

As in cognitive and biological psychology, laboratory experiments in the learning approach are conducted on both humans and animals. Some are natural experiments, such as those comparing boys and girls, other are true experiments such as comparing the effects of reinforcement (or not) on social learning. Where the IV can be manipulated and participants can be randomly allocated to groups the findings of experiments are likely to be more valid. However, other factors affect the credibility of findings. One of these is the level of control over the experimental situation. Many laboratory experiments in the learning approach have been conducted on animals with much higher levels of control than would be possible with humans. Testing environments such as the Skinner box are a good example of this – the findings are highly reliable.

Figure 6.11
Our belief in the dangers of ladders is reinforced every time we walk around one

Uncontrollable reinforcers and learning to be superstitious

Studies such as Skinner's and the work of Pickens & Thompson (1968) have illustrated the importance of contingency – the reinforcer should be dependent on the performance of the behaviour. This suggests that when a positive consequence follows a behaviour we would tend to repeat that behaviour even if it was not the cause of the reward. Positive consequences that occur regardless of our behaviour are called *uncontrollable reinforcers* – 'uncontrollable' because they occur regardless of our behaviour and 'reinforcers' because they increase the probability of the behaviour being performed at the time being repeated. The power of uncontrollable reinforcers was first demonstrated by Skinner (1948) (see Classic Research). The behaviours that arise as a consequence of such reinforcement are called *superstitious* behaviours. We would expect that superstition, the belief in a relationship which does not in fact exist, to be uniquely human as we assume that animals do not have beliefs. However, Skinner designed this experiment to demonstrate that superstitious behaviours could be acquired by animals. He proposed that superstitious behaviours simply arise because they are accidentally reinforced by some consequence which is *not* dependent upon that response.

More recently, Helena Matute has examined the role of uncontrollable reinforcers in human behaviour. In one study, Matute (1996) tested whether a superstitious behaviour can arise because we fail to test the possibility that a positive outcome can occur irrespective of our behaviour. Participants worked on computers, some of which periodically emitted beeps. If the participants had the opportunity to discover that doing nothing led to the beep stopping on its own, they learned to wait. However, when they were instructed to try to stop the beep, the participants acquired superstitious responses. In an attempt to stop the noise they tried pressing particular buttons, and learned (wrongly) that it was this button that made the noise stop.

" " Discussion of operant conditioning

Operant conditioning is well supported by experimental evidence and clearly operates in many situations with humans as well as animals. The range of processes that affect operant conditioning, such as the schedule of

Classic research

Optional

Skinner, B.F. (1948)

'Superstition in the pigeon'

Journal of Experimental Psychology, 38: 168–72.

Pigeons are superstitious!

Aim: To demonstrate that superstitious behaviours could be acquired by animals.

Procedure: Eight pigeons were given limited food to reduce them to 75% of their normal weight to ensure that they were hungry. Each was placed individually in a Skinner box for a few minutes a day and received a food pellet every 15 seconds regardless of its behaviour. After several days of conditioning, two independent observers recorded the birds' behaviour. The time interval between pellets was increased to one minute and the frequency of responding was recorded again. Finally the pigeons were given time for acquired behaviours to extinguish by stopping the release of pellets. In one pigeon 15-second interval food pellets were reintroduced after 20 minutes of extinction.

Findings: Of the eight pigeons, six developed repetitive behaviours that they performed between the arrival of pellets. These included turning anti-clockwise, hopping, head tossing and pendulum swings of the head, none of which were exhibited before the experiment. This behaviour was so clear to see that the observers agreed perfectly about the records of behaviour. None of these behaviours had been observed in the birds before. Most of the new behaviours were performed in the same part of the cage each time and quite frequently, at a rate of about 5–6 times between each reinforcement. When the time between reinforcers (food pellets) was extended to one minute the pigeons' behaviour increased until they became frantic. Extinction of these new behaviours was slow. For example, the bird that had acquired hopping behaviour performed over 10,000 responses before extinction occurred. When this bird began to receive pellets at 15-second intervals again it rapidly began hopping (see Figure 6.12).

Conclusion: The pigeons behaved as though they believed that the delivery of food pellets depended upon their response even though it did not, as people do when they hold superstitions. Since reinforcement was intermittent, the pigeons' behaviour, like that of superstitious humans, was difficult to extinguish. When extinction did occur, the behaviour could then be readily reconditioned.

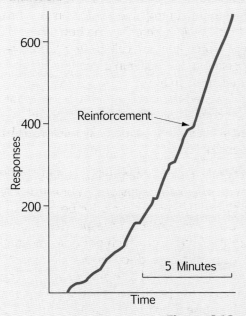

Figure 6.12
Positive reinforcement leads to an increase in the frequency of a behaviour even when the rewards are not dependent on the behaviour performed

reinforcement and the effect of uncontrolled reinforcers helps to explain a wide range of observations about behaviour. Operant conditioning, unlike classical conditioning, can explain how completely new behaviours can be acquired and offers ways to deliberately alter behaviour through shaping. One aspect of learning that operant conditioning cannot account for is the way that behaviour changes in response to observing the actions of others. We will consider this influence later in the chapter.

The learning approach and therapy

Learning theory can be used in clinical settings to change people's behaviour. The clinical application of classical conditioning is called behaviour therapy, operant conditioning has given rise to behaviour modification. We will look at an example of each.

Aversion therapy: a therapy using classical conditioning

Some behaviours are seen as undesirable and **aversion therapy** may be used to eliminate them. For example, smokers and alcoholics may undergo aversion therapy to cure their addictions. Aversion therapy works through classical conditioning. Prior to treatment a UCS – which will become part of the treatment – produces an unpleasant, i.e. aversive, UCR. During treatment this unpleasant response becomes associated with the stimulus to be avoided, this is the CS. An association is built up which causes the client's behaviour to change as the maladaptive habit (e.g. smoking or drinking) becomes linked to the unpleasant response (the CR) (see Box 6.1).

Box 6.1 **Aversion therapy**

Aversion therapy is used to treat alcoholism. The drug Antabuse causes vomiting if it is combined with alcohol and, through classical conditioning, the response of drinking alcohol is removed:

UCS (Antabuse) $\longrightarrow$ UCR (vomiting)

UCS + NS (alcohol) $\longrightarrow$ UCR (unpleasant expectation accompanying vomiting)

CS (alcohol) $\longrightarrow$ CR (unpleasant expectation)

As the CR is aversive the individual stops drinking alcohol.

Aversion therapy has been used in many different ways. For example, Duker & Seys (2000) reduced self-injury in 41 children with learning difficulties using aversion therapy. The aim was to prevent harmful behaviours such as refusing food, vomiting, head banging and hair-pulling. Non-aversive therapies and milder aversive stimuli (such as unpleasant tastes and water sprays) had been used with the children without success. Following extensive physical health evaluations and ethical approval, small electric shocks were used as aversive stimuli. The shock was administered though an electrode attached to the individual's body (e.g. hand or foot) and was applied using a remote control device if the individual began to self-harm. This treatment successfully reduced self-harming behaviour over the experimental period and beyond.

However, long term follow-up (up to 108 months later) showed that in some individuals the behaviours reappeared. This extinction suggests that the learned suppression of the behaviour is in some instances lost over time.

Weinrott *et al.* (1997) used aversion therapy with sex offenders to eliminate conditioned responses of sexual arousal. Young sex offenders listened to an audiotaped crime scenario that evoked deviant sexual arousal. They were then immediately exposed to a videotaped aversive stimulus – the negative social, emotional, physical and legal consequences of sex offences. Weinrott *et al.* found that the offenders' physiological arousal and self-reported measures of arousal reduced following this treatment.

Howard (2001) tested the effectiveness of aversion therapy with 82 alcoholic patients who were given a 10-day treatment programme with a drug which induced nausea with alcohol. They were tested before and after the programme on how confident they were that they could avoid consuming alcohol in difficult situations where they would normally be tempted to drink. They were also checked to ensure that any effect of conditioning was specific to alcoholic drinks. After treatment the patients were more confident that they would be able to resist drinking alcohol even in high-risk situations showing that the conditioning had worked. However, this effect was less strong in patients with a longer history of alcohol-associated nausea and more anti-social behaviour. Using pulse rate as an indicator, the aversion was found to be specific to alcoholic beverages.

Figure 6.13
Aversion therapy using drugs such as Antabuse can be used to help alcoholics

Aversion therapy clearly has useful applications but it also has disadvantages. It can be misused, for example in misguided attempts to 'cure' homosexual tendencies. There is also a risk of spontaneous recovery. This is where the old (maladaptive) response reappears over time. The patient may also revert to their previous maladaptive behaviour if the new (adaptive) response undergoes extinction. It can also only be used when trying to eradicate a behaviour – rather than introduce a new one – and for those responses for which a suitable aversive stimulus exists.

Token economy: a therapy using operant conditioning

This approach to therapy uses both positive reinforcement and shaping. In an institutional setting (such as a mental hospital) the frequency with which particular behaviours are performed can be increased. The desired responses are positively reinforced with coin-like tokens or punches on a card. These tokens are secondary reinforcers, that is, they have reinforcing powers because they have been linked to a positive reinforcer by classical conditioning. The tokens are saved up and exchanged for privileges or goods (e.g. luxury food) – these are the primary reinforcers. The use of tokens as indirect rewards allows for immediate reinforcement of appropriate behaviour. This means that, even though patients cannot continuously be given primary reinforcers such as food, they can be positively reinforced straight away which increases the chances of the desired behaviour being repeated. Shaped behaviours can include better socialisation, self-care (such as washing) or reduced aggression.

media watch

Scientists put price on addicts' treatment

Della Fok

yaledailynews.com 11 October 2006

Yale scientists have put a price on incentive-based treatments for drugs abusers, helping to clarify the programs' costs and benefits.

Researchers from the Yale Department of Epidemiology and Public Health and the University of Connecticut Health Center found that it costs an additional $258 per patient to use prize-based incentives, which past research has shown can encourage patients to remain drug-free. The study, conducted by Yale research scientist Todd Olmstead and professor Jody Sindelar, along with University of Connecticut researcher Nancy Petry, was recently published in the September issue of Drug and Alcohol Dependence.

The researchers gathered data from eight clinics serving a variety of patients across the country, focusing on treatment for addiction to cocaine, amphetamine and methamphetamine. The incentive method they explored was a supplemental program used alongside traditional treatment.

If the patients submitted drug-free urine samples, they earned chances to draw from a fishbowl with 500 chips, representing different levels of prizes. Out of 500 chips, 250 said 'Good job,' 209 were for small items worth about $1, 40 were for larger prizes worth $20, and one was for the jumbo prize worth $100. The longer the patients remained drug-free, the more draws they earned.

'The incentive is to have continuous days of abstinence, which encourages long periods of abstinence,' Sindelar said. 'This escalates the number of consecutive days and weeks patients stay clean, which mimics getting out of the habit.'

Petry, who designed the prize-based incentive technique, compared it to traditional behavior modification methods such as giving children allowances to encourage them to do a particular task more often.

Previous studies have proven that these types of treatment supplements are effective in helping substance abuse patients stay abstinent for longer periods of time, Olmstead said.

Although he said he wasn't surprised by the effectiveness of the method, he was surprised by the amount of money required for the administration. Including inventory, restocking and shopping for the items, the cost of the administration totaled almost as much as that of the prizes themselves.

'The next question is how to improve cost-effectiveness, streamline administration and improve efficiency,' Olmstead said.

While the researchers said it remains to be proven whether or not this strategy makes financial sense, they said they believe spending the extra $258 will cut back on some of the negative consequences of drug use, including crime and lost work days.

'Substance abuse treatment is becoming less punitive,' Petry said. 'It's becoming more of a positive experience, so the patients now like going to treatment because they get prizes and get to stay clean longer. It changes the atmosphere of the whole treatment.'

1. The treatment programme described above works like a token economy programme as the chance to enter the draw can lead to a range of different reinforcers. What are the primary and secondary reinforcers being used?
2. How is behaviour being shaped by this programme?
3. Identify two advantages of this treatment programme mentioned in the text.
4. Suggest two disadvantages of this programme.

In general, a token economy system is cheap to administer and effective in a range of situations. For example, Ayllon & Azrin (1968) used it successfully for reinforcing self-care in schizophrenic patients in a psychiatric hospital. Petry *et al.* (2006) found the use of reward of entries to a prize draw as tokens with alcoholics to be highly effective. Sindelar *et al.* (2007) demonstrated similar success with the same programme with 120 cocaine abusers on a 12-week programme (see Media watch). When payouts were bigger ($240 rather than $80 pay-out) the participants provided a higher percentage of drug-free urine samples, stayed clean for longer and were more likely to complete the treatment programme. Even though the prizes were of higher value, the overall cost-effectiveness of the programme was better than when prizes were of a lower value.

Furthermore, token economies are preferable to other methods, such as aversion therapy, because it is a more ethical way to modify behaviour because it is less distressing. However, token economies may lead to dependency, for example, patients may expect to be rewarded for everyday activities which would make coping outside the institutional environment difficult. A disadvantage from the ethical viewpoint arises because the decision about which behaviours are 'desirable' and which are not is made by the institution. As a consequence, differences of opinion may arise if individuals are being deprived of privileges that others see as rights.

For & Against
behavioural therapies

FOR Evidence suggests that these techniques are extremely effective. For example, the aversion therapy used by Duker & Seys (2000) and the token economy used by Sindelar (2007) have made significant improvements to the lives of individuals on the programmes.

FOR The changes in behaviour that are produced are based on sound experimental evidence and are the result of observable learning processes which makes the techniques credible.

AGAINST In cases where genes (see Chapter 5) or family relationships (see Chapter 4) have played a role in the development of symptoms behavioural treatments, which just alleviate symptoms, cannot be considered cures. Techniques such as aversion therapy and token economies only alter the performance of behaviours, they do not solve the cause of the problem.

AGAINST Sometimes behavioural treatments can be unpleasant for patients. The benefit of the treatment needs to be balanced against this trauma. For example, in Duker & Seys' use of electric shocks, other possible methods have to have been tried and strict ethical guidelines for treatment adhered to.

Gender development

At the beginning of the previous chapter we described how genes determine sex. This is one way to look at gender – simply as biological sex. But, as we also saw in Chapter 5, biological sex is not clear-cut in every case. All individuals nevertheless have an internal concept of whether they are male of female, this is their **gender identity** (see p. 104). One way that we characterise maleness and femaleness is through behaviour and social roles (think back to the efforts to make 'Bruce' female – see pp. 142–43). **Gender stereotypes** refer to the beliefs people hold about the way that males and females behave. In this section we look at the importance of learning on the acquisition of gender identity and **sex-typed behaviours**, that is, the performance of actions that fit in with gender stereotypes.

One gender stereotype that has been investigated is social aggression. Whilst stereotypes suggest that males are generally more aggressive than females, social aggression, for example engaging in malicious gossip, is believed to be more typically female. Underwood *et al.* (2004) investigated how boys and girls differ in their response to a difficult play partner. They observed 146 friendship pairs (aged between 10 and 14 years) playing Pictionary (a board game). Each pair was with a same-gender child-confederate trained to be a difficult play partner (by bragging, messing up the game and asking irrelevant questions). Observers recorded the children's vocalisations and gestures, identifying indicators of social exclusion, verbal aggression and verbal assertion. There were few differences, although boys tended to socially exclude the actor more and to be more verbally aggressive than girls. Girls, in contrast, employed a wider range of non-verbal behaviours, including glaring, rolling their eyes and turning away from the confederate and were more negative when the confederate was absent.

Modelling

Social learning theory proposes that learning can occur when one individual (the learner) observes and imitates another, the model. For example, a young girl may watch an older one putting on make up and try to copy her. According to Bandura (1977) modelling will occur when the observer pays attention, is able to remember and reproduce what they have observed and when they are motivated to do so. This motivation may be an external reward or some inner drive. Internal motivation may be generated by the model and this can explain why there are differences in the effectiveness of different models.

Figure 6.14
Children are motivated to imitate adult models as they are seen as powerful. However, same-sex models are preferred and we may acquire sex-typed behaviours by observation and imitating them

Pennington (1986) identifies three categories of variable that affect imitation:

- characteristics of the model
- characteristics of the observer
- the consequences of the behaviour for the model.

Bandura *et al.* (1961) indicated one important characteristic of the model, their sex. Others include age and status. A model who is of similar age and high in status is more likely to be imitated. For example, young people who perceive drug-users as high in status may be drawn into drug taking because the sight of high status people taking drugs is more influential than the threats of their parents. The effect of status is one reason why girls are more likely to copy boys' behaviour than vice versa. The status of males in society makes stereotypically male attributes more valuable, thus to be brave or dominant may be seen as more positive than being safe or placatory. For the observer, their own level of self-esteem is an important determinant of imitation. One important consequence for the model is whether they are reinforced. If the observer sees the model receiving positive reinforcement for their actions they are more likely to imitate them. This effect is called *vicarious reinforcement*.

Observations

When psychologists want to record the behaviour of participants (including children and animals as well as adults) they can use observations. In some studies, such as Bandura *et al.* (1961) the observations are simply a way to record the dependent variable in an experiment. In other situations, the observation itself is the research method. For example, two studies have video-taped children's free play in the playground, focusing on the levels of real aggression and play fighting. In both cases this was later compared to the children's testosterone level. Sánchez-Martín *et al.* (2000) found that boys with higher levels of testosterone were also those observed to engage in more acts of aggression. Similarly, Ahedo *et al.* (2002) found a positive correlation between observed levels of playful aggression and testosterone. In both studies, the levels of aggression (serious and playful) were much lower in girls.

The examples described above illustrate several differences in the way an observation can be carried out. When the observer is not part of the group (as in Sánchez-Martín *et al.* and Ahedo *et al.*) the observer is described as non-participant. This makes recording easier as the observer can readily focus on different individuals or behaviours without drawing attention to them as would happen if the observer were part of the social group. They also retain their objectivity, unlike an observer who is involved whose observations may become subjective. However, when the observer is participant, that is involved in the situation, they can benefit from understanding more about the feelings of the participants and the reasons for their behaviour. For example, Marsh *et al.* (1978) observed the 'careers' of football hooligans at Oxford United football club by being an active supporter of the team. In this situation, the participants, that is the football hooligans, were unaware that they were being observed. This is an example of a covert observation. This means that the observer is hidden from the participants. This was traditionally achieved by observing from behind a one-way mirror (e.g. in Bandura *et al.*, 1961). Modern research tends to use video recording (as in the Ahedo *et al.* (2002)

above and Underwood *et al.* (2004), p. 180) or a one-way dark grey glass screen. Even though the participants are likely to have been invited behind the screen to see the observation area, so they would know they were being observed, having a screen or hidden camera helps to reduce the impact of the presence of the observers and their equipment. Because they cannot see the observer they are less likely to be affected by demand characteristics. This is especially important for children who may respond to being watched, for instance by 'showing off'. There is also, however, the disadvantage that in some covert observations it is difficult to ask the participants for their informed consent without making the observation obvious. The alternative is to be an overt observer, that is, to be obvious to the participants. This has both ethical and practical advantages. It avoids the need for deception and means that the observers can follow a particular individual and do not have to disguise the fact that they are making recordings.

When conducted in the participants' normal surroundings, observations are naturalistic. This applied to Marsh's study of the football supporters and to Ahedo *et al.* (2002) and Underwood *et al.* (2004) studies of children's free play in the playground. In the case of Bandura, however, the children had been brought into a special laboratory designed to look like a playroom but with a one-way mirror in one wall. Their behaviour was also manipulated by frustrating them. This type of observation is contrived rather than naturalistic. Naturalistic observations in contrast are highly representative of real behaviour, that is they are valid because they reflect the way people would behave in actual situations. However, they are harder to control and observer subjectivity and ethical issues are harder to deal with.

So, when conducting observations there are important practical decisions to be made about the relationship between the observer and the observed. Another practical decision relates to the recording of observations. Particular behaviours have to be selected for observation and these, like the variables in an experiment, need to be operationally defined. This is especially important if there is more than one observer as it is essential that they record the same information when observing the same events, that is that they have high inter-observer reliability. Finally, the observer must decide how their observational recordings will be made. The simplest method is to make a checklist. This is used for event sampling in which each occurrence of a behaviour on the list is recorded. This would produce quantitative data about the frequency of each behaviour. Records of the length of time spent on each behaviour would also produce quantitative data. When results are obtained in this way descriptive and inferential statistics can then be applied. This would be useful for comparing different behaviours or looking at which behaviours occur most in different situations. For example, the frequency of aggressive behaviour in boys compared to girls could be measured by counting the number of aggressive acts by each gender. Alternatively, observational recordings can be qualitative. In ths case, detailed records are made of specific events. This may be a direct written record or can be transcribed, that is written out from a more complete record such as a continuous description spoken into a recorder or a video recording of the observational session. In this case, the aim is to preserve the detail in the results. Similarities between the nature of patterns of behaviour can be identified in different settings or between different individuals. These would then be identified as key 'themes' as is done in other qualitative methods. For example, in an observation of aggression in boys and girls, the kind of behaviours used could be observed in detail. For example, girls might use subtle body language to exclude others rather than being physically aggressive. Detailed attention to an individual could be used to reveal how and when this is done.

There are also several ethical concerns raised by observations. As in any study, we would expect participants to be given the opportunity to offer their informed consent and this should be done whenever possible. In practice, this is impractical and unnecessary in many naturalistic settings where participants may be unaware that they are being watched. It is important therefore that such observations only take place in situations where the individuals would expect to be on public display. In such environments there may also be privacy issues relating to the location itself. So places such as shops, although essentially 'public' in that we might expect to be seen by others, are owned and permission must be sought from appropriate management sources to avoid infringing the privacy of their customers.

When observing children, particular caution is necessary. Children should not be observed in public places and never without the consent of their guardians. In a school or playgroup, permission from the institution as well as the guardians is essential. Children themselves should be asked for their consent if they are aware that they are being watched and should also have the right to withdraw. Researchers need to be mindful that children may express their desire to leave a study in different ways from adults, such as by not wanting to join in or walking away. It is important that such indicators are recognised and responded to.

Modelling, reinforcement and shaping in gender development

One key feature of a model is their gender. The findings of Bandura et al. (1961) (see Classic Research p. 182) suggest that same-sex models are more effective than opposite-sex models for increasing aggressive behaviour in children. Is the same pattern found in the acquisition of gender-stereotyped behaviours? Before we can answer this question, we need to know a little about what the stereotyped expectations might be. Williams & Best (1990) have shown that beliefs about maleness and femaleness are fairly consistent across cultures. Golombok & Fivush (1994) suggest the essence of these stereotypes are:

- male: being instrumental, that is acting on things in the world to make things happen
- female: being relational, that is having a concern for interactions between people and how they feel.

These differences are then reflected in identifiable beliefs and expectations in society, for example that:

- males will be: aggressive, active and competitive
- females will be: nurturing, passive and cooperative.

Note that, just because these stereotypes are widely believed does not mean that they represent real differences between the sexes. One difference is clear however that, in general, traits associated with maleness are more highly valued in society.

A child will be exposed to models of both sexes. As Bandura has shown, they are more likely to imitate same-sex models. Learning theory, however, encompasses more than just modelling. When children copy gender-matching behaviour they are likely to be reinforced, for example by parents or by same-gender peers. For example, a girl may be encouraged when playing with dolls but ignored, laughed at or told off for playing with guns. The reverse is often the case for boys. This selective reinforcement shapes their behaviour to conform to gender stereotypes. Because the child is reinforced more for same-sex activities than opposite-sex ones, they learn to value sex-typed behaviours for their own gender more than those for the opposite gender. This effect is also evident in the way children treat one another. Pre-teenage children who do not conform to gender stereotypes are less popular with their peers than those who do (Sroufe *et al.*, 1993). Even in adulthood such influences are still powerful. An assertive woman may be described as 'pushy', a caring man as a 'wimp'. These represent significant pressures to behave in what society dictates to be 'gender-appropriate' ways.

Evidence suggests that both selective imitation and reinforcement do occur. Lytton and Romney (1991) meta-analysed evidence relating to the way that parents treat male and female children. They found that sex-typed behaviour was encouraged in both genders, e.g. shaping children's choices of activities and interests. However, there were also many similarities in the way that boys and girls were raised and they concluded that it was unlikely that differences in reinforcement could account for differences in the acquisition of sex-typed behaviour.

The models to which children are exposed are not simply their parents. One focus of research has been on gender representation in children's books. Although books are much less stereotyped than they were, significant differences in representation still exist. Evans & Davies (2000) looked at the books published in 1997 for children in the first, third and fifth grade at school. They found that, although there were approximately equal numbers of males (54%) and females (46%) represented, the characters were still somewhat stereotypical (see Table 6.01). Similarly, Milburn *et al.* (2001), in an analysis of males and females in computer clip art, found that males are more often portrayed as active and non-nurturing than females.

Table 6.1
Evans & Davies (2000)

Trait	Males	Females
Aggressive	24	5
Competitive	36	11
Emotionally expressive	14	33
Passive	8	30

interactive angles

Are these clip art images stereotyped?

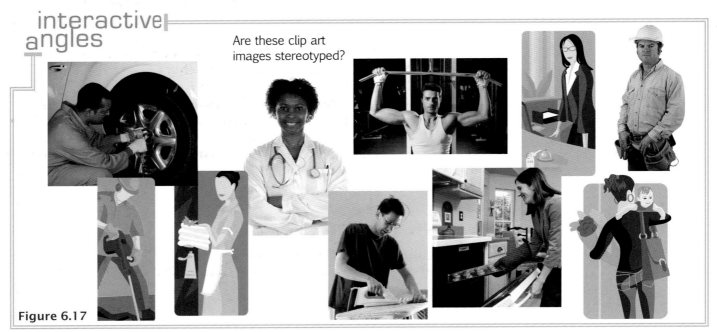

Figure 6.17

Using the chi-squared test

One way to be sure about the effect in a study that has produced numerical data is to conduct a statistical test. You have already encountered, the Spearman Rank Order Correlation (Chapter 4) and the Mann–Whitney (Chapter 5). In a study such as one comparing the number of gender-stereotyped behaviours illustrated in advertisements an appropriate test is the chi-squared test of association. You do not have to learn the formula for this test, work it out by hand or do it in an exam, but you do need to have used it. To run a chi-squared test online, go to http://faculty.vassar.edu/lowry/VassarStats.html. Follow the link to 'frequency data' on the navigation bar, scroll down to 'Chi-Square, Cramer's V, and Lambda' (ignoring the link for 'Chi-Square "Goodness of Fit" Test') and click on it. The first thing you will have to do is select the number of rows and columns. Click on 2 rows and 3 columns then enter the following data into the rows provided:

Type of behaviour illustrated ⟶ Gender of illustration ↓	Gender-consistent	Gender–inconsistent	Gender neutral
Males	61	15	24
Females	27	25	38

Click on 'Calculate' and look for the chi square box. The figure here is your observed value for chi-squared, in this case 18.32. The figure for chi-squared is usually represented by the symbol χ^2. So, in this case, we would say that the observed value of $\chi^2 = 18.32$. Two other figures are given to you. The one labelled 'df' is important. 'df' stands for Degrees of Freedom and is used for looking up the critical value in a table. It is calculated using the following formula: (rows – 1) × (columns – 1). In this case, it is $(2 - 1) \times (3 - 1) = 2$, as it says in the box beside the chi-squared value, so we would say that df = 2.

The table below contains an extract from a table of critical values for chi-squared. Before conducting their research, an experimenter would have decided on a level of significance. In this case it would be $p \leq 0.05$ as we have evidence to suggest what will happen in studies such as this, that is that there will be gender differences. The researchers would also have a null hypothesis and an alternative hypothesis, which could be directional or non-directional. Let's assume in this case it was a non-directional hypothesis such as 'There is a difference in stereotyping between illustrations of males and females in advertisements'. A suitable null hypothesis would be 'There is no difference between the stereotyping in illustrations of males and females in advertisements'. We now have all the information we need to look up the critical value:

- df = 2
- $p \leq 0.05$
- two-tailed test

To look up the correct critical value for our test, we need to find the row corresponding to df = 2, then the column for a two-tailed test at $p \leq 0.05$.

	Level of significance for a two-tailed test				
	0.2	0.1	0.05	0.02	0.001
	Level of significance for a one-tailed test				
df	0.1	0.05	0.025	0.01	0.0005
1	2.706	3.841	5.024	6.635	7.879
2	4.605	5.991	7.378	9.210	10.597
3	6.251	7.815	9.348	11.345	12.838
4	7.779	9.488	11.143	13.277	14.860

The critical value is 7.378. In order to decide what the results mean, this must be compared to the observed value. If the observed value is greater than or equal to the critical value, then the pattern in the results is significant. Since the observed chi-squared value, $\chi^2 = 13.05$, is greater than the critical value (7.378), we can conclude that there is a significant pattern. This means that the null hypothesis can be rejected and the alternative hypothesis can be accepted. We can therefore conclude that 'There is a difference in stereotyping between illustrations of males and females in advertisements'.

how science works

Research Methods

Choosing a statistical test

There are two decisions to be made when choosing between the three statistical tests that you know. These are illustrated on the flowchart below.

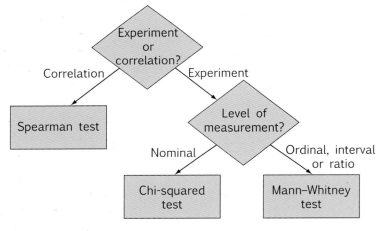

Figure 6.18
Choosing a statistical test

- Bandura, Ross & Ross (1961) used a Chi-squared to test the effect of models on physical aggression. Was the method used an experiment or a correlation?
- In a study similar to Kippin (2000), Coria-Avila *et al.* (2005) used a chi-squared test in an experimental design to test classical conditioning to odour for female mate preference. What would you expect their level of measurement to have been?
- To assess the similarity between twins in twin studies the Spearman test is used. Why?
- In studies comparing males and females on measures of the volume of different parts of the brain, which test would be used?

We have seen that children copy same-sex models from the media and other sources. It is also clear that they may experience selective reinforcement. But is there any evidence that such an environment does affect children's gender behaviour? The evidence seems to be inconclusive. Several studies (e.g. Morgan, 1982; Morgan & Rothschild, 1983 and Williams, 1986) have demonstrated that when children watch more television they are likely to hold more stereotypical views about sex roles. However, these findings tend to be difficult to interpret as other variables such as IQ are also important. Research does show however, that children do have very gender-stereotyped views and that exposure to counter-stereotypical examples in real life is important in reducing these.

Cordua *et al.* (1979) were interested in whether young children's gender stereotypes affect their memories. A total of 128 white, middle-class American children aged five years to six years eight months were recruited from church-affiliated kindergartens. Each child was shown four films that illustrated each of the possible combinations of female and male doctors and nurses. The children's memory for gender-consistent illustrations of occupations were typically good. However, when faced with counter stereotypes, the children tended to mis-recall them as male doctors and/or female nurses. Only 22% of the children who saw a male nurse and a female doctor correctly identified both roles when tested later. The tendency to relabel was stronger for the male nurse than for the female doctor. This suggests that the children's gender schema affected their recall. Neither sex, age nor number of recent visits to a doctor affected their accuracy. The participants' mothers' job, and whether they had encountered male nurses in real life, did however affect correct identification.

Figure 6.19
Children's gender stereotypes are affected by their experiences of gender consistent examples and counter stereotypes

Often, results of studies looking at TV viewing and stereotyping are correlational. This means that it is impossible to establish cause and effect between exposure to stereotyped models on television and views about males and females. It is equally possible that factors in a child's home life are responsible for both their TV viewing and their beliefs. Cherney & London (2006) found that boys and girls change in terms of their TV viewing and other activities over time.

Cherney & London (2006) looked for gender differences in the choices of leisure activity of 60 boys and 60 girls aged five to twelve years. Using questionnaires and interviews they found out about each child's favourite toys, television shows, computer games and outdoor activities and how much time they spent on each. They were given a pencil in thanks for participation. The children's activities were rated on a 7-point Likert scale for gender stereotypicality by ten male and ten female graduate students who were unaware of the purpose of the study. The findings showed that boys spent more time on leisure activities than girls, mostly on sports, then watching television and playing computer games. Girls spent most time watching television, followed by sports and computer games. Both boys and girls displayed a preference for own-gender toys although this preference decreased in girls as they grew older. Conversely, in their television choices, girls became more feminine with age. It appears that in some respects children's behaviour becomes more sex-typed as they grow older, but in other respects it becomes less so.

If possible, try to work in a group for this activity. Each individual needs to choose a time and channel of television to watch and the group needs to agree definitions for sex-typed behaviours. Your aim is to compare aspects of television programmes with regard to gender stereotypes. You might consider, when it is shown: whether the programme is directed at adults or children; whether males or females are cast in high-status roles; and whether males and females are represented in male, female or gender-neutral roles. If you have more than one person viewing the same programmes, you can assess their records for inter-observer reliability.

Alternatively, try to replicate Milburn *et al.* (2001) who examined gender stereotyping in clip art (see p. 186). As above, you will need to decide which version(s) of clip art will be sampled, how many images will be used, what search terms will be used to find them and how you will classify them as gender-stereotyped or gender-neutral. You could conduct this research on your own or, if you work in a group, you will need to consider reliability between individuals rating the images.

If evidence shows that television affects children's gender stereotypes, then programmes with a balanced outlook should have a positive effect. This also seems to be the case. Johnston & Ettema (1982) compared nine- to twelve-year olds before and after watching 26 episodes of a drama *Freestyle*, which was designed to challenge gender stereotypes. They reported a significant reduction in stereotyping after watching the programmes. For example, their questionnaire responses showed that girls became more interested in sports and in roles that were traditionally male, such as being a mechanic or an engineer. Likewise, boys were more accepting of girls' participation in these activities. These effects were, however, very small unless viewing was backed up by classroom discussion.

" " Discussion of social learning and gender development

Social learning theory can clearly help us to understand some aspects of the acquisition of gender stereotypes. There is considerable evidence to suggest that gender stereotyped models exist and that children are responsive to them. This evidence is, however, somewhat conflicting with studies demonstrating fairly small effects and indicating that other factors, such as IQ and socio-economic status, are important in stereotyping. One interesting finding from Morgan (1982) was that girls with the heaviest TV viewing had the highest expectations of themselves. This is counter to expectations based on the negative effects of gender-stereotyped viewing but was predicted by Morgan on the basis that female role models with professional status are well represented on television.

Although much evidence does support the sex-typed portrayal of males and females, this appears to be changing. Yanowitz & Weathers (2004) used content analysis to investigate the representation of males and females in undergraduate level educational textbooks. They looked at the way real and fictitious males and females were represented in scenarios. Like previous researchers, they found some evidence of a bias in the way men and women are portrayed but they also found many similarities. They concluded that there was a very positive representation of both genders, for example in illustrating both genders acting bravely and being caring. This too suggests that modelling is important, but that it can have positive as well as negative influences.

Dad, lad, gay icon, player – why Beckham is Britain's model man

Denis Campbell
The Observer 2 February 2003

David Beckham has overcome the hostility and endless jokes he inspires to emerge as the most influential man in Britain, according to a new academic study. An analysis of the effects of the England captain's global fame portrays him as a bold crusader who is making the world a better place by single-handedly transforming men's attitudes towards sex, love, babies, nights out with the lads and even homosexuality.

'David Beckham is a hugely important figure in popular culture and now probably the most influential male figure for anyone in Britain aged five to 60,' said Dr Andrew Parker of Warwick University, co-author of the research. 'By defying expectations in areas such as what clothes men are allowed to wear, he has helped create a complex new concept of masculinity. That has already begun to change male behaviour and has the potential to encourage a whole generation of young men who admire him to act more like him.'

The academics praise Beckham as a trailblazer for subverting male stereotypes by showing an interest in ballet and fashion, publicly confessing his love for his wife Victoria and daring to acknowledge his large gay following. 'He has broken so many strict traditional working class masculine codes of behaviour that he has the potential to influence lots of boys and young men to do the same, for example accepting homosexuality as part of life.'

Figure 6.20
A potent role model

1. What characteristics might make Beckham such a powerful role model?
2. Explain using social learning theory the process by which a young man might be influenced by David Beckham.

For & Against
learning theory as an explanation of gender behaviour

FOR   classical conditioning can explain the acquisition of some gender-related behaviours such as fetishes. This means that behaviours as well as emotions and attitudes to gender, such as stereotypes, may be affected by classical conditioning.

FOR   operant conditioning can explain how children are selectively reinforced for sex-typed behaviour, for example by pressure from peers or approval from parents. Peers will tend to positively reinforce gender-consistent behaviour and punish gender-inconsistent behaviour, e.g. by ignoring or teasing children who display them.

AGAINST · however, there is also powerful reinforcement of male behaviours for both sexes as maleness has higher status. This would tend to cause female children who are 'tomboyish' to be tolerated more readily than male children who are 'cissies' so this can only be partly responsible for gender differences.

FOR · social learning can explain the acquisition of sex-typed behaviours through observation. Bandura showed how children are more likely to copy same-sex models, so this is likely to affect their gender behaviours as children may observe gender-stereotyped models in the home as well as in the media.

FOR · social learning is further reinforced by observing reinforcement in the model, that is vicariously. This can also explain why gender stereotypes as such differences are often reinforced in the media, for example through stereotyped advertising.

AGAINST · however, not all media models are stereotypical and in some instances, such as the many roles for professional women on TV, they run counter to gender stereotypes. This would tend to reduce the effect of learning on the acquisition of gender role behaviours.

Bringing it together: gender development

In common with the psychodynamic approach, the learning approach says that other people play a part in the development of gender behaviour. Whereas the psychodynamic approach focuses predominantly on the parents whose effects are confined to the early years of childhood, the learning approach suggests that the influences are much wider. Although our parents would be important role models for gender behaviour, children are also exposed to and affected by peers and the media. The psychodynamic approach also suggests that both the mother and father are important to the child's progress through the Oedipus conflict, although the child finally identifies with the same sex parent. In social learning, too, the same-sex parent will be the critical role model for gender

Figure 6.21
Parents, especially the same gender parent, are role models for their children

behaviours although either parent (or other people, such as school friends) could be sources of reinforcement for sex-typed behaviour.

The biological approach suggests that gender identity is governed by genetic sex. This is a nature argument, saying that inherited, biological factors determine behaviour. This directly contradicts the view of the learning approach, which says that behaviour can change and that models and consequences influence the way a child behaves. Clearly both of these factors are important. We know that biology is vital from the case of David Reimer, but it is also clear that environmental factors are important too. Children tend to imitate same sex models and will be more likely do so if they are high status and are reinforced. These environmental factors contribute to the nurture side of this argument.

REALlives

Key

You have now explored a selection of ideas and studies from the learning approach to psychology. We have come across some real life issues that can be examined using a learning theory perspective. The aim of this section is to show in some detail how we can take an issue of real world importance and apply learning theory to understand it. We will do this for you with one issue then challenge you to do the same with a different situation.

Media violence

Is violence in the media – in television programmes, videos and computer games – really the cause of children's aggression? Children certainly see a lot of media violence and they pay attention to what they see, even when very young. Troseth (2003) showed that children as young as two years old could use information they had seen on a video. For two weeks some children were allowed to watch themselves 'live' on the family television. They later saw, on video, a toy being hidden in another room and were asked to find it. Children at this age generally find tasks like this very difficult. These children, however, were successful, suggesting that they had learned to reproduce behaviours they had viewed on TV.

interactive angles

If possible, try to work in a group for this activity. Each individual needs to choose a time and channel of television to watch and the group needs to agree definitions for aggressive behaviour. Your aim is to compare aspects of television programmes with regard to violence. Plan and conduct an observation. In your planning you might consider: when the programmes are shown; whether the aggression is verbal, physical or both; whether it is perpetrated and/or directed towards males, females or inanimate objects; whether the perpetrator is a powerful character and so on. If you have more than one person viewing the same programmes, you can assess their records for inter-observer reliability.

Applying learning theory to understanding the effects of media violence

We have seen that people in real life can be important as role models for gender stereotyping and that media role models may be important too. In the acquisition of aggression, Bandura showed that adults can influence children's behaviour. What evidence is there to suggest the learning of aggressive behaviour can be attributed to the media?

Imitation of role models

When characters on TV use violence they are modelling aggression. Recall that, for behaviour to be acquired by social learning, four processes take place: attention, retention, reproduction and reinforcement. By watching TV and following a storyline, we are paying attention. If the violence seen is distinctive and arousing this means it is likely to be retained. Children may be impressed by the violence used, motivating them to reproduce it later. This is particularly true if the model is rewarded for their actions (vicarious reinforcement).

Operant conditioning

There may also be direct positive reinforcement for imitated violence. Children who are aggressive may be rewarded for their behaviour by obtaining benefits through threatening others, such as taking their sweets. Positive reinforcement may also be experienced through the feeling of power over others, or via increased status. Simply being able to imitate the voice or actions of a popular TV character may increase a child's popularity. Any of these examples would act as reinforcers and could increase the frequency with which the aggressive behaviours are performed.

Identification with role models

TV heroes are designed to have the precise features that make them effective models. They have high social status, are likeable and powerful. Take the on-screen persona of Jean-Claude Van Damme or Vin Diesel. These are just the sort of characters that young males aspire to be like, therefore they identify with them. This identification makes imitation more likely.

Figure 6.22
Cartoon characters are powerful models for children's aggression

Thinking critically

If we accept that there really is a link between media violence and aggressive behaviour then learning theory provides an extremely neat explanation. However, we need to think a little critically about whether such a link exists.

Eron *et al.* (1972) measured the level of violence in TV programmes watched by seven- to eight-year-olds and measured their aggressiveness. They found a positive correlation between the two. By their teenage years, Eron *et al.* found an even stronger positive correlation of violence viewed and aggressiveness in boys (though not girls). And, the more violence the boys had watched on television as children, the more likely they were to be violent criminals as adults (Eron & Huesmann, 1986). Of course, these findings are based on data from several decades ago and not all of the sample were available for the follow-up work so the results may not be generalisable. This study was also correlational raising doubts about cause and effect. The level of aggression may not be caused by the individuals' viewing habits – it is possible that both the watching of violence and the aggressive behaviour may have been caused by some other variable such as harsh parental punishment. This can be countered, however, by experimental evidence. Bandura *et al.* (1963) compared the effect of an adult model and a film of the same adult, dressed as a cartoon cat. Using a procedure similar to Bandura *et al.* (1961), they found that aggressive behaviour modelled by the cartoon cat produced the highest levels of imitated aggression.

Some studies have failed to find a link between aggression and TV viewing. For example Hagell & Newbury (1994) found that young offenders watched no more violent television than a school control group. The delinquents were also less focused on television viewing, being less able to name favourite programmes or television character they imitated and were more likely to be on the streets getting into trouble than indoors watching television. In a natural experiment, Charlton *et al.* (2000) showed that media violence does not necessarily lead to aggression. They recorded levels of playground aggression on the island of St Helena in the South Atlantic, before and after the introduction of satellite television in March 1995. Prior to the introduction, the younger children were exceptionally well behaved and, even though the violent content of the programmes was slightly higher than in the UK (46% as opposed to 41%) they did not seen to be affected negatively. The amount of hitting, kicking, pushing and pinching stayed the same and teachers rated the children to be as hard-working and cooperative as they had been before.

exercise

Key

Look at the following two extracts from newspaper articles. on this page and the next one The first illustrates how the media may influence males and females differently. The second one describes a woman with a phobia.

1. Ofsted chief praises Buffy the gender bias slayer

By John Clare *Daily Telegraph* 6 March 2004 [edited]

More television programmes such as Buffy the Vampire Slayer would help ensure that the superior achievements of girls at school and university were mirrored later in careers, David Bell, the head of Ofsted, said yesterday.

Why, he asked, did girls, having secured an early head-start, most notably at GCSE and A-level, fail to gain the golden prizes at the finishing line in terms of jobs and salaries? The answer was gender bias. It influenced the choices girls made at school, which led more women than men to enter the 'caring professions' of social work, nursing and teaching that had historically lower rates of pay.

One solution was to boost the number of strong female role models such as Buffy, played by Sarah Michelle Gellar on BBC and Sky, portrayed in the media.

Gender bias also meant that many girls were automatically excluded from scientific and technological professions because they did not specialise at an early age.

Mr Bell said: "We have to be alert to differences [between girls and boys] that are conditioned and which actually mean that one gender does better or worse than the other, really for no good reason and certainly not for one that is 'natural'. It is not 'political correctness gone mad' to want to ensure that different kinds of characters of both genders are well represented in the media."

Figure 6.23
Buffy: an important role model for girls

How does the learning approach suggest that more strong female roles such as Buffy could change the number of women in senior jobs?

2. STOP THE PIGEON!

By Beth Neil *Daily Mirror* 12 April 2007

MY stomach lurches. My heart beats faster. A chill runs through my body. The enemy is approaching, I'm alone and there's nowhere to run, nowhere to hide. But I'm not facing a gang of knife-wielding Asbo hoodies. No. Hopping about menacingly in front of me is, in fact ... a pigeon.

For years I've had a crippling fear of our disease-riddled feathered friends but I've finally decided to get some help with my phobia. My pigeon horror stems from a traumatic ordeal at Trafalgar Square during a family trip to London. I was eight years old and thoroughly enjoying my first visit to the capital. But then came the doomed visit to Nelson's Column. While my brother and sister dashed about chasing the winged rats which infest London's famous landmark, I freaked out. Thanks so much for that mum and dad!

From that day on I've been physically repulsed by every single one of the 18 million feral pigeons we share our country with. I cross the road to avoid them. Sometimes I'll stop dead in the middle of the street, standing still until the threat has passed. It's become a source of hilarity among my friends but to me the blighters are the bane of my life.

Figure 6.24
Nelson's Column

Classical conditioning, operant conditioning and social learning could each provide explanations of how phobias might be learned. Use any aspect(s) of learning theory to explain how a fear of pigeons may be acquired.

over to you

Your practical exercise for the learning approach is to carry out an observation. This can be conducted either using participants in real life or from another source, such as on the television. Two television observations have been suggested earlier in the chapter (see pp. 190 and 193). These would be suitable as they will fulfil the criteria that your study needs to meet. It must:

- be based on an aspect of learning theory (e.g. reinforcement or modelling)
- gather quantitative data
- have a design that will produce data suitable for analysis using a chi-squared test.

Some other appropriate examples for observations include:

- observing lessons such as PE in which you can record changes in participants' behaviour in relation to reinforcement. Does praise alter the number of times a behaviour is performed?
- observing children's play, for example comparing boys' and girls' choices when presented with stereotypically 'boys'' and 'girls'' toys or gender-neutral toys
- observing adults in a large store. How much time do men and women spend looking at stereotypically 'male' and 'female' goods?
- observing adult gender-stereotyped behaviours such as child care or driving in a location such as a car park or shopping centre.

It is vital that you consider the ethical issues that observations raise. If you are observing children in a school or nursery, make sure that you have the permission of their parents and the staff. If you are observing in an area such as a store or shopping centre you will need permission from the appropriate management.

Figure 6.25
Remember that there are special ethical considerations when observing children

You can be asked questions about this task in your exam, so make sure that you understand the following as you design and conduct your observation:

- What are you aiming to find from your observation?
- What behaviours will you observe?
- As you will be collecting nominal data, what are the categories that you will be recording?
- How will they be operationalised?
- What observation technique will you use (e.g. checklisting)?
- Will you observe behaviour directly or not (e.g. use video or recorded materials such as television)?
- Will you be a participant or non-participant observer?
- Will you be overt or covert?
- If there is more than one observer, what will you do to improve inter-observer reliability?
- What sample will you use and how will it be selected?
- What ethical issues does your observation raise and how will you solve them?
- What will you do to raise the validity and reliability of your findings?

- To what extent are your findings credible and generalisible?
- How did you use the chi-squared test to analyse your findings and what did you conclude? (Remember, you can use http://faculty. vassar.edu/lowry/VassarStats.html to conduct a chi-squared test on your data.)

Make sure that when you have carried out your observation you keep a record of your answers to these questions and a record of your findings as part of your learning approach notes.

Conclusions

The learning theory approach to psychology is based on the importance of the processes of classical and operant conditioning and social learning in the acquisition of new behaviours. Because the learning approach sees humans and other animals as learning by similar processes it is often easier to study animals and then apply the results to humans. The learning approach has given rise to behavioural therapies which are designed to help people learn new and healthier behaviours in place of maladaptive ones. We have looked in particular at aversion therapy, which is based on classical conditioning, and token economies which are based on operant conditioning.

We have applied the principles of conditioning and social learning to understanding real life issues, importantly gender development and the role of the media in aggressive behaviour. We have also learned about research methodology, including observations and inferential statistics. Observations provide us with a way to study behaviour in a natural context but, with that opportunity, a range of practical and ethical issues present themselves and these must be dealt with in order to use the method effectively.

What do I know?

1. From the list of concepts below, choose the correct term for each of the examples given and write them into the correct spaces in a copy of the table.

Concept	Example
	a pigeon receives a food pellet every time it pecks a disc so it learns to peck the disc more often.
	a rat in a Skinner box which has learned to press the lever for food is then given an electric shock each time it approaches the lever. It stops pressing the lever.
	a rat in a Skinner box is exposed to a loud noise. Every time it presses the lever the loud noise stops. It learns to press the lever.

    - positive reinforcement
    - negative reinforcement
    - punishment

    [3]

2. (a) Define the following terms:

    (i) Extinction [1]

    (ii) Spontaneous recovery. [1]

    (b) What is the difference between primary and secondary reinforcement? [2]

3. (a) (i) Identify **one** study, other than Bandura, Ross & Ross (1961), from the learning approach. [1]

    (ii) Outline the procedure of the study you identified in part a (i). [5]

    (b) (i) Identify one study from the learning approach (it may be the same study as in 1a(i)).

    (ii) Evaluate the study you have identified in part b (i). [5]

4. One explanation for the development of gender behaviour is social learning theory.

    (a) Describe the social learning theory. [5]

    (b) Evaluate social learning theory as an explanation for gender behaviour. [4]

5. Operant and classical conditioning have both been used to provide therapies or treatments for mental disorders such as phobias or addictions.

    (a) Describe one therapy or treatment based on **either** classical **or** operant conditioning. Explain how the therapy works using the appropriate theory of conditioning. [5]

    (b) Evaluate the theory you have described in part (a). [4]

what's ahead

By the end of this chapter I should be able to:

- understand how my AS-level will be examined
- know how and what to revise
- answer exam-style questions
- refer to sample questions and answers to see how they are marked
- see how can I improve my marks
- revise for the exam

How is my AS examined?

You will be required to take two written examinations to assess your knowledge and understanding of the material covered in the AS specification.

Unit 1: Social and Cognitive Psychology

You may sit this examination in January or in June. As its title indicates, this examination covers the material from Chapters 2 and 3 in this book, the Social Approach and the Cognitive Approach. About half the marks will be allocated to each topic. The paper will be marked out of 60 and the examination will last for 1 hour and 20 minutes.

Unit 2: Understanding the Individual

This unit is only available in June. It covers the remaining three approaches, Biological, Psychodynamic and Learning. This is a slightly longer examination at 1 hour and 40 minutes, it is marked out of 80 and once more the marks are divided up so that the number available for each approach is similar.

What skills does the examination aim to assess?

All the examinations you take throughout the course are designed to assess three different skills. The term 'Assessment Object' means that a particular question or task is designed to develop or assess a particular skill. The three skills that the course aims to develop and assess are therefore known as AO (for Assessment Objective) 1, 2 and 3. Here is what they mean in the context of an examination:

- AO1: This is knowledge of the subject. These questions will be asking you to identify correct answers to factual questions, describe material you have learned about and show you understand this material by using it accurately to respond to questions set.
- AO2: Evaluation is the key idea here. If a question is asking for AO2 skills it may ask you to consider strengths or weaknesses, to compare one theory or study with another, to judge the usefulness of a piece of research or suggest how it might be applied in the real world. These questions will often follow on from an AO1 question where you have been asked to describe something.
- AO3: Here you will be asked to demonstrate your understanding of research methods. Questions can be drawn from the sections on the specification on 'How science works' as well as 'Evidence of practice'.

All three assessment objectives are tested in both Unit 1 and Unit 2.

Structure of the examinations

Both units are divided up into three parts (see Figure 7.1). The amount of time you spend on each section should depend on the number of marks it is worth. There will be an indication at the start of each section of how many minutes you are recommended to spend on that section. This time includes the time you will need to read and think about the questions as well as the time needed to answer them.

Part A: This is a set of multiple-choice questions. You will be given several answers to choose from. These questions will assess both AO1 and AO3 skills.

Part B: Here you will be asked to provide short answers to a series of questions. A question may either be asking you to use AO1, AO2 or AO3 skills, but there will not be a mixture within a particular question. This means that if, for example, you put some description (AO1) in an AO2 question it cannot gain any marks.

However, there may be a series of questions that are linked together by a common theme. Some of these assess AO1 skills and others AO2 skills.

Part C: This is the extended writing section and here you will be asked to develop a line of argument more fully to show the examiner you are able to combine the knowledge you have gained in the course with the evaluation skills you have developed. There are likely to be two questions here and one of them may well be awarded a mixture of AO1 and AO2 marks. In this case you should expect to focus effort equally between the two skills.

Questions in this section could also ask about AO3 skills, but this is unlikely.

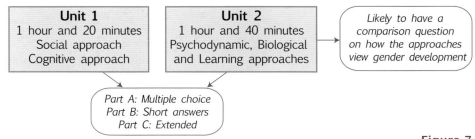

Figure 7.1
The structure of the two units is similar in many ways

How and what to revise

There is no single correct way to revise. Most people develop revision strategies based on trial and error. They try out different ways and then repeat the ones that work best for them. However many of you will find that the strategies you need to revise effectively for AS and A level examinations differ from those you used successfully at GCSE. This is because the kind of understanding you are asked to demonstrate changes as you progress.

In the past you have mainly been asked questions that test how much knowledge you have about a topic. At AS level there is more emphasis on using that knowledge in some way rather than just demonstrating that you know the facts. If you continue into the A2 topics you will find that this shift becomes even more pronounced. This change means that although memorising information is important you also need to practise using the material to answer questions in different ways.

Try to use the material you are revising to answer practice questions. When you studied cognitive psychology you learned about the levels of processing theory. You can now put that into practice. By using the material to answer practice questions you are semantically processing it and will learn it better. If you just read it through you are likely to use just visual processing, and you will not learn the material so well.

Questions can and will be asked on all aspects of the specification. That means it is very unwise to 'miss a bit out' when revising, even if it was on the last paper. To help you plan what you need to know, and in how much detail, there are summary tables for each of the approaches to help you.

When planning exactly what to revise and in how much detail there are two factors that you need to keep in mind. Firstly, you will find that often one piece of information can be used for more than one purpose, for example, Hofling *et al.*'s (1966) study into obedience in nurses is one of your studies in detail for Social Psychology but it can also be used to illustrate a variety of methodological issues. Secondly, when revising ensure that you have an appropriate amount of detail to gain all the marks that are likely to be available on a particular topic.

When answering a question do ensure that you

- give enough detail to clearly gain the mark(s)
- create balance in your answer (e.g. one good example is useful, but multiple examples of the same issue will not gain more credit)
- give a little bit more than you think you need for the marks.

One way to use the summaries of the five approaches is to use them to create a checklist for revision. Let us look at how this could be used for the very first part of the Social Psychology summary.

Social

Define social psychology	Influence of	Example	Cultural differences
	Individuals	A person may tell us we must do something. We are likely to do so if they are in authority over us. This is because we are brought up to believe obedience to authority figures is generally good.	Levels of obedience vary from one culture to another and also over time. People question authority more now than they did 50 years ago.
	Groups	We tend to act in a positive way towards people in a group of which we are a member. It also works if it is a group we admire even if not a member. In contrast we may act negatively towards groups we do not identify with.	Attitudes towards members of other groups vary in how negative they are depending on culture. In a very prejudiced culture attitudes and actions may be very aggressive whereas in a more tolerant culture the reactions to other groups will be very mild.
	Society	Society has norms that members are expected to abide by. We are socialised into these norms as we grow up through processes such as social learning. Approval by others for abiding by norms also reinforces behaviour.	Each society has its own set of norms, e.g. in Britain it is seen as wrong to walk into someone's house and just borrow something without asking, but that is the norm on the Solomon Islands.

What you need to know

Summaries of the five approaches from the specification. Remember the 'How much' column is the <u>minimum</u> amount you need. If you go into the examination knowing less than this you will not know enough to answer the questions.

Unit 1: Social Psychology

Specification	What you need to know	How much?
Define social psychology	The way an individual's behaviour is influenced by those around them, including other individuals, groups and society. Be able to show how these might be affected by cultural differences.	1 example for each of the influences that can be elaborated for 3 marks.
Define terms	Definitions and an example of each of the following: agentic state autonomous state moral strain in-group/out-group social categorisation social identification social comparison obedience	2–3 marks for a simple definition plus 2 marks for an example that makes it clearer what you mean.
Studies	Milgram's (1963) study of obedience One variation on the original study also done by Milgram A study of obedience from a country other than the USA Hofling *et al.*'s (1966) study of obedience in nurses *Either* Sherif's 'Robbers' Cave' (1961/1988) study *or* Tajfel's (1970) study of minimal groups *or* Reicher & Haslam's (2002) Learning from The Experiment	Detailed method and results for each study (5 marks for each). Overview including aims and conclusions. Evaluations: at least 2 strengths, 2 weaknesses.
Content	Agency Theory (Milgram 1973) Social Identity Theory (Tajfel 1970)	Describe theory and components. Evaluate theory.
Methodology	Surveys: questionnaires and interviews Designing surveys Unstructured, semi-structured and structured interviews Open and closed questions Alternative hypotheses Reliability, validity and subjectivity applied to the survey method Ethical guidelines Sampling methods (random, stratified, volunteer, self-selecting and opportunity) Qualitative and quantitative data Ways of analysing qualitative data Evidence of your own practice	Description of each in detail including use of appropriate examples. Descriptions should focus on what it is, not what it is not. Apply/identify in a novel scenario. Evaluate strengths, weaknesses, usefulness, practicality, generalisability, reliability, validity, applications as appropriate.
Key issue	Apply either agency theory or social identity theory to a situation.	How effective is the theory and consider alternatives.

Unit 1: Cognitive Psychology

Specification	What you need to know	How much?
Define cognitive psychology	Explain the term cognition and be able to relate to processes such as memory, learning and language.	2–3 marks for an explanation plus a relevant example.
Define terms	Definitions and an example of each of the following: information processing memory forgetting storage retrieval	2–3 marks for a simple definition plus 2 marks for an example that makes it clearer what you mean.
Studies	Godden & Baddeley's (1975) study on cue dependent memory *Either* Peterson & Peterson (1959) Suppression of rehearsal *or* Craik & Tulving (1975) Levels of processing *or* Ramponi *et al.* (2004) Levels of processing and age.	Detailed method and results for each study (5 marks for each). Overview including aims and conclusions. Evaluations: at least 2 strengths, 2 weaknesses.
Content	Levels of processing (Craik & Lockhart 1972) One other theory of memory Cue-dependent theory of forgetting (Tulving 1974) One other theory of forgetting.	Describe theory and components. Evaluate theories. Compare theories.
Methodology	Experiments: natural, field and laboratory Repeated measures, matched pairs and independent group designs Independent and dependent variables Operationalisation of variables Experimental hypotheses (directional and non-directional) Randomisation Counterbalancing Order effects Experimental control Situational and participant variables Reliability and validity in experiments Experimenter effects Demand characteristics Ways of analysing quantitative data: central tendency, spread and graphs Evidence of your own practice	Description of each in detail including use of appropriate examples. Descriptions should focus on what it is, not what it is not. Apply/identify in a novel scenario. Evaluate strengths, weaknesses, usefulness, practicality generalisability, reliability, validity, applications as appropriate.
Key issue	Apply theories of memory/forgetting to a key issue.	How effective is the theory and consider alternatives.

Unit 2: Psychodynamic Approach

Specification	What you need to know	How much?
Define the psychodynamic approach	Define the term psychodynamic. Explain the influence of unconscious processes on behaviour and the role of early childhood experiences	2–3 marks for definition and 2–3 marks for an explanation of each influence plus relevant examples.
Define terms	Definitions and examples for each of the following: id, ego and superego psychosexual stages of development (oral, anal, phallic, latent and genital) Oedipus complex defence mechanisms including repression conscious, unconscious and preconscious	2–3 marks for a clear definition plus 2 marks for an example that takes the explanation further.
Studies	Freud's study of Little Hans (1909) *Either* Axline's (1964/1990) study of Dibs *or* Bachrach et al. (1991) Effectiveness of psychodynamic therapies *or* Cramer (1997) Identity, personality and defence mechanisms	Detailed procedure and findings for each study (5 marks for each). Overview including aims and conclusions. Evaluations: at least 2 strengths, 2 weaknesses.
Content	Freud's theory of psychosexual development How stages link to development of personality Repression and one other defence mechanism Use of theory to explain gender development	Describe stages of theory. Evaluate theory. Compare development of gender with biological/learning approaches.
Methodology	Credibility of Freud's theory Case study Self reports Rating scales Analysis of qualitative data including issues of reliability, validity, subjectivity, objectivity and generalisability Ethics and credibility of personal data in case studies Cross sectional and longitudinal research methods Correlational method/design Positive and negative correlations and strength of correlation Sampling methods (random, stratified, volunteer, self selecting and opportunity) Scattergram Spearman's test Evidence of your own practice	Description of each in detail. Descriptions should focus on what it is, not what it is not. Apply/identify in a novel scenario. Evaluate strengths, weaknesses, usefulness, practicality generalisability, reliability, validity, applications as appropriate.
Key issue	Apply psychodynamic explanations to a topic relevant in today's society.	Describe, evaluate, other explanations.

Unit 2: Biological Approach

Specification	What you need to know	How much?
Define biological approach	Define biological approach and explain the role of both genes and the nervous system in individual differences.	2–3 marks for definition plus 2–3 marks for each role plus relevant examples.
Define terms	Definitions and an example of each of the following: central nervous system synapse and receptor neurone and neurotransmitter genes hormones brain lateralisation	2–3 marks for a simple definition plus 2 marks for an example that makes it clearer what you mean.
Studies	Money (1975) Ablatio penis study and subsequent testimony of David Reimer *Either* Gottesman & Shields (1966) Schizophrenia in twins *or* Raine *et al.* (1997) PET scans of murderers *or* De Bellis *et al.* (2001) Sex differences in brain maturation	Detailed method and results for each (5 marks for each). Overview including aims/conclusions. Evaluations: at least 2 strengths, 2 weaknesses.
Content	Roles of central nervous system, neurotransmitters and genes Nature–nurture debate with regard to genes Role of genes, hormones and brain lateralisation on gender Effect of biological factors on gender development Animal research Methodological issues	Describe each role for 4 marks. At least 2 arguments on each side of nature–nurture, each with elaboration and example. Evaluate factors and compare with psychodynamic and learning approach.
Methodology	Twin and adoption studies PET and MRI scanning techniques Alternative, experimental and null hypotheses One- and two-tailed tests of significance Levels of significance and *p* values critical and observed values Mann–Whitney U test IV, DV and control groups Sampling and allocation to groups Levels of measurement Credibility, ethical and practical issues regarding the use of animals in biological psychology Reliability, validity and generalisability of lab experiments Evidence of your own practice	Description of each in detail including use of appropriate examples. Apply/identify in a novel scenario. Evaluate strengths, weaknesses, usefulness, practicality generalisability, reliability, validity, applications as appropriate.
Key issue	Apply biological theories/concepts to a key issue	Explain and evaluate.

Unit 2: Learning Approach

Specification	What you need to know	How much?
Define learning approach	Define learning approach Explain the effects of conditioning, reinforcement and social learning on organisms	2–3 marks for definition. 2–3 marks for each explanation plus relevant examples.
Define terms	Definitions and an example of each of the following: Classical conditioning, extinction and spontaneous recovery Operant conditioning, positive and negative reinforcement, primary and secondary reinforcement, punishment Social learning, imitation, modelling, observation and vicarious reinforcement Stimulus and response	2–3 marks for a simple definition plus 2 marks for an example that makes it clearer what you mean.
Studies	Bandura, Ross & Ross (1961) Imitation of aggression *Either* Watson & Rayner (1920) Little Albert *or* Skinner (1948) Superstitious pigeons *or* Pickens & Thompson (1968) Cocaine-reinforced behaviour in rats	Detailed method and results for each study (5 marks for each). Overview including aims and conclusions. Evaluations: at least 2 strengths, 2 weaknesses.
Content	Classical conditioning Operant conditioning A therapy derived from classical or operant conditioning Social Learning Theory	Describe theory and components. Evaluate theories. Use to explain gender behaviour and compare.
Methodology	Reliability, validity and generalisability Credibility Overt/covert Non-participant/participant Qualitative and quantitative Laboratory experiment Chi-squared (χ^2)test Levels of measurement Levels of significance Critical and observed value Naturalistic observations Ethical issues Evidence of your own practice	Description of each in detail including use of appropriate examples. Descriptions should focus on what it is, not what it is not. Apply/identify in a novel scenario. Evaluate strengths, weaknesses, usefulness, practicality generalisability, reliability, validity, applications as appropriate.
Key issue	Apply theories of learning to a key issue	How effective is the theory and consider alternatives.

How to answer questions

You will be expected to answer the questions on the examination paper in the same booklet as the questions appear. In the case of the multiple choice questions you will be asked to indicate, by putting crosses in the boxes provided, which answers you wish to select. For all other questions there will be a lined space after the question. The amount of space provided is a reflection of the amount examiners expect you to write. However it is important to remember that unless you have exceptionally large writing you are unlikely to need all the space provided. It is quite possible to get all the marks available for a question using less than half the space, even with normal-sized handwriting.

Remember a correct answer will not necessarily use up all the space available:

> Identify one theory of forgetting other than the cue-dependent theory that you have studied.
>
> (1)

> One theory of forgetting is Interference theory

The number of marks available is the best indicator of how much to write. If a question asks for two strengths of a theory and is worth four marks you will need to give each strength and then elaborate sufficiently to get the second mark. Never assume there will be a mark for just identifying or naming anything unless that is indicated by the question. If a question is worth 4 or 5 marks then make sure you have at least that number of points made. These may all be independent points, or some of the things you write may be an elaboration on something already stated. One problem is that often students think they have made four different points for four marks, however an examiner may feel that two of the points are very similar and only worthy of one mark. It is therefore advisable, as suggested earlier, to give a little more than seems essential to get the marks.

An elaboration point clearly made is worth a second mark, however if the same idea is given in slightly different words it is considered repetition.

> Explain two strengths of the Levels of Processing theory.
>
> (4)

> One strength of Levels of Processing theory is it can explain how we remember things even when we have not apparently learned them, this is because if we ✓ have used the material in a meaningful way it may have been encoded because of the depth of processing. ✓
>
> Another strength is it explains why processing information helps it to stick even though we have not rehearsed the material. **Repetition**

The 'injunction' in a question is important for two reasons. It is the word that instructs you what to do in a question, but it is also useful in guiding you on how much to write. For example the injunction 'outline' means something shorter than the term 'describe'. While the list below can only be a guide it covers most of the injunctions you are likely to encounter. Use these words as cues to help you practice your skills at answering questions. As they are all terms you may encounter in examination questions it is important you understand what each term means.

Below is a list of injunctions you are likely to encounter in examination questions.

- **identify** – show knowledge by making something recognisable
- **name** – identify by referring to something or someone such as a title or author(s)
- **state** – show awareness of one specific point in a brief, clear way
- **define** – explain what is meant by a particular term
- **outline** – briefly give details without explanation, give most important points
- **describe** – give a detailed account without explanation, give all main points
- **explain** – give a clear account of why and how something is so
- **what is meant by** – give a brief description then explain it
- **evaluate** – look at the value or effectiveness of something in terms of advantages and disadvantages, or how true and/or useful it is
- **assess** – determine the value of, weigh up, the quality of a topic or issue
- **discuss** – give a reasoned account of the topic, balancing different points of view
- **distinguish** – give relevant differences between two ideas or situations
- **compare** – look for similarities and differences, possibly reach a conclusion
- **apply** – explain how a concept can be used when considering everyday issues or novel situations

Sample questions and answers

This book is being written before anyone has taken the examinations for this revised specification so we cannot give you real candidates' answers, nor can we provide you with real past questions. However, the questions are very similar to the sort of questions you will be asked and the answers draw on a great deal of experience in teaching, reading and marking examination questions. This section will look at the different ways in which questions may be asked, and provide answers similar to those you might expect to see for these questions, with comments on the questions and answers.

You may recall that earlier in this chapter the different parts of the examination paper were mentioned – A, B and C. In addition, in the summary of 'what you need to know' for each approach headings were used to indicate the nature of the material. Here you will find these two pieces of information have been put together so you can see what type of questions you are likely to encounter as well as how to go about answering them.

Defining approaches and terms

There are two ways in which you may be required to use this material. Some questions not directly related to the definition of approaches or terms will require knowledge of these terms. These tend to be questions on content or a key issue. You will find your knowledge of this section will be valuable in interpreting such questions. However, there will be some questions that ask you directly about this material. Many of these questions will be multiple-choice where you will be given several options to choose from. It is likely that at least two of the options will need careful thought. These questions will usually have one correct answer for one mark. Sometimes there may be variations such as two correct responses for two marks. The instructions with the questions will make it clear what you are required to do. Make sure you read these.

Here is an example of how a multiple-choice question might be asked:

Choose an answer, A, B, C or D and put a cross in the box (✗). If you change your mind put a line through the box (—), and then put a cross in another box (✗).

1. The Central Nervous System (CNS) is important in controlling the body. Which statement best describes what components make up the CNS?

   ☐ A   The brain, spinal cord and major nerve bundles to the limbs

   ☒ B   The brain and the spinal cord

   ☐ C   The spinal cord and the major nerve bundles to the limbs

   ☐ D   All of the nerve pathways from the brain to all areas of the body

   (1/1)

Remember

- **Do** read through choices you are given carefully, it is easy to misread and make a mistake.
- **Do** think about multiple choice answers carefully.
- **Don't** leave a question unanswered, if you genuinely don't know you may as well make a best guess.

The other type of question that will ask you about definitions and approaches will be short answer questions. These will typically be worth at least two marks but no more than five. They are most likely to be AO1 questions.

Here is an example of a short answer question and some possible responses:

---

1. During your course you have studied the Learning Approach. Define what is meant by the Learning Approach in psychology.

   (3)

Answer (i)

The Learning Approach is about how people learn, it includes conditioning.

0/3

Answer (ii)

The Learning approach believes behaviour is mainly a result of experiences in our environment. ✓ It uses the ideas of classical conditioning, operant conditioning and social learning theory to explain how behaviour comes about. ✓

2/3

Answer (iii)

> The Learning Approach sees learning and the environment as the main means of behaviour change. ✓ The mechanisms involved are classical conditioning where new stimuli can produce a behaviour, e.g. a bell producing salivation, ✓ operant conditioning where new behaviour is created, e.g. a dog sitting up and begging ✓ and social learning where an individual observes the behaviour of others and imitates it. (✓)
>
> 3/3

Comment

Answer (i) is very weak. Saying that the approach is about learning gets no credit as it merely repeats the question. Even the comment on conditioning is too weak. It says nothing about the nature of conditioning or the type of conditioning. Answer (ii) is better, the first sentence is worthy of a mark as it links learning to the environment. Because it is comprehensive, the list of types of learning studied in the learning approach is also worthy of a mark. However there is no development of any of these ideas. Note as well that listing like this does not get you credit for each individual item. By contrast, answer (iii) is a thorough response to the question. If there were a fourth mark available this would get it. There is a mark for environment and behaviour change and a potential mark for each of the three mechanisms as they are clearly explained.

Remember

- **Do** give an example to elaborate your answer when possible as it shows you really understand what you are writing.
- **Do** make sure you have made at least as many points as there are marks available.
- **Don't** use a key word from the question as an explanation.

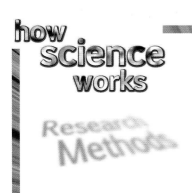

Methodology and evidence of practice

Questions related to these topics will assess your understanding of how research is conducted within psychology. These topics are put together here even though evidence of practice is in a different place in the specification from how science works/methodology. This is because the material covered under the two headings in any one approach is linked, with most items occurring in both. Some questions will relate to terminology, some will ask you to apply your knowledge and understanding, others will draw on your own experience of conducting and writing up the short tasks included in the evidence of practice sections. There are likely to be both multiple choice and short answer questions. Questions tapping into this area of your learning will primarily be AO3.

Here are examples of how a multiple-choice question might be asked.

Choose an answer, A, B, C or D and put a cross in the box (✗). If you change your mind put a line through the box (—), and then put a cross in another box (✗).

1. Counterbalancing is a technique used by researchers when conducting a repeated measures design. The purpose of counterbalancing is to

    ☐ A make sure all participants have an equal chance of getting the answers right

    ☐ B reduce the possibility of individual differences affecting results

    ☒ C ensure order effects do not affect results

    ☐ D remove the need for a control group

    (1/1)

Sometimes the question may require application of your knowledge rather than just remembering information.

---

2. A researcher is to undertake an observational study into imitation of gender role models on children aged from six to eight years old at a local sports centre. Under ethical guidelines, who would the researcher need to ask for consent in order to protect the participants?

    ☐ A Manager of the sports centre and the parents of the children

    ☐ B Manager of the sports centre, the parents of the children and the children

    ☐ C Manager of the sports centre and the children

    ☒ D The parents of the children and the children

    (1/1)

You will encounter a range of short answer questions within this area. Remember it is to do with research so covers quite a broad area. It will also often include a question that relies on you having conducted some of your own research as part of the course. Questions may be prompted by stimulus material, where you are given a short description of a real or fictional study. Other questions may ask you more directly about something. Here are some examples to show the variety of ways that questions may be asked.

1. Researchers investigating whether decisions about education were related to parental experiences requested all the students at a sixth-form college to complete a questionnaire on whether they intended to apply to university. The questionnaire also asked what stage their parents had reached when ending their education. Out of 800 students the researchers received replies from 500. The table below summarised the data collected.

		Parental education ended at		
		GCSE	A level	Higher level
Students post A level choice	Job	185	55	10
	University	165	45	40

The researchers carried out a χ^2 test on the data. The observed value was calculated as 20.14, and there were 2 df. The table of critical values is shown here.

	Levels of significance for a one tailed test					
	0.10	0.05	0.025	0.01	0.005	0.0005
	Levels of significance for a two tailed test					
df	0.20	0.10	0.05	0.02	0.01	0.001
2	3.22	4.60	5.99	7.82	9.21	13.81

(a) The researchers decided to use a two-tailed test as their hypothesis was non-directional. Using the table explain whether or not they can accept their alternative (experimental) hypothesis and why.

(3)

Answer (i)

The researchers can accept their hypothesis as the observed value is greater than the critical value ✓

1/3

Answer (ii)

The observed value of 20.14 is greater than the critical value of 5.99 at $p = 0.05$ for a two-tailed test and 2 df. ✓✓ Therefore the researchers can accept the alternative hypothesis. ✓ In fact they could accept the hypothesis at $p = 0.001$ as the observed value is greater than 13.81

3/3

The first answer here gets credit only for saying whether the hypothesis is accepted or not. To mention the observed and critical values without giving figures is not sufficient for a second mark. In contrast the second answer is very thorough. It gives the relevant observed and critical values and explains why this particular critical value has been selected, and is explicit about the conclusion to accept the alternative hypothesis.

Remember

- **Do** state both the observed values and critical values.
- **Do** explain why you have selected this particular critical value.
- **Do** explain which hypothesis should be accepted or rejected and why.
- **Do** give the p value at which this decision has been made.

(b) Write a suitable alternative (experimental) hypothesis for this study

(2)

Answer (i)

There will be no relationship between whether a student decides to go to university and what level of education their parents had.

0/2

Answer (ii)

There will be a relationship between a student deciding to attend university or go straight into work and whether their parent(s) studied to GCSE, A level or a higher level of education. ✓✓

2/2

Comment

The first of these answers is a null hypothesis, and as such it will score nothing as it is not an appropriate hypothesis for the question. It does not matter whether the variables have been operationalised or not. By contrast not only is the second answer an appropriate hypothesis, that is a non-directional alternative (experimental) hypothesis, but it also successfully identifies the variables accurately so gains both marks.

Remember

- **Do** try and use wording that the stimulus material provides.
- **Do** check if what your answer states suits the clues you are given about whether the hypothesis should be directional or non-directional.
- **Do** ensure that you operationalise the variables as appropriate, for example, parental education as the level their education ended at GCSE, A level or higher.

(c) The researchers received replies from 500 students out of the total of 800 at the college. Explain possible reasons why the return rate may be this low.

(3)

Answer (i)

> Some of the students probably thought it wasn't important so didn't bother filling it in.✓ Because they didn't get a big return the results are not valid but this is better than the return rate on many questionnaires.
>
> 1/3

Answer (ii)

> Students who didn't reply may have felt the study wasn't important enough to spend time on. ✓ Filling in questionnaires is time consuming and unless it was made very easy to complete and return they may not bother. ✓ It might be the questionnaire was done when there were a lot of absentees from college, e.g. a trip out or lots of people ill. ✓ Some students may not want to fill in the information as they have not decided what to do. (✓)
>
> 3/3

Comment

In the first answer although the comments in the second sentence are true they do not answer the question, so cannot gain credit. Make sure when you answer that you keep the question in mind. In contrast the second answer does keep focused on the question. In fact, if there were another mark available this response could get it as it clearly states four possible reasons.

Remember

- **Do** try and elaborate your answer to make the points clearer.
- **Do** ensure you make at least as many points as there are marks available.
- **Do** make the answer relevant to the stimulus material provided.

> (d) Identify one ethical guideline the researchers should abide by and suggest how this might have been implemented.
>
> (4)

Answer (i)

> Confidentiality is one ethical guideline that should be used. ✓ The researchers should make sure that they do not ask students to put their names on the questionnaires. ✓ They should reassure the students by explaining on the questionnaire that the data are confidential and if they do not wish to answer a particular question they may leave it blank. ✓ Although they probably had a list of all the students so they could ensure everyone got a copy of the questionnaire, such a list should be destroyed once it is longer necessary ✓ and until then kept in a secure place.
>
> 4/4

Answer (ii)

> Right to withdraw. ✓ They should tell participants they have the right to withdraw at any time during the study.
>
> 1/4

The first of these answers is thorough. It identifies the guideline then explains in detail exactly how it could be applied to this particular study, gaining all 4 marks with ease. In contrast the second answer does nothing to show how it might be implemented in this study. To obtain any mark beyond that for identifying the guideline it would need to explain how this right to withdraw may be implemented as part of the questionnaire design.

Remember
- **Do** make sure you know the BPS ethical guidelines.
- **Do** be able to explain why each guideline is important.
- **Do** show you know how it can be implemented.
- **Do** know what precautions need to be taken if a guideline cannot be fully implemented.

> 2. As part of your course you undertook an experiment within the cognitive approach. Identify the independent variable (IV) in your study and explain how it was operationalised.
>
> (3)

Answer (i)

> The independent variable was if participants did an interference task or not ✓
>
> 1/3

Answer (ii)

> The independent variable was the two levels of processing, semantic and structural. ✓ Semantic was operationalised by asking participants if the word fitted into a sentence e.g. Does 'bird' fit into the sentence 'The … flew away'. ✓ Structural was operationalised by asking if the word was typed in italics, underlined, bold or in normal print. ✓
>
> 3/3

The first of these answers does not operationalise the IV so only gets 1 mark. The second answer identifies the IV and then gives a full explanation so gains all 3 marks. The amount written in the second answer is much better, clearly giving the different conditions and an example of how it was operationalised in each case.

Remember

- **Do** ensure you revise the little projects you did for each approach as questions will be asked on them.
- **Do** give detail, the questions will be designed to credit answers which prove you really did the study yourself.
- **Do** remember there will be little quirky details that will bring your answer 'alive' – use them.

Studies in detail

You are expected to be able to describe and evaluate several studies, some in each approach. In all cases you do need to know quite a lot of detail. This is because you may be asked about one particular part of the study, or one particular aspect to the evaluation. Most of these questions are likely to be short answer questions. You may also find you are asked to relate a study to a particular theory. Just because theories come under 'content' and studies have a separate heading does not mean the two will never crop up together. Equally, you may find that some of the points you wish to make when evaluating a study overlap with methodological issues. That is quite reasonable, and will still gain you credit in these sorts of questions.

1.

(a) Describe the method used by Hofling *et al.* (1966) in their study of obedience in nurses.

(5)

Answer (i)

Hofling phoned nurses ✓ and told them to give twice the maximum dose of a medication to a patient. ✓ All except one nurse obeyed even though the doctor hadn't signed the paperwork.

2/5

Answer (ii)

It was a field study taking place on hospital wards. ✓ A dummy medication labelled Astroten had been placed in the drugs cabinet. ✓ Nurses, who were alone at the time received a phone call from a 'doctor' ✓ telling them to administer twice the maximum dose of this drug to a particular patient ✓ and he would sign the relevant paperwork when he arrived on the ward. ✓

5/5

Comment

This is typical of the type of question you can expect on a named study, so do make sure you have enough detail to answer a question like this. The first of these answers is unclear. Hofling did not do the phoning up, but at least the fact that a phone call was made is there so that gets credit, as does the information that the dose to be given was twice the maximum. No credit can be given for the second sentence as it concerns the results, not the method. The paperwork comment is a good example of a piece of information that *could* have been given credit. However, in this answer there is no information to suggest why paperwork would be important. In other words *nothing has been done* with the information. The second answer is a good answer, it is not comprehensive, more could be written, but it is sufficient for the marks available. It covers all the major points and keeps to the method.

Remember
- **Do** make sure you know all the prescribed studies and at least one optional study in detail for each approach.
- **Do** learn the overall information so you can give a general summary.
- **Do** ensure you can go into detail on the method, results and conclusions.
- **Don't** use a study other than the ones given in the specification.

> (b) Assess the importance of the findings of the Hofling *et al.* (1966) study.
>
> (4)

Answer (i)

> Hofling showed that nurses would obey doctors even when it broke the hospital rules. ✓ 21 out of the 22 nurses obeyed the instructions which is a lot.
>
> 1/4

Answer (ii)

> Hofling's results were important as it showed the level of obedience to doctors by the nurses was so high that they were prepared to break hospital rules. ✓ The nurses reported that many doctors got angry if they were not obeyed which suggested that nurses need to be trained to resist pressure from doctors. ✓ Because it was a field study the results have higher validity than most other studies of obedience. ✓ The study showed that authority figures in the workplace need to be trained not to abuse their position. ✓
>
> 4/4

This is quite a tricky question and needs to be thought about carefully. It is asking you to assess so is an AO2 question, therefore a description of the results cannot get credit. In the first answer if that second sentence had gone on to explain why having a lot of obedient nurses was an important finding, e.g. as it showed that it was easy for nurses to fall into an agentic state when dealing with doctors, it would have gained a mark. The second answer is quite full and makes several different clear points, each one of which is addressing the question.

The word *assess* means the question requires you to weigh up, in this case, the importance of the finding. So points need to relate to the impact the findings may have had. Another word that might be used in this type of question is *implications*. This type of question is designed to try and get you to think about your answer in the examination. There is no way that you can pre-prepare every answer for this type of question. In fact many of the questions are deliberately structured to make you think. However, provided you have understood and practiced what skills the question wishes you to use, and you know the study thoroughly, then a little thought means you can create the answer in the examination.

Remember
- **Do** ensure you know all your studies well enough to be able to evaluate.
- **Do** use a technique such as a mnemonic to help you remember what things you can use as evaluation points.
- **Do** make points fully and clearly and expand a basic point to explain why.

Content

Questions aimed at assessing the content of the specification will appear as multiple choice questions, short answer questions and also as extended writing questions. In addition to the material that is listed under content you should expect to draw extensively on definitions, methodology and studies in detail to flesh out answers appropriately. This means that to do well on these questions you must know the other areas too. While much of the content is theory there are other items that appear there that will also be assessed.

In each of the approaches some of the content is specified and there is also an element of choice. For example in the Social Approach you must learn about a study of obedience from a country other than the USA, but it can be any study from any country. As long as you can describe the study and compare it to Milgram's 1963 study in a cross-cultural way it does not matter which country it is from.

It may be that at different sittings of an examination, questions on a particular topic may appear in any of the three sections, A, B or C. So, on one examination paper there may be a multiple-choice question asking you to select from a set of statements which best describes the difference between prejudice and discrimination. Another time, a short answer question may ask you to distinguish between prejudice and discrimination, while an extended writing piece may give you some stimulus material about prejudice and discrimination against migrant workers and ask you to explain what is happening in terms of Social Identity Theory.

Examples of how multiple-choice questions might be asked

Choose an answer, A, B, or C and put a cross in the box (✗). If you change your mind put a line through the box (—), and then put a cross in another box (✗).

1. Susie and Amina were walking home from college along a tree-lined road. It had been raining and as they walked they kept getting large drips of water falling onto them from the leaves above. They decided to cross over to the other side of the road to avoid the drips. Avoiding the drips is an example of

   ☐ A   positive reinforcement

   ☒ B   negative reinforcement

   ☐ C   a punishment

   (1/1)

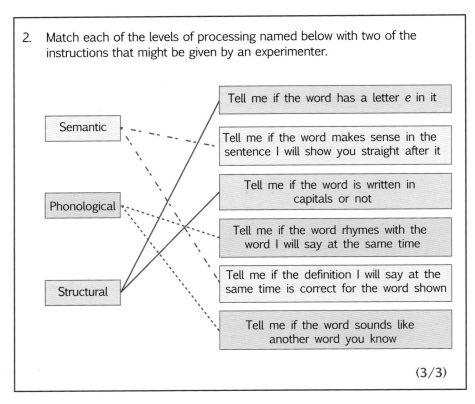

2. Match each of the levels of processing named below with two of the instructions that might be given by an experimenter.

Semantic

Phonological

Structural

Tell me if the word has a letter *e* in it

Tell me if the word makes sense in the sentence I will show you straight after it

Tell me if the word is written in capitals or not

Tell me if the word rhymes with the word I will say at the same time

Tell me if the definition I will say at the same time is correct for the word shown

Tell me if the word sounds like another word you know

(3/3)

Both of these questions expect you to think and work out the answer, it is very unlikely that the exact examples given would match completely anything you have learned through the course. This is an example of using your knowledge and understanding to think out what is the most appropriate answer.

Remember

- **Do** check you are answering the question in the way you are asked to. Instructions will be provided, it is important to read them carefully.
- **Don't** try to be too clever and put in too many line connections as this will lose you marks.
- If you change your mind clearly cross out the line you wish the examiner to ignore and replace it with a new line.
- **Do** think about your answers.

Now for some short answer questions. Remember these will be found in Section B of the examination paper and can be either asking you what you know about the content (AO1) or asking you to evaluate or apply that knowledge in some way (AO2).

(a) According to Freud we use defence mechanisms to protect our ego. Identify and describe one defence mechanism other than repression.

(3)

Answer (i)

> Displacement. ✓ This is where the feelings generated by a particular person or situation are expressed towards someone else. ✓ E.g. someone is upset and angry because they feel that their boss has treated them unfairly, but instead of reacting towards the boss in an angry manner they go home and fall out with the family. ✓
>
> 3/3

Answer (ii)

> Regression. ✓ Regression is when the person goes back to an earlier stage in their lives.
>
> 1/3

Comment

The first example here is a clear, and well-focused answer. As the question asks you to 'identify' this shows there will be a mark for naming the defence mechanism. The other two marks are for the description. The example is good because it makes the description clearer. The second answer by contrast gains only the identification mark. The statement of going back to an earlier stage is neither sufficiently accurate nor sufficiently detailed to gain a mark.

Remember

- The injunction tells you how detailed the answer needs to be.
- **Do** give enough material for all the marks available.
- **Do** make sure points are fully and accurately made.

> (b) Evaluate Freud's theory of the personality having three parts, the id, ego and superego.
>
> (4)

Answer (i)

> Most people would agree that there is a selfish component to personality which dominates us when we are babies. ✓ There is also a commonsense appeal to the idea of the two components of the superego, guilt and the ego ideal. Most people aspire to be better in some way than they are and feel guilty when they believe they have let down someone that matters to them. ✓ The concept of part of the personality being in the conscious and part in the unconscious also fits with evidence from cognitive psychology as it is clear that many thought processes are undertaken without us being aware of them until the answer is 'popped' into the conscious part of our mind. ✓
>
> 3/4

Answer (ii)

> Freud claimed personality is split into three parts. The id is in the unconscious, both the ego and the superego are in both the conscious and the unconscious. Jarvis suggests that Freud's theory is the most complete in trying to understand what influences personality ✓
>
> 1/4

Comment

The first of these two answers is good, making several clear points. It is good to use the evidence from cognitive psychology, though the point takes rather a long time to make. It lacks evidence from studies or other sources. Finding these is difficult with Freud's theory but Jarvis (see Chapter 4) could be used, for example. The first part of the second answer describes the tripartite system of Freud's theory. As this is an AO2 question it gets no credit. However, the final sentence is creditworthy, although the point could well have gained a second mark if it had been better developed.

Remember

- **Do** provide both positive and negative evaluation points whenever possible.
- **Do** use psychological evidence either from studies or from real life. However, if from real life the comment must be described and developed to show it is useful and not just an anecdote.
- **Do** read questions carefully so that you are sure that you are using the correct type of evaluation.

In addition to short answer questions it is possible that a piece of extended writing may be requested. Extended writing, as the name implies, asks you to write more about something. These questions will be found in part C of the paper. Some of the questions will require you to make both AO1 and AO2 points in the same answer. These questions will clearly use two injunctions such as 'describe and evaluate'. Other questions will, as in the short answer questions, be separated into two parts, one of which will ask you to use AO1 skills, and the other will be using AO2 skills. This means it is particularly important to read these questions carefully.

Extended writing

Most of the extended writing questions will be marked in a slightly different way to the short answer questions. An examiner will take into account the number of relevant points made, and also the quality of your written communication. Both these factors will be used to assign a mark. If a question is using this type of marking there will be an asterisk (*) by the question number.

Marks awarded for the quality of written communication will take into account whether your answer is focused on the question or goes off the point. In the case of questions asking you to use both AO1 and AO2 skills together, marking will take into account whether you have attempted to keep a reasonable balance between the two skills. In addition, whether you have communicated your ideas clearly and competently, used appropriate language and developed ideas sufficiently will also be assessed.

Criteria for the awarding of marks in these questions are organised into bands. Here is a brief summary to explain what you need to do to gain a mark in any particular band. There will always be five levels of band from 0 to 4. Band 0 will be 0 marks. The other bands will normally be equally spaced. The exact number of marks will be determined by the total number of marks available for that question. This will become clearer in the examples that follow.

Note also that in the following worked examples, as with real answers, even those reaching the top band are not necessarily perfect.

Level of band	Description
0	No material worthy of a mark.
1	Answer short. It will be related to the question but statements will be simple and lack development. Evidence will be either absent or irrelevant. Answer will lack clarity and organisation. Spelling and grammar poor. Poor use of psychological terms.
2	Statements will be mostly related to the question and there will be some development in the form of evaluation / analysis / comparison to suit the question. Limited evidence will be presented. Answer will have parts that lack clarity and organisation. Frequent errors in spelling and/or grammar. Some use of psychological terms.
3	Answer will show good understanding of the focus of the question. Analysis, evaluation and comparisons will be included. A range of evidence will be presented. Evidence of some conclusions though ideas not always fully developed. Some lapses in spelling and/or grammar apparent. Appropriate psychological terms used.
4	Answer well focused and arguments developed appropriately. Coverage of topic will demonstrate awareness of main issues. Accurate reporting of material and good use of evidence demonstrated. Evidence of excellent organisation and planning. Coherent presentation of material and arguments. Few spelling and/or grammatical errors and good use of psychological terms.

An example of a question that asks for just AO2, would be one that asks for some type of evaluation or application. Note however that because this question uses a banding system the number of marks given and the number of ticks will not necessarily be the same.

---

*1. Carmel just could not remember where she had left her folder. She had it during Psychology that morning, but now she could not recall where she had left it. Use the Cue-dependent Theory and one other theory of forgetting to explain why Carmel cannot recall where her folder is and suggest how she might use her knowledge of these theories to find it.

(8)

> Cue-dependent forgetting can explain why Carmel can't remember where her folder is as the cues are no longer present. This is a good explanation because as it is later in the day she won't be in the same place as she was when she last had it. ✓ The best way to use this knowledge to help her find it is to reinstate the situation. ✓ This can be done either in her head or for real. ✓ If Carmel retraces her day since the Psychology lesson she might remember where it is, it will work even better if she recalls the mood she was in. ✓ So if at lunchtime she was feeling really happy until someone broke some really bad news if she thinks about this mood it might help recall those events and whether her folder was there. ✓
>
> My second theory is interference theory. Interference theory can explain why when Carmel tries to find her folder she goes back to the library where she was using a different folder later in the day. It is particularly useful for explaining how two memories can get confused with one another. ✓ Sometimes the information can be from earlier memories such as where she left her folder last week. Amalgamating earlier memories with current ones has a similar effect.
>
> Band 3

Level of band	Mark	Description
0	0	No material worthy of a mark.
1	1–2	Answer short. It will be related to the question but statements will be simple and lack development. May talk about memory in general. Will leave parts of the question unanswered, e.g. just one theory. Evidence will be either absent or irrelevant. Answer will lack clarity and organisation. Spelling and grammar poor. Poor use of psychological terms.
2	3–4	Statements will be mostly related to the question and there will be some development in the form of evaluation of theory and/or application. Limited evidence will be presented. May only address one theory. Answer will have parts that lack clarity and organisation. Frequent errors in spelling and/or grammar. Some use of psychological terms.
3	5–6	Answer will show good understanding of the focus of the question. Evaluation and application will both be included. A range of evidence will be presented. Both theories will be addressed and the answer will be balanced. Evidence of some conclusions though ideas not always fully developed. Some lapses in spelling and/or grammar apparent. Appropriate psychological terms used.
4	7–8	Answer well focused and arguments developed appropriately. Coverage of topic will demonstrate awareness of main issues. Accurate reporting of material and good use of evidence demonstrated. All parts of the question will be addressed. Evidence of excellent organisation and planning. Coherent presentation of material and arguments. Few spelling and/or grammatical errors and good use of psychological terms.

Comment

In this question there are 8 marks available and two theories need to be covered. This means the top two bands will only be available if both theories have been tackled. In a similar way this question asks for both evaluation and application of the theories, so both need to be tackled to ensure the upper bands are achieved.

This answer is quite typical as it is not as tightly linked into the question as would be ideal. There is a lot of description here that cannot gain credit but it has taken up time and effort by the student. Avoiding this problem in an examination can be difficult as there is not a great deal of time to reflect on the question. Two things that may help are to do a brief plan to help you to think through what you need to include. The second thing to do is to start with the question and, from time to time, refer back to it in your answer. This particular answer has been put into Band 3. If we have a closer look at the criteria in the description for Band 3 we can see that it shows 'good understanding of the focus of the question', it also gives both evaluation and application. Indeed it could be argued that this answer meets the criterion of well focused indicated for Band 4. This answer does not get into the top band because it does not mention if and how interference theory might be used to recover the folder, despite the clear instruction in the question that both theories should be used in this way. It also does not use very much evidence, relying on general knowledge of the theories rather than mentioning that, for example, police reconstructions are used to reinstate context in the hope of triggering memories.

We mentioned earlier that planning can help keep the focus of a question much tighter and that referring back to the question can also help. Let's see what happens if we use these strategies to answer a different question.

---

*2. Assess research into obedience.

(8)

Plan: why study it? ethics of studies – harm v greater good, repeated. Practicality – any alternative? Milgram, Hofling. Agency theory – evaluate

---

Research into obedience started because people were concerned about people obeying bad orders and wanted to understand why it happened. One of the problems with obedience studies is the ethical implications. Often participants were lied to and put into traumatising situations so the studies could be conducted, and this was repeated time and time again. ✓ However without the deception a true measure of willingness to obey would have been impossible. ✓ If participants knew the true nature of the study behaviour would change, ✓ and it would not have been possible to produce valid results. ✓ The findings of studies shocked people as no-one had anticipated such a high level of obedience, so it helped to explain how atrocities can happen. ✓ However it is probably the case that, for example, Milgram did not need to use so many participants in so many variations of the study in order to show the impact of obedience on behaviour. ✓

Hofling in 1966 used a less traumatising and more realistic type of study, testing the willingness of nurses to obey a doctor even when this contravened both hospital procedures and the maximum stated dose of the drug. ✓ This work was also better as it was a very realistic field study, unlike Milgram's very contrived research. ✓ It too showed strong evidence for obedience having the potential to cause harm because the individual doesn't question authority figures. ✓

Agency theory seems a realistic way of explaining obedience. It has been shown that suspension of our own values because we are being directed by an authority figure does happen but can be countered by encouraging independent thinking. ✓

Band 4

Level of band	Mark	Description
0	0	No material worthy of a mark.
1	1–2	Answer short. It will be related to the question but statements will be simple and lack development. May talk about obedience in general, or fail to assess either theory or studies. Will leave parts of the question unanswered. Evidence will be either absent or irrelevant. Answer will lack clarity and organisation. Spelling and grammar poor. Poor use of psychological terms.
2	3–4	Statements will be mostly related to the question and there will be some development in the form of assessment. Limited evidence will be presented. Answer will have parts that lack clarity and organisation. Frequent errors in spelling and/or grammar. Some use of psychological terms.
3	5–6	Answer will show good understanding of the focus of the question. Will weigh up value of some of evaluations effectively. A range of evidence will be presented. Evidence of some conclusions though ideas not always fully developed. Some lapses in spelling and/or grammar apparent. Appropriate psychological terms used.
4	7–8	Answer well focused and arguments developed appropriately. Coverage of topic will demonstrate awareness of main issues. Accurate reporting of material and good use of evidence demonstrated. Will show understanding of both positive and negative aspects. Evidence of excellent organisation and planning. Coherent presentation of material and arguments. Few spelling and/or grammatical errors and good use of psychological terms.

Comment

This answer achieves the top band. Just planning the outline of the answer beforehand allows thinking through to be done before writing. It makes it easier to remember that the injunction is *assess*, and this is done well throughout the essay. It links back to the question by using terms such as 'problems', that is words that refer to assessing the research. The answer looks at both studies and theory, both of which can be included under the term research. It looks at positive and negative points, ethics and practicality. It does not confine itself to Milgram but provides a well-rounded and broad-reaching assessment, hence the top band.

Remember

- **Do** plan extended writing; planning saves time in the long run.
- **Do** make sure you address every aspect of the question, however briefly.
- **Do** spend time thinking about how as well as what you write.
- **Don't** use lists or note form if you run out of time.
- **Do** make a point properly.

As explained earlier it is also possible that you could be asked an extended writing question on the content of the approaches that expects you to use both AO1 and AO2 skills. The wording of the question will make it clear that this is required. Again, because there are more marks involved it will take longer to write than a short answer question so it is worth planning your answer before attempting to write. Unless you are clearly told otherwise you should assume that you need to give similar weight to the description and the evaluation in the essay. Band marking will again be employed.

*3. Describe and evaluate one theory or model of memory other than Levels of Processing

(12)

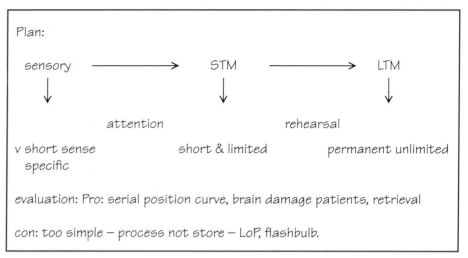

Plan:

sensory ⟶ STM ⟶ LTM

attention   rehearsal

v short sense   short & limited   permanent unlimited
specific

evaluation: Pro: serial position curve, brain damage patients, retrieval

con: too simple – process not store – LoP, flashbulb.

There are two answers below, each using the same plan – but at different levels

Answer (i)

The multi-store model of memory says that memory is divided up into 3 separate parts. These are the sensory, short- and long-term memories. ✓ Sensory memory lasts for a very short time and then decays. STM lasts a bit longer but is of limited capacity whereas LTM lasts forever and is limitless. ✓ Information moves from one store to the other by the processes of attention and rehearsal. ✓

This is a good theory of memory as there is proof that STM and LTM are different from studies like Glanzer and Cunitz who showed the serial position curve effect. We can prove that the stores are different. ✓ Brain damaged patients also prove there are different parts to memory as they only lose some functions. ✓ The levels of processing theory is better as it doesn't rely on rehearsal to move information from STM to LTM but it still doesn't explain flashbulb memory. ✓

Band 2

Answer (ii)

The multi-store model of memory sees memory as having different stages. The first stage is sensory memory. Each sense has a memory of its own which is of extremely short duration. ✓ Studies such as Sperling's work suggest that visual sensory memory lasts only a couple of seconds. There is far more material received into sensory memory than we can handle so we only process into the next stage, short-term memory (STM) information that we pay attention to. ✓

Once in STM information will be quickly lost unless we rehearse it as STM is of limited capacity and duration. Miller claimed the capacity was 7+/-2 items and the Brown-Peterson technique suggests duration is a maximum of 20 seconds. ✓✓ Without rehearsal information is lost. Rehearsal can retain information in STM or process it through into long-term memory (LTM) ✓ Once in LTM information can be permanently stored for the rest of our lives as there seems to be no limit on either capacity or duration. ✓

Evidence to support the separate stage of memory comes from studies such as Glanzer and Cunitz on the serial position curve. Material at the start of the list has moved into LTM and is retained well whereas the last few items that are still in STM are vulnerable to decay if an interpolated task is given before recall. ✓ If memory was all the same this would not happen. ✓ There is also evidence from studies into brain damaged patients such as HM where the ability to create new LTM is affected though STM seems intact. ✓ This suggests that STM and LTM are located in different places in the brain as the brain damage has only affected one type of memory. ✓

Further evidence for the separate stores comes from the nature of errors that are made by participants in studies using lists of words and retrieval from STM or LTM. When words are retrieved from STM errors tend to be acoustic whereas errors in words retrieved from LTM are semantic. ✓

However there is evidence that the multi-store model is over simplistic. Craik and Lockhart showed that rehearsal is not necessary for information to transfer from STM to LTM, level of processing can influence this. ✓ Similarly flashbulb memory syndrome (Brown & Kulik) shows how a very traumatic experience seems to bypass STM and go straight into LTM in detail. ✓ However the criticisms of the multi-store model are more to do with making it better and introducing more complexity into it rather than a fundamental disagreement with how it works and it has given us a very good idea of how memory is likely to work. ✓

Band 4

Level of band	Mark	Description
0	0	No material worthy of a mark.
1	1–3	Answer short. It will be related to the question but statements will be simple and lack development. Evidence will be either absent or irrelevant. Likely to be only description or evaluation. Answer will lack clarity and organisation. Spelling and grammar poor. Poor use of psychological terms.
2	4–6	Statements will be mostly related to the question and there will be some development in the form of evaluation. Limited evidence will be presented and points not developed. Answer will have parts that lack clarity and organisation. Frequent errors in spelling and/or grammar. Some use of psychological terms.
3	7–9	Answer will show good understanding of the focus of the question. Evaluation will be balanced. A range of evidence will be presented. Evidence of some conclusions though ideas not always fully developed. Some lapses in spelling and/or grammar. Appropriate psychological terms used.
4	10–12	Answer well focused and arguments developed appropriately. Coverage of theory will demonstrate awareness of main features and issues. Accurate reporting of material, good use of evidence and a balance between positive and negative points. Evidence of excellent organisation and planning. Coherent presentation of material and arguments. Few spelling and/or grammatical errors and good use of psychological terms.

Comment

These two answers are a sharp reminder that although a plan can help, it cannot answer the question for you: how you use the plan is important. In Answer (i) there is little attempt to develop points, something that is essential if you are to get into the higher bands of marks. The description of the multi-store model is rudimentary, doing little more than identifying the different stores. In contrast Answer (ii) develops each of the steps, giving a brief but accurate description of the key features of each memory and explains the transition of information through the system. On the basis of the descriptive part of the answer, Answer (i) would be in Band 1 whereas Answer (ii) would be in Band 4.

The evaluation in Answer (i), though not well developed, has some variety. It mentions serial position curve and evidence from brain-damaged patients in support and levels of processing as criticism. This aspect of the answer is at the very top of Band 2, or the very bottom of Band 3. If we balance this against the descriptive part of the essay it suggests it belongs in the middle of Band 2. It is difficult to demonstrate differences in spelling and grammar in answers like this, but by comparing the language used you should gain some idea of what is required.

In Answer (ii) each of the evaluation points is backed up with some evidence and most are developed. There are still areas where the answer falls short of ideal. For example the nature of the errors made in short- and long-term memory could be better explained and there could be a reference to research. It is important to appreciate that perfect answers do not happen in examinations. Students are recalling everything from memory and they are working under pressure so they are not going to produce a comprehensive answer. Provided the answer gives a range of evidence and a reasonable number of points are developed then the top bands are achievable.

Remember

Ways to boost your marks into the higher bands

- **Do** develop points so that you are demonstrating your knowledge fully.
- **Do** try and give a thorough description of the main points.
- **Do** give both strengths and weaknesses.
- **Do** give evidence either from theories or studies to back up most of your evaluation points.

Gender in Unit 2

One particular topic that may well appear as an essay on Unit 2 will be a question asking you to draw comparisons between the different approaches and their views on the development of gender. The specification uses gender development as a running theme through the approaches of Unit 2. You will have learned how the psychodynamic, biological and learning approaches all say quite different things regarding the development of gender. Questions may centre on one, two or all three of the approaches, asking you to compare them, to use one to evaluate another and so on.

Here is an extended writing question where the material has been split into two parts. This means it is important to read both parts carefully, before you start the question. Note that the two sections, (a) and (b) are linked. If you answered part (a) before thinking through part (b) you may find it difficult to do part (b) or find yourself needing to re-write part (a) so you can use the explanations you want in part (b).

As part of Unit 2 you have studied explanations for the development of gender behaviour from the learning, biological and psychodynamic approaches. Such explanations may be evaluated by giving their strengths and weaknesses. These explanations can also be compared by showing both their similarities and differences.

(a) Describe one explanation for gender behaviour.

(4)

Freud explained gender behaviour as caused by the way children identify with their same sex parent, so a boy identifies with his father and adopts the appropriate gender role. ✓ This happens through the Oedipus complex. A little boy has castration anxiety, believing his father will castrate him as punishment for wishing to replace his father in his mothers affections ✓ By identifying with his father and acting like him he is less likely to be castrated, his mother will love him because he is like his father. ✓

3/4

Comment

This is a reasonably good answer. The first sentence sets the scene by summarising what this explanation is about. It gains marks because it uses the term identify, so it is summarising but it is also giving an important bit of the explanation. The description could have been done in several ways – a detailed explanation of the Oedipus complex would not be appropriate as that would be explaining the development of the superego, nor is just mentioning the Oedipus complex enough to gain a mark as it does not link it to gender behaviour. The focus of the question on gender development means it is necessary to emphasise the consequences at the resolution of the conflict when the child identifies with the same-sex parent. This answer does not include Freud's ideas on what happens in the resolution of the female Oedipus complex. Such an explanation would be worthy of marks if used instead of or as well as the male story. The description fails to mention that this conflict is played out in the unconscious part of the child's mind.

(b) Evaluate the explanation for gender behaviour you have described in part (a) and compare it with one other explanation.

(12)

Plan: Eval: single parent families, opposite sex genitals, no evidence, too complex

Compare with biological. Overt signs of sex Differ on how used. Freud unconscious Bio genes.

One of the problems with psychodynamic explanations for the development of gender identity is it cannot explain how children brought up in single parent households, or gay households are able to successfully develop their gender identity. ✓ Children of 3 years old are not always aware of the genitals of the opposite sex and castration anxiety relies on knowing the difference. ✓ Freud's theory of gender development is based on the study of Little Hans. This data for this study was collected by Hans' father and sent to Freud in letters which means it is not reliable.

I am going to compare the psychodynamic approach to gender development with the biological approach. Both rely on the biological aspect of sexuality as a starting point for gender differences. However whereas the biological approach sees the genitals as an overt sign of the underlying mechanisms triggered by the genes and hormones the psychodynamic approach sees it as the stimulus for the development of the Oedipus complex. ✓ Both approaches see the development of gender as something of which the individual is unaware and which is also hidden from those around the child as the biological approach sees it being the genes that produce gender while the psychodynamic approach thinks it is psychological conflict in the unconscious that is responsible for gender development . ✓ The biological approach sees gender as predetermined and stable whereas the psychodynamic approach sees it developing because of experiences. ✓

7/12 Band 3

Level of band	Mark	Description
0	0	No material worthy of a mark.
1	1–3	Answer short. It will be related to the question but statements will be simple and lack development, points will fail to gain credit as not fully explained. May write about gender behaviour in general, but will not evaluate and compare. Evidence will be either absent or irrelevant. Answer will lack clarity and organisation. Spelling and grammar poor. Poor use of psychological terms.
2	4–6	Statements will be mostly related to the question and there will be some development in the form of either evaluation and/or comparisons. However points will be limited in scope. Limited evidence will be presented. Answer will have parts that lack clarity and organisation. Frequent errors in spelling and/or grammar. Some use of psychological terms.
3	7–9	Answer will show good understanding of the focus of the question. Answer will both evaluate first explanation and compare it with a different explanation. A range of evidence will be presented. Points may lack full development. Evidence of some conclusions though ideas not always fully developed. Some lapses in spelling and/or grammar apparent. Appropriate psychological terms used.
4	10–12	Answer well focused and arguments developed appropriately. Coverage of topic will demonstrate awareness of main issues. Accurate reporting of material and good use of evidence demonstrated. Will give both positive and negative evaluation points as well as similarities and differences between the two theories. Evidence of excellent organisation and planning. Coherent presentation of material and arguments. Few spelling and/or grammatical errors and good use of psychological terms.

Comment

This answer just squeezes into the bottom of Band 3. The saving grace for this answer is that it does both the evaluation and the comparison. However, there is also evidence that the student does not know the material well. There is a lack of detail and the comment made about the source of the data for the Little Hans study incorrectly identifies the nature of the problem as being one of reliability. Provided that Hans' father was not creating these stories in his imagination the data are reliable, the problems arose because of the interpretation of the dreams and fears – this is a question of validity. In the comparison part of the answer many of the points are not fully developed so fail to gain credit. This is an example of an answer that suggests the student knows quite a lot, but has not said enough to gain the marks. Refer back to the advice at the end of the essay on the multi-store model for ways in which the student could have improved this essay.

Key issues

The key issues sections of the specification are where you are asked to apply the knowledge and understanding you have acquired in an approach and apply it to a real world situation. While you will have studied a key issue within the course and may be asked to use this in the examination it is equally likely that you will be given a novel scenario and asked to explain it using the theories you have learned about from a particular approach.

It is likely that most of the questions on key issues will be extended writing; there may, occasionally be a short answer question. All the comments about how extended writing questions may be asked and how answers are marked that have been made previously also apply here.

How can I improve my marks?

Now that we have had a look at both the sort of questions that might come up and different answers to the questions, it is useful to look at how marks can be boosted.

First of all, some general points to remember.

In preparation for the examination:

- revise material thoroughly
- make sure you have revised everything for the relevant approaches
- have enough detail for the likely number of marks available on different questions
- practice writing answers to examination type questions
- practice answering questions when not using notes
- practice writing answers using a time limit
- do not learn 'model' answers off by heart
- use your psychology knowledge to improve your learning.

In the examination:

- read the questions carefully so what you write is an answer to the question set
- on short answer questions make sure you have made sufficient points
- use a relevant example if it helps to explain more clearly what you mean
- plan extended writing questions
- aim to keep AO1 and AO2 in balance in essays that are assessing both skills
- use evidence to support points made
- make sure that a point made is fully made
- for essays in particular, read through the essay at least once after writing it and ask yourself does it say what you intended to say?

Revising for the exam

Revision is best if it is planned and carried out spaced out over the course. You can make a big difference to how much work is required to prepare well for the examination by one simple routine. At the end of each week go through all the notes from that week's lessons and 'do' something with them. What precisely you do will depend on your personal style but any of the following options will help to consolidate that week's learning.

- Rewrite or type up on the computer all the notes from that week with additional points added in as you go through it.
- Read the class text or use the Internet to get some additional notes and integrate those into the class notes.
- Go through the class notes and use highlighter pens to colour code key ideas, facts, theories, studies.
- Write a summary of what that week's work is about so that you can produce an index/contents page for your notes as you go through the year.

If you do this, when you come to the main revision period in the run up to the examination the task will be much easier as you will discover you know a lot more than you realised you did.

Motivating yourself to revise

Many people find the prospect of revision daunting. Because of this, some leave it until the last minute. As a result they do not know the material well enough and do not do as well as they could in the exam. If you want to do yourself justice in the exam then good revision is the key. Doing good revision means you need to be motivated. Here are some tips on how to improve your motivation.

Have a positive approach to both revision and the forthcoming exam – a 'can do' mentality will keep you motivated far better. Keep in mind the reasons why you want to do well. It is far better if you are trying to achieve because you want to, not because someone else wants you to. If you feel in control of your situation you will feel far more motivated than if you feel someone else is writing your agenda.

Beware of putting things off. Everyone is guilty of doing this at times, it is called procrastination, and when it comes to revision it can be a disaster. You need to decide on a firm date to start your revision and stick to it. And once you start the revision process make sure that you keep to a timetable so you have time to go through everything sufficiently thoroughly.

Practical tips

Decide when you can start the main period of revision and plan out the days from then until the exam with days and times when you can revise. This should be at the latest from the start of the Christmas holidays if you are taking a January examination and it may well be as early as Easter for the May examinations. If you are revising during a holiday period it enables you to plan your time more effectively and ensures you can do something almost every day.

- When you sit down to revise you should have a target that you aim to achieve, but make sure it is achievable in a reasonable amount of time.
- Reward yourself once you have achieved that target by a short enjoyable break.
- Avoid long uninterrupted periods of revising as you will find you become progressively less productive.
- Decide before you start a revision session how long/how much you will do before a break and how long and what sort of breaks you will give yourself, and keep to it (this is hard but well worth it in the end).
- Avoid suddenly finding an essential bit of tidying up to do. This is procrastinating, you know you never normally tidy up!
- Do make sure you ring the changes both in what you revise and how you revise.
- If something just isn't sticking, change topic. Go back to the problem area another time.

Motivation questionnaire

Answer the following questions as honestly as you can. The questionnaire is designed to assess your current state of motivation and should enable you to decide whether you are on the right track, or whether your motivation needs a boost.

		True	False
1.	I usually get what I want out of life	☐	☐
2.	If I don't succeed in a task I usually give up as it doesn't matter that much	☐	☐
3.	I work best at the last minute when the pressure is on	☐	☐
4.	I like to get my room in order before starting a task	☐	☐
5.	The amount of work I do has no effect on my grades	☐	☐
6.	I never try anything I am not sure of	☐	☐
7.	I know what I have to do but frequently find that I have done something else	☐	☐
8.	I carry my books/work around with me but rarely open them	☐	☐
9.	I think that I could easily win the national lottery	☐	☐
10.	I do not really believe that I can achieve all my goals	☐	☐
11.	I have been too tired, nervous or upset to carry out the difficult task that faces me	☐	☐
12.	I have often found that what is going to happen will happen	☐	☐
13.	I don't think I ever have enough time to study	☐	☐
14.	I can't do well in my exams because I don't have long-term career goals	☐	☐
15.	I don't think there is enough time between now and my exams to get enough revision done	☐	☐
16.	Most of the people in my group are more clever than me, so I can never do as well as them	☐	☐
17.	I think there is too much material for me to cover it all	☐	☐
18.	I don't think there is any point in studying hard as I won't get anything out of it anyway	☐	☐
19.	My life feels like a series of random events	☐	☐
20.	Any success I have is mainly a matter of chance	☐	☐

If you have answered 'True' to a lot of these questions it suggests your motivation still needs improving. Reassess your motivation by answering the following questions honestly:

Do I want to do well?

Do I feel in control of my learning and revision?

Do I feel optimistic?

Do I feel I can get on with things now?

Look at the ones you answered 'no' to, as those identify where the work to improve your motivation needs to focus. Wanting to do well is easier if you have a clear target in mind. This is simpler if you know you want to get a particular grade, but you can set yourself a target. Even promising yourself a treat if you achieve a certain level will help here.

Taking control of your own revision and learning can be made easier by making a few decisions and sticking to them even when there is pressure from someone else to give way. So if you have decided to stay in and revise on Thursday night don't let friends tempt you out until you've done the revision you promised yourself you would do. Equally important don't let someone like your part-time employer bully you into working an extra shift. Your exam results might not matter to them but they do to you.

Feeling optimistic is a matter of starting to believe you can achieve. Set a few small achievable targets and once you start to succeed then your confidence will build and your optimism will grow.

Finding it hard to get started now? Get out that calendar or draw yourself one on the computer and create a timetable. But don't procrastinate by making the timetable very colourful and intricate! Once you have that timetable sorted out – and it shouldn't take very long – put up three copies of it. Put one in your room near where you relax, another one by the desk you work at and the other one in the kitchen, ideally on or by the fridge. Every time you have completed a session of revision put a big tick against the session on the timetable. If you really want to help yourself achieve you might even use three different levels. A gold tick for an ace revision session, a silver tick for one that was OK and bronze for the one that wasn't so good. See if you can get the gold ticks to increase in number over a period of a few days.

The exam
- Once you have done all the revision and done all the preparation you can you will be taking the exam.
- Do make sure you have a careful note of when and where the exam is to be held.
- Check on the exam timetable at college or school to make sure you are going to turn up at the right place, at the right time, prepared to sit the right exam.
- Make sure you take at least one spare pen into the exam with you, preferably two and any other equipment you know you may need.
- Make sure your pens are black or blue.
- Once you have gone into the examination room and sat down make sure you have everything to hand and nothing on you that is forbidden such as a mobile phone. If there is a problem tell the person in charge of the exam (invigilator) straight away.
- Once the examination papers are handed out while you are waiting to be told you may start, read the instructions on the front cover. They are there to help you.
- Fill in the details on the front cover as requested.
- Once you have been told to start spend a short time quickly reading through all the questions first so you can identify those questions that you will find tricky and those that you feel are easy. It is often worth starting with the questions you feel most comfortable with and leaving trickier questions until you are in the swing of the exam.
- Make sure you put your name on every sheet of paper you use.
- Make sure you keep your writing on the lines provided and within the black frame on each page.

- If you run out of lines use extra space in the booklet and direct the examiner to the page; if you run out of space use an extra sheet provided by the invigilator. Do not squeeze answers at the bottom or sides as the examiner will not be able to read these properly.
- If you wish to make notes on a separate piece of paper, you must use a sheet obtained from the invigilator.
- Remember to take time to read through your answers. They should make sense. If you cannot understand what you have written there is not much hope that the examiner will.
- If you decide to rewrite an answer or part of an answer because you are not happy with it do the new answer then cross out the one you do not want marked. **Never use Tippex**, and don't cross out an answer until you have got something you are happier with to replace it.

Final words

Hopefully this chapter has helped you to prepare for the examination and understand what to expect in the exam a little better. We are all aware, psychologists more than most, that the examination process is a very artificial and less than perfect system for assessing a student's ability. Nonetheless it is the system we have and it is better than some other systems. If you prepare thoroughly you will have the chance to show what you are capable of. This chapter should have helped you improve your level of preparation. Now it is up to you.

References

Abe, N., Suzuki, M., Tsukiura, T., Mori, E., Yamaguchi, K., Itoh, M. & Fujii, T. (2006) 'Dissociable roles of prefrontal and anterior cingulate cortices in deception'. *Cerebral Cortex* 16(2): 192–9.

Adams, C.E., Rathbone, .J, Thornley, B., Clarke, M., Borrill, J., Wahlbeck, K. & Awad, A.G. (2005) 'Chlorpromazine for schizophrenia: a Cochrane systematic review of 50 years of randomised controlled trials'. *BMC Medicine*, 3: 15.

Adams, H., Wright, L. & Lohr, B. (1996) 'Is homophobia associated with homosexual arousal?' *Journal of Abnormal Psychology,* 105: 440–5.

Ahedo, L., Cardas, A., Azpiroz, P., Brain, F. & Sanchez-Martin, J.R. (2002) 'Social behavior in male and female 5-year-olds and its relation to salivary testosterone levels'. Paper presented at the XV World Meeting of the International Society for Research on Aggression.

Allport, G.W. & Postman, L. (1947) *The Psychology of Rumour.* New York, Holt, Rhinehart and Winston.

Atkinson, R.C. & Shiffrin, R.M. (1968) 'Human memory: a proposed system and its control mechanisms'. In Spence, K.W. & Spence, J.T. (eds) *The Psychology of Learning and Motivation, Volume II.* London, Academic Press.

Axline, V.M. (1964) *Dibs in Search of Self.* London: Penguin.

Ayllon, T. & Azrin, N.H. (1968) *The Token Economy: A Motivated System for Therapy and Rehabilitation.* New York: Appleton-Century Crofts.

Bachrach, H.M., Galatzer-Levy, R., Skolnikoff, A. & Waldron, S. (1991) 'On the efficacy of psychoanalysis'. *Journal of the American Psychoanalytic Association,* 39: 871–913.

Bailey, J.M. & Pillard, R.C. (1991) 'A genetic study of male sexual orientation'. *Archives of Genetic Psychiatry*, 48(12): 1089–96.

Bailey, J.M. & Pillard, R.C. (1995) 'Genetics of human sexual orientation'. *Annual Review of Sex Research,* 6: 126–50.

Bailey, J.M., Dunne, M.P. & Martin, N.G. (2000) 'Genetic and environmental influences on sexual orientation and its correlates in an Australian twin sample'. *Journal of Personality and Social Psychology,* 78(3): 524–36.

Baker, J.R., Bezance, J.B., Zellaby, E. & Aggleton, J.P. (2004) 'Chewing gum can produce context-dependent effects ,n memory'. *Appetite,* 43: 207–10.

Bandura, A. (1977) *Social Learning Theory.* Englewood Cliffs, NJ: Prentice-Hall .

Bandura, A., Ross, D. & Ross, S.A. (1961) 'Transmission of aggression through imitation of aggressive models'. *Journal of Abnormal and Social Psychology,* 63: 575–82.

Bandura, A., Ross, D. & Ross, S.A. (1963) 'Imitation of film-mediated aggressive models'. *Journal of Abnormal and Social Psychology*, 66: 3–11.

Bartlett, F.C. (1932) *Remembering.* Cambridge: Cambridge University Press.

Bateman, A. & Holmes, J. (1995) *An Introduction to Psychoanalysis.* London: Routledge.

Bateson, P. (1986) 'When to experiment on animals'. *New Scientist*, 1496: 30–2.

Bergan-Gander, R. & von Kurthy, H. (2006) 'Sexual orientation and occupation: gay men and women's lived experiences of occupational participation'. *British Journal of Occupational Therapy*, 69: 402–8.

Berntsen, D. (2002) 'Tunnel memories for autobiographical events'. *Memory and Cognition,* 30: 1010–20.

Blass, T. (1996) 'Attribution of responsibility and trust in the Milgram obedience experiment' *Journal of Applied Social Psychology,* 26: 1529–35.

Blass, T. & Schmitt, C. (2001) 'The nature of perceived authority in the Milgram paradigm: Two replications'. *Current Psychology,* 20: 115–21.

Bornstein, R.F., Hilsenroth, M.J., Padawer, J.R. & Fowler, J.C. (2000) 'Interpersonal dependency and personality pathology: variations in Rorschach Oral Dependency scores across Axis II diagnoses'. *Journal of Personality Assessment*, 75: 478–91.

Breuer, J. & Freud, S. (1896) *Studies on Hysteria. The Complete Works of Sigmund Freud, Volume II.* London: Hogarth.

British Psychological Society (2006) *Ethical Principles for conducting Research with Human Participants: Introduction to the revised principles.* Leicester: BPS.

Brown, R. & Kulik, J. (1977) 'Flashbulb memories'. *Cognition*, 5: 73–99.

Brown, D. & Pedder, J. (1991) *Introduction to Psychotherapy.* London: Routledge.

Carli, L.L. (1999) 'Cognitive reconstruction, hindsight and reactions to victims and perpetrators'. *Personality and Social Psychology Bulletin,* 25: 966–79.

Cassaday, H.J., Bloomfield, R.E. & Hayward, N. (2002) 'Relaxed conditions can provide memory cues in both undergraduates and primary school children'. *British Journal of Educational Psychology,* 72: 531–47.

Charlton. T., Gunter, B. & Hannan, A. (eds) (2000) *Broadcast Television Effects in a Remote Community.* Mahway, NJ: Lawrence Erlbaum Associates.

Cherney, I. & London, K. (2006) 'Gender-linked differences in the toys, television shows, computer games, and outdoor activities of 5- to 13-year-old children'. *Sex Roles*, 54: 717–26.

Conners, F.A., Rosenquist, C.J., Atwell, J.A., and Klinger, L.G. (2000) 'Cognitive strengths and weaknesses associated with Prader-Willi syndrome'. *Education and Training in Mental Retardation and Developmental Disabilities.*

Cordua, G.D., McGraw, K.O., and Drabman, R.S. (1979) 'Doctor or nurse: children's perception of sex-typed occupations'. *Child Development*, 50(2): 590–3.

Coria-Avila, G.A., Ouimet, A.J., Pacheco, P., Manzo, J. & Pfaus, J.G. (2006) 'Olfactory conditioned partner preference in the female rat'. *Behavioral Neuroscience*, 119(3): 716–25.

Craik, F.I.M. (1973) 'A levels of analysis view of memory'. In Pliner, P., Krames, L. & Alloway, T.M. (eds) *Communication and Affect: Language and Thought*. London: Academic Press.

Craik, F.I.M. & Lockhart, B. (1972) Levels of processing. *Journal of Verbal Learning and Verbal Behaviour*, 11: 671–84.

Craik, F.I.M. & Tulving, E. (1975) 'Depth of processing and retention of words in episodic memory'. *Journal of Experimental Psychology*, 104: 268–94.

Cramer, P. (1997) 'Identity, personality and defence mechanisms: an observer-based study'. *Journal of Research in Personality*, 31: 58–77.

Dai, X., Thavundayil, J. & Gianoulakis, C. (2005) 'Differences in the peripheral levels of beta-endorphin in response to alcohol and stress as a function of alcohol dependence and family history of alcoholism'. *Alcoholism: Clinical and Experimental Research*, 29(11): 1965–75.

De Bellis MD, Keshavan, M.S., Beers, S.R., Hall, J., Frustaci, K., Masalehdan, A., Noll, J. & Boring, A.M. (2001). 'Sex differences in brain maturation during childhood and adolescence.' *Cerebral Cortex*, 11(6): 552–7.

de Lago, E., de Miguel, R., Lastres-Becker, I., Ramos, J.A., Fernández-Ruiz, J. (2004) 'Involvement of vanilloid-like receptors in the effects of anandamide on motor behavior and nigrostriatal dopaminergic activity: in vivo and in vitro evidence'. *Brain Research*: 1007(1–2): 152–9.

Delfabbro, P.H. & Winefield, A.H. (1999) 'Poker-machine gambling: an analysis of within session characteristics'. *British Journal of Psychology*, 90: 425–39.

Diamond, M. & Sigmundson, K. (1997) 'Sex reassignment at birth: a long term review and clinical implications'. *Archives of Pediatrics and Adolescent Medicine*, 151(3).

Diseth, A. & Martinsen, O. (2003) 'Approaches to learning. Cognitive style and motives as predictors of academic achievement', *Educational Psychology*, 23: 195–207.

Djordjevic, J., Zatorre, R.J., Petrides, M., Boyle, J.A. & Jones-Gotman, M. (2005) 'Functional neuroimaging of odor imagery'. *Neuroimage*, 24(3): 791–801.

Dobbs, M. & Crano, W.D. (2001) 'Outgroup accountability in the minimal group paradigm: implications for aversive discrimination and social identity theory'. *Personality and Social Psychology Bulletin*, 27: 355–64.

Domínguez-Salazar, E., Portillo, W., Baum, M.J., Bakker, J. & Paredes, R.G. (2002) 'Effect of prenatal androgen receptor antagonist or aromatase inhibitor on sexual behaviour, partner preference and neuronal Fos responses to estrous female odors in the rat accessory olfactory system'. *Physiology and Behavior*, 75(3): 337–46.

Duka, T., Weissenborn, R. & Dienes, Z. (2001) 'State-dependent effects of alcohol on recollective experience, familiaruty and awareness on memories', *Psychopharmacology*, 153: 295–306.

Duker, P.C. & Seys, D.M. (2000) 'A quasi-experimental study on the effect of electrical aversion treatment on imposed mechanical restraint for severe self-injurous behaviour'. *Research in Developmental Disabilities*, 21: 235–42.

Entwistle, N. & Tait, H. (1996). *Approaches and Study Skills Inventory for Students*. Centre for Research on Learning and Instruction. University of Edinburgh.

Eron, L.D. & Huesmann, L.R. (1986) 'The role of television in the development of antisocial and prosocial behavior'. In Olweus, D., Block, J. & Radke-Yarrom, M. (eds) *Development of Antisocial and Prosocial Behaviour, Theories and Issues*. New York: Academic Press.

Eron, L.D., Huesmann, L.R., Leftowitz, M.M. & Walder, L.O. (1972) 'Does television violence cause aggression?' *American Psychologist*, 27: 253–63.

Evans, L. & Davies, K. (2000) 'No sissy boys here: a content analysis of the representation of masculinity in elementary school reading books'. *Sex Roles*, 42: 255–70.

Eysenck, H.J. (1952) 'The effects of psychotherapy: an evaluation'. *Journal of Consulting Psychology*, 16: 319–24.

Eysenck, M. (1998) 'Memory'. In Eysenck, M. (ed.) *Psychology, an integrated approach*. Harlow: Addison-Wesley Longman.

Fagot, B.I., and Leinbach, M.D. (1993) 'Gender-role development in young children: from discrimination to labeling'. *Developmental Review*, 13: 205–24.

Fineberg, N.A., Tonnoir, B., Lemming, O. & Stein, D.J. (2007) 'Escitalopram prevents relapse of obsessive-compulsive disorder'. *European Neuropsychopharmacology*, 17(6–7): 430–9.

Fink, J.M., Willemsen, G. & Boomsma, D.I. (2003) 'The association of current smoking behavior with the smoking behavior of parents, siblings, friends and spouses'. *Addiction*, 98(7): 923–31.

Fisher, R.P. & Geiselman, R.E. (1988) 'Enhancing eyewitness memory with the cognitive interview'. In Gruneberg, M., Morris, P. & Sykes, R.N. (eds) *Practical Aspects of Memory: Current Research and Issues. Volume 1*. Chichester: Wiley.

Forde, E.M.E. & Humphreys, G.W. (2002) 'The role of semantic knowledge in short-term memory'. *Neurocase*, 8: 13–27.

Frankland, A. & Cohen, L. (1999) 'Working with recovered memories'. *The Psychologist*, 12: 106–7.

Freud, A. (1936) *The Ego and the Mechanisms of Defence*. London: Hogarth.

Freud, S. (1894) *The Defence Neuropsychoses*. Standard Edition volume I. London: Hogarth.

Freud, S. (1900) *The Interpretation of Dreams*. London: Hogarth.

Freud, S. (1905) *Three Essays on Sexuality*. London: Hogarth.

Freud, S. (1909) 'Analysis of a phobia in a five-year-old boy'. *Collected Papers* vol. III, 149–295.

Freud, S. (1914) *Psychopathology of Everyday Life*. London: Benn.

Freud, S. (1915) *Introductory Lectures on Psychoanalysis*. London: Hogarth.

Freud, S. (1923) *The Ego and the Id*. London: Hogarth.

Freud, S. (1925) *An Autobiographical Study*. London: Hogarth.

Freud, S. (1933) *New Introductory Lectures on Psychoanalysis*. London: Hogarth.

Frost, J.A., Binder, J.R., Springer, J.A., Hammeke, T.A., Bellgowan, P.S., Rao, S.M. & Cox, R.W. (1999) 'Language processing is strongly left lateralized in both sexes. Evidence from functional MRI'. *Brain*, 122(2): 199–208.

Frovenholt, J., Bragesjo, M., Clinton, D. & Sandell, R. (2007) 'How do experiences of psychiatric care affect the credibility of different forms of psychotherapy?' *Psychology and Psychotherapy*, 80: 205–16.

Galynker, I.I., Watras-Ganz, S., Miner, C., Rosenthal, R.N., Des Jarlais, D.C., Richman, B.L. & London, E. (2000) 'Cerebral metabolism in opiate-dependent subjects: effects of methadone maintenance'. *Mount Sinai Journal of Medicine*, 67(5–6): 381–7.

Gardiner, J.M., Brandt, K., Vargha-Khadem, F., Baddeley, A. & Mishkin, M. (2006) 'Effects of level of processing but not of task enactment on recognition memory in a case of developmental amnesia', *Cognitive Neuropsychology*, 23: 930–48.

Gee, C.G., Ryan, A., Laflamme, D.J. & Holt, J. (2006) 'Self-reported discrimination and mental health status among African descendants, Mexican Americans, and Other Latinos in the New Hampshire REACH 2010 Initiative: the added dimension of immigration'. *American Journal of Public Health*, 96: 1821–8.

Gelkopf, M. & Zakai, D. (1991) 'One more criticism of the multistore model of memory: an experiment on the first-in-first-out (FIFO) principle'. *Journal of Psychology*, 125: 497–9.

Gigi, A., Babai, R., Katzav, E., Atkins, S. & Hendler, T. (2007) Prefrontal and parietal regions are involved in naming of objects seen from unusual viewpoints. *Behavioral Neuroscience*, 121(5): 836–44.

Glanzer, M. & Cunitz, A.R. (1966) 'Two storage mechanisms in free recall'. *Journal of Verbal Learning and Verbal Behaviour*, 6: 928–35.

Godden, D.R. & Baddeley, A.D. (1975) 'Context-dependent memory in two natural environments: on land and underwater'. *British Journal of Psychology*, 66: 325–31.

Golombok, S. & Fivush, R. (1994) *Gender Development*. Cambridge: Cambridge University Press.

Golombok, S. (2000) *Parenting: What Really Counts?* Philadelphia: Taylor & Francis.

Gorno Tempini, M.L. & Price, C.J. (2001) 'Identification of famous faces and buildings: A functional neuroimaging study of semantically unique items'. *Brain*, 124: 2087–97.

Gottesman, I. (1991) *Schizophrenia Genesis: The Origins of Madness*. New York: Freeman.

Gottesman, I.I. & Shields, J. (1966) 'Schizophrenia in twins: 16 years' consecutive admissions to a psychiatric clinic'. *British Journal of Psychiatry*, 112: 809–18.

Griffith, C.T. (1999) 'A study of stress and cognitive distortions in adolescent male offenders and non-offenders'. *Dissertation Abstracts International*, 59: 5083.

Hadley, C.B. & MacKay, D.G. (2007) 'Does emotion help or hinder memory? Arousal versus priority binding mechanisms'. *Journal of Experimental Psychology*, 32, 79–88.

Hagell, A. & Newbury, T. (1994) *Young offenders and the Media*. London: Policy Studies Institute.

Hamer, D.H., Hu, S., Magnuson, V.L., Hu, N. & Pattatucci, A.M.L. (1993) 'A linkage between DNA markers on the X chromosome and male sexual orientation'. *Science*, 261: 321–7.

Hamilton, V.L. & Sanders, J. (1995) 'Crimes of obedience and conformity in the workplace: surveys of Americans, Russians and Japanese'. *Journal of Social Issues*, 51: 67–88.

Hellerstein, J.K., Neumark, D. & Troske, K.R. (2002) 'Market forces and sex discrimination'. *The Journal of Human Resources*, 37: 353–80.

Heston, L.L. (1966) 'Psychiatric disorders in foster home reared children of schizophrenic mothers'. *British Journal of Psychiatry*, 112: 819–25.

Hettema, J.M., Annas, P., Neale, M.C., Kendler, K.S. & Fredrikson, M. (2003) 'A twin study of the genetics of fear conditioning'. *Archives of General Psychiatry*, 60(7): 702–8.

Hofling C.K., Brotzman, E., Dalrymple, S., Graves, N. & Pierce, C.M. (1966) 'An experimental study in nurse–physician relationships'. *Journal of Nervous and Mental Disease*, 143: 171–80.

Howard, M.O. (2001) 'Pharmacological aversion treatment of alcohol dependence. I. Production and prediction of conditioned alcohol aversion'. *American Journal of Drug and Alcohol Abuse*, 27(3): 561–85.

Hu, S., Pattatucci, A. M., Patterson,C., Li, L., Fulker, D.W., Cherny, S.S., Kruglyak, L. & Hamer, D.H. (1995) 'Linkage between sexual orientation and chromosome Xq28 in males but not in females'. *Nature Genetics*, 11(3): 248–56.

Huprich S.K., Gacono, C.B., Schneider, R.B. & Bridges, R.M. (2004) 'Rorschach oral dependency in psychopaths, sexual homicide perpetrators and non-violent paedophiles'. *Behavioural Sciences and the Law*, 22: 345–56.

Jaeger, J.J., Lockwood, A.H., Van Valin, R.D., Kemmerer, D.L., Murphy, B.W. & Wack, D.S. (1998) 'Sex differences in brain regions activated by grammatical and reading tasks'. *Neuroreport*, 9(12): 2803–7.

Jarvis, M. (2004) *Psychodynamic Psychology: Classic Theory and Contemporary Research*. London: Thomson.

Jarvis, M. (2006) 'Learning strategies and achievement in AS-level psychology: an exploratory study'. Paper presented at the *11th Annual Conference of the European Learning Styles Information Network*. June 2006, University of Oslo.

Jerabek, I. & Standing, L. (1992) 'Imagined test situations produce contextual memory enhancement'. *Perceptual and Motor Skills*, 75: 400.

Johnston, J. & Ettema, J.S. (1982) *Positive Images: Breaking Stereotypes with Children's Television*. Beverley Hills: Sage.

Kanaan, R.A., Craig, T.K.J., Wesseley, S.C. & David, A.S. (2007) 'Imaging repressed memories in motor conversion disorder'. *Psychosomatic Medicine*, 69: 202–5.

Kendler, K.S., Thornton, L.M., Gilman, S.E. & Kessler, R.C. (2000) 'Sexual orientation in a US national sample of twin and nontwin sibling pairs'. *American Journal of Psychiatry*, 157: 1843–6.

Kilberg, R.R. (2004) 'When shadows fall: using psychodynamic approaches in executive coaching'. *Consulting Psychology Journal*, 56: 246–68.

Kimble, G.A. (1961) *Hilgard and Marquis' Conditioning and Learning*. New York: Appleton-Century-Crofts.

Kippin, T.E. (2000) 'Olfactory-conditioned ejaculatory preference in the male rat: implications for the role of learning in sexual partner preferences'. *Dissertation Abstracts International: Section B: The Sciences and Engineering*, 61(3-B): 1678.

Koehler, T., Thiede, G. & Thoens, M. (2002) 'Long and short-term forgetting of word associations. An experimental study of the Freudian concepts of resistance and repression'. *Zeitschrift fuer Klinische Psychologie, Psychiatrie und Psychotherapie*, 50: 328–33.

Koh, A.S. & Ross, L.K. (2006) 'Mental health issues a comparison of lesbian, bisexual and heterosexual women'. *Journal of Homosexuality*, 51: 33–57.

Koopman, P., Gubbay, J., Vivian, N., Goodfellow, P. & Lovell-Badge, R. (1991) 'Male development of chromosomally female mice transgenic for Sry'. *Nature*, 351: 117–21.

Krackow, A. & Blass, T. (1995) 'When nurses obey or defy inappropriate physician orders: attributional differences'. *Journal of Social behaviour and Personality*, 10: 585–94.

Kulynych, J.J., Vladar, K., Jones, D.W. & Weinberger, D.R. (1992) 'Gender differences in the normal lateralization of the supratemporal cortex: MRI surface-rendering morphometry of Heschl's gyrus and the planum temporale'. *Brain*, 115: 1521–41.

Leichsenring, F. & Falk, E. (2007) 'Psychodynamic therapy: a systematic review of techniques, implications and empirical evidence'. *Psychology and Psychotherapy*, 80: 217–28.

Levine, M., Prosser, A., Evans, D. & Reicher, S. (2005) 'Identity and emergency intervention: how social group membership and inclusiveness of group boundaries shape helping behaviour'. *Personality and Social Psychology Bulletin*, 31: 443–53.

Loehlin, J.C. (1992) *Genes and Environment in Personality Development*. Newbury Park: Sage.

Loftus, E.F. (1975) 'Leading questions and the eyewitness report'. *Cognitive Psychology*, 7: 560–72.

Lüttke, H.B. (2004) 'Experiments within the Milgram Paradigm/Experimente Unter Dem Milgram-Paradigma'. *Gruppendynamik und Organisationsberatung*, 35: 431–64.

Lytton, H. & Romney, D. M. (1991). 'Parents' differential socialization of boys and girls: a meta-analysis'. *Psychological Bulletin*, 109: 267–96.

Maltby, J. & Price, J. (1999) 'Conservatism and defence style'. *Journal of Genetic Psychology*, 160: 389–96.

Marcia, J. (1980) 'Identity in adolescence' In Adelson, J. (ed.) *Handbook of Adolescent Psychology*, Wiley: New York.

Marsh, P., Harre, R. & Rosser, E. (1978) *The Rules of Disorder*. London: Routledge.

Massie, H. & Szeinberg, N. (2002) 'The relationship between mothering in infancy, childhood experience and adult mental health'. *International Journal of Psychoanalysis*, 83: 35–55.

Matute, H. (1996) 'The illusion of control: detecting response-outcome independence in analytic but not naturalistic conditions'. *Psychological Science*, 7: 289–93.

McGlone, J. (1978) 'Sex differences in functional brain asymmetry'. *Cortex*, 14: 122–8.

Meeus, W.H.J. & Raaijmakers, Q.A.W. (1986) 'Administrative obedience: carrying out orders to use psychological-administrative violence'. *European Journal of Social Psychology*, 16: 311–24.

Memon, A. & Wright, D.B. (1999) 'Eyewitness testimony and the Oklahoma bombing'. *The Psychologist*, 12: 292–5.

Milburn, S.S., Carney, D.R. & Ramirez, A.M. (2001) 'Even in modern media, the picture is still the same: a content analysis of clipart images'. *Sex Roles*, 44: 277–94.

Milgram, S. (1963) 'Behavioural study of obedience'. *Journal of Abnormal and Social Psychology*, 67: 371–8.

Milgram, S. (1965) 'Liberating effects of group pressure'. *Journal of Personality and Social Psychology*, 1: 127–34.

Milgram, S. (1974) *Obedience to Authority*. New York: Harper & Rowe.

Money, J. (1975) 'Ablatio penis: normal male infant sex-reassignment as a girl'. *Archives of Sexual Behavior*, 4(1): 65–71.

Morgan, M. (1982) 'Television and adolescents' sex-role stereotypes: a longitudinal study'. *Journal of Personality and Social Psychology*, 43(5): 947–55.

Morgan, M. & Rothschild, N. (1983) 'Impact of the new television technology: cable TV, peers and sex-role cultivation in the electronic environment'. *Youth and Society*, 15(1): 33–50.

Mystkowski, J.L., Mineka, S., Vernon, L.L. & Zinbarg, R.E. (2003) 'Changes in caffeine states enhance return of fear in spider phobia'. *Journal of Consulting and Clinical Psychology*, 71: 243–50.

Nyberg, L. (2002) 'Levels of processing: a view from functional brain imaging'. *Memory*, 10: 345–8.

O'Neill, R.M., Greenberg, R.P. & Fisher, S. (1992) 'Humour and anality'. *Humour: International Journal of Humour Research*, 5: 283–91.

Olson, J.M., Vernon, P.A., Harris, J.A. & Jang, K.L. (2001) 'The heritability of attitudes: a study of twins'. *Journal of Personality and Social Psychology*, 80(6): 845–60.

Olson, M.A. & Fazio, R.H. (2001) 'Implicit attitude formation through classical conditioning'. *Psychological Science*, 12(5): 413–7.

Pate, J.E. & Gabbard, G.O. (2003) 'Adult baby syndrome'. *American Journal of Psychiatry*, 160: 1932–6.

Paterson, H.M. & Kemp, R.I. (2006) 'Comparing methods of encountering post-event information: the power of co-witness suggestion'. *Applied Cognitive Psychology*, 20: 1083–99.

Pavlov, I.P. (1927) *Conditioned Reflexes*. Oxford: Oxford University Press.

Pavlov, I.P. (1955) *Selected Works*. Moscow: Foreign Languages Publishing House.

Pennington, D.C. (1986) *Essential Social Psychology*. London: Edward Arnold.

Peters, K. & Richards, P. (1998) '"Why we fight:" Voices of youth combatants in Sierra Leone', *Africa*, 68: 183–210.

Peterson, L.R. & Peterson, M.J. (1959) Short-term retention of individual items'. *Journal of Experimental Psychology*, 58: 193–8.

Petry, N.M., Kolodner, K.B., Li, R., Peirce, J.M., Roll, J.M., Stitzer, M.L. & Hamilton, J.A. (2006) 'Prize-based contingency management does not increase gambling'. *Drug and Alcohol Dependence*, 83(3): 269–73.

Pezdek, K. (2002) 'Memory for the terrorists' attack on New York 9/11/01'. Paper delivered at the *Tsukuba International Conference on Memory*, March 2002.

Pickens, R. & Thompson, T. (1968) 'Cocaine-reinforced behaviour in rats: effects of reinforcement magnitude and fixed-ratio size'. *The Journal of Pharmacology and Experimental Therapeutics*, 161(1): 122–9.

Piolino, P., Giffard-Quillon, G., Desgranges, B., Chételat, G., Baron, J-C. & Eustache, F. (2004) 'Re-experiencing old memories via hippocampus: a PET study of autobiographical memory'. *NeuroImage*, 22(3): 1371–83.

Platow, M.J., McClintock, and Liebrand, W.B. (1990) 'Predicting intergroup fairness and in-group bias in the minimal group paradigm'. *European Journal of Social Psychology*, 20: 221–39.

Poppe, E. & Linssen, H. (1999) 'In-group favouritism and the reflection of realistic dimensions of difference between national states in Central and Eastern European nationality stereotypes'. *British Journal of Social Psychology*, 38: 85–102.

Pugh, K.R., Shaywitz, B.A., Shaywitz, S.E., Constable, R.T., Skudlarski, P., Fulbright, R.K., Bronen, R.A., Shankweiler, D.P., Katz, L., Fletcher, J.M. & Gore, J.C. (1995) 'Cerebral organization of component processes in reading'. *Brain*, 119: 1221–38.

Raine, A., Buchsbaum, M. & LaCasse, L. (1997) 'Brain abnormalities in murderers indicated by positron emission tomography'. *Biological Psychiatry*, 42: 495–508.

Ramos, S. (2003) 'Revisiting Anna O: a case of chemical dependence'. *History of Psychology*, 6: 239–50.

Ramponi, C., Richardson-Klavehn, A. & Gardiner, J.M. (2004) 'Level of processing and age affect involuntary conceptual priming of weak but not strong associates'. *Experimental Psychology*, 51: 159–64.

Reason, J. (2000) 'The Freudian slip revisited'. *The Psychologist*, 13: 610–11.

Reber, R., Perrig, W.J., Flammer, A. & Walter, D. (1994) 'Levels of processing and memory for emotional words'. *Schweizerische Zeitschrift fuer Psychologie*, 53: 78–85.

Reicher, S. & Haslam, S.A. (2002) 'Learning from The Experiment'. *The Psychologist*, 15: 344–5.

Reicher, S. & Haslam, S.A. (2006) 'Rethinking the psychology of tyranny: the BBC Prison Study'. *British Journal of Social Psychology*, 45: 1–40.

Riniolo, T.C., Koledin, M., Drakulic, G.M. & Payne, R.A. (2003) 'An archival study of eyewitness memory of the Titanic's final plunge'. *Journal of General Psychology*, 130: 89–95.

Rossell, S.L., Bullmore, E.T., Williams, S.C.T. & David, A.S. (2002) 'Sex differences in functional brain activation during a lexical visual field task'. *Brain and Language*, 80: 97–105.

Rung, J.P., Carlsson, A., Markinhuhta, R. & Carlsson, M.L. (2005a) '(+)-MK-801 induced social withdrawal in rats; a model for negative symptoms in schizophrenia'. *Progress in Neuropsychopharmacology and Biological Psychiatry*, 29(5): 827–32.

Rung, J.P., Carlsson, A., Markinhuhta, R. & Carlsson, M.L. (2005b) 'The dopaminergic stabilizers (-)-OSU6162 and ACR16 reverse (+)-MK-801-induced social withdrawal in rats'. *Progress in Neuropsychopharmacology and Biological Psychiatry*, 29(5): 833–9.

Sagger, S. & Drean, J. (2001) *British Public Attitudes and Ethnic Minorities*. London: Cabinet Office.

Sánchez-Martín, J.R., Fano, E., Ahedo, L., Cardas, J., Brain, P.F., Azpíroz, A. (2000) 'Relating testosterone levels and free play social behavior in male and female preschool children'. *Psychoneuroendocrinology*, 25(8): 773–83.

Scoville, W.B. & Milner, B. (1957) 'The loss of recent memory after bilateral hippocampal lesions'. *Journal of Neurology, Neurosurgery and Psychiatry*, 20: 11–21.

Seitz, K. & Schumann-Hengsteler, R. (2000) 'Mental multiplication and working memory'. *European Journal of Cognitive Psychology*, 12: 552–70.

Shaywitz, B.A., Shaywitz, S.E., Pugh, K.R., Constable, R.T., Skudlarski, P., Fulbright, R.K., Bronen, R.A., Fletcher, J.M., Shankweiler, D.P., Katz, L. & Gore, J.C. (1995) 'Sex differences in the organization of the brain for language'. *Nature*, 373: 607–9.

Sherif, M., Harvey, O.J., White, B.J., Hood, W.R. & Sherif, C.W. (1961) *Intergroup Conflict and Co-operation: The Robber's Cave Experiment*. Norman: University of Oklahoma Press.

Sindelar, J., Elbel, B., Petry, N.M. (2007) 'What do we get for our money? Cost-effectiveness of adding contingency management'. *Addiction*, 102(2): 309–16.

Skinner, B.F. (1938) *The Behavior of Organisms*. New York: Appleton-Century-Crofts.

Skinner, B.F. (1948) 'Superstition in the pigeon'. *Journal of Experimental Psychology*, 38: 168–72.

Slater, M., Antley, A., Davison, A., Swapp, D., Guger, C., Barker, C., Pistrang, N. & Sanchez-Vives, M. (2006) 'A virtual reprise of the Stanley Milgram obedience experiments'. *PLOS One*, np.

Smythe, J.W. & Costall, B. (2003) 'Mobile phone use facilitates memory in male but not female subjects'. *Neuroreport*, 14: 243–6.

Solms, M. (2000) 'Freudian dream theory today'. *The Psychologist*, 13: 618–9.

Sroufe, L.A., Bennett, C., Englund, M., Urban, J. & Shulman, S. (1993) 'The significance of gender boundaries in preadolescence: contemporary correlates and antecedents of boundary violation and maintenance'. *Child Development*, 64(2): 455–66.

Stonewall (2005) *Tackling Homophobia in Schools*. London, Stonewall.

Sullivan, P.F., Keefe, R.S., Lange, L.A., Lange, E.M., Stroup, T.S., Lieberman, J. & Maness, P.F. (2007) 'NCAM1 and neurocognition in schizophrenia'. *Biological Psychiatry*, 61(7): 902–10.

Tajfel, H. (1970) 'Experiments in intergroup discrimination'. *Scientific American*, 223: 96–102.

Tajfel, H. & Turner, J.C. (1979) 'An integrative theory of intergroup conflict'. In Austin, W.G. & Worchel, S. (eds) *The Social Psychology of Intergroup Relations*. Cambridge, Cambridge University Press.

Thorndike, E.L. (1911) *Animal Intelligence: Experimental Studies*. New York: Macmillan.

Tienari, P. (1992) 'Implications of adoption studies on schizophrenia'. *British Journal of Psychiatry*, 161(supplement 18): 52–8.

Torrey, E.F., Fuller, E.H., Bracha, H.S., Bowler, A.E., McNeil, T.F., Rawlings, R.R., Quinn, P.O., Bigelow, L.B., Rickler, K. & Sjostrom, K. (1994) 'Prenatal origins of schizophrenia in a subgroup of discordant monozygotic twins'. *Schizophrenia Bulletin*, 20: 423–32.

Trivedi, M.H., Rush, A.J., Wisniewski, S.R., Nierenberg, A.A., Warden, D., Ritz, L., Norquist, G., Howland, R.H., Lebowitz, B., McGrath, P.J., Shores-Wilson, K., Biggs, M.M., Balasubramani, G.K. & Fava, M. (2006) 'Evaluation of outcomes with citalopram for depression using measurement-based care in STAR*D: implications for clinical practice'. *American Journal of Psychiatry*, 163: 28–40.

Troseth, G.L. (2003) 'Two-year-old children learn to use video as a source of information'. *Developmental Psychology*, 39(1): 140–50.

Tulving, E. (1972) 'Episodic and semantic memory'. In Tulving, E. & Donaldson, W. (eds) *Organisation of Memory*. London: Academic Press.

Tulving, E. & Pearlstone, Z. (1966) 'Availability vs accessibility of information in memory for words'. *Journal of Verbal Learning and Verbal Behaviour*, 5: 389–91.

Underwood, M.K., Scott, B.L., Galperin, M.B., Bjornstad, G.J. & Sexton, A.M. (2004) 'An observational study of social exclusion under varied conditions: gender and developmental differences'. *Child Development*, 75(5): 1538–55.

Verkooijen, K.T., de Vries, N.K. & Nielsen, G.A. (2007) 'Youth crowds and substance use: the impact of perceived group norm and multiple group identification'. *Psychology of Addictive Behaviours*, 21: 55–61.

Volpicelli, J., Balaraman, G., Hahn, J., Wallace, H. & Bux, D. (1999) 'The role of uncontrollable trauma in the development of PTSD and alcohol addiction'. *Alcohol Research and Health*, 23(4): 256–62.

Voyer, D. (1996) 'On the magnitude of laterality effects and sex differences in functional lateralities'. *Laterality*, 1: 51–83.

Wada, J.A., Clark, R. & Hamm, A. (1975) 'Cerebral hemisphere asymmetry in humans'. *Archives of Neurology*, 32: 239–46.

Walker, W.R., Vogel, R.J. & Thompson, C.P. (1997) 'Autobiographical memory: unpleasantness fades faster than pleasantness over time'. *Applied Cognitive Psychology*, 11: 399–413.

Watanabe, T., Yagishita, S. & Kikyo, H. (2008) 'Memory of music: roles of right hippocampus and left inferior frontal gyrus'. *Neuroimage*, 39(1): 483–91.

Watson, J.B. & Rayner, R. (1920) 'Conditioned emotional responses'. *Journal of Experimental Psychology*, 3(1): 1–14, details from laboratory notes reported in Watson, J.B. (1924) *Behaviorism*, New York: Norton.

Weinrott, M.R., Riggan, M. & Frothingham, S. (1997) 'Reducing deviant arousal in juvenile sex offenders using vicarious sensitisation'. *Journal of Interpersonal Violence*, 12: 704–28.

Williams, J.E. & Best, D.L. (1990) *Measuring Sex Stereotypes: A Multi-Nation Study*. Newbury Park, CA: Sage Publications.

Williams, T.M. (ed.) (1986) *The Impact of Television: A Natural Experiment in Three Communities*. Orlando, FL: Academic Press.

Willick, M.S. (1995) 'Defense', In Moore, B., and Fine, B. (eds) *Psychoanalysis: the Major Concepts*, New Haven: Yale University Press, 485–93.

Wood, G.K., Tomasiewicz, H., Rutishauser, U., Magnuson, T., Quirion, R., Rochford, J. & Srivastava, L.K. (1998) 'NCAM-180 knockout mice display increased lateral ventricle size and reduced prepulse inhibition of startle'. *Neuroreport*, 9(3): 461–6.

Wynn, V.E. & Logie, R.H. (1998) 'The veracity of long-term memory: did Bartlett get it right?' *Applied Cognitive Psychology*, 12: 1–20.

Yanowitz, K.L. & Weathers, K.J. (2004) 'Do boys and girls act differently in the classroom? A content analysis of student characters in educational psychology textbooks'. *Sex Roles: A Journal of Research*, 51: 101–7.

Yuille, J.C. & Cutshall, J.L. (1986) 'A case study of eyewitness memory of a crime'. *Journal of Applied Psychology*, 71: 291–301.

Index

Acknowledgements

Matt and Julia would like to thank Rick Jackman who, as always, has been an excellent guide on this project, also the team at Folens who have provided terrific support.

The authors and publishers are grateful to the following for permissions to reproduce copyright material.

p. 2, © James Steidl/Shutterstock; p. 7, © The Gallery Collection/Corbis; p. 10, © James Thew/Shutterstock; p. 12, © photogl/Shutterstock; p. 13 (top, bottom), from the film Obedience © 1968 by Stanley Milgram, © renewed 1993 by Alexandra Milgram, and distributed by Penn State Media Sales; p. 18, Figure 1 from Slater M et al. (2006) A Virtual Reprise of the Stanley Milgram Obedience Experiments.PLoS ONE 1(1):e39. doi:10.1371/journal.pone.0000039; p. 19, © Cryptos/Shutterstock; p. 21, © Marcin Balcerzak/Shutterstock; p. 23, courtesy of Philip Zimbardo; p. 32, courtesy of Alex Haslam; p. 33 (top, middle), courtesy of Alex Haslam; p. 33 (bottom), © MedioImages/Corbis; p. 35, © Vasily Smirnov/Shutterstock; p. 39, © David Burrows/Shutterstock; p. 42, © Tomasz Szymanski/Shutterstock; p. 44, © Bruce Rolff/Shutterstock; p. 50 (top), © Chad Littlejohn/Shutterstock; p. 50 (bottom), © Yuri Arcurs/Shutterstock; p. 54, © iofoto/Shutterstock; p. 64, © Jacques Langevin/Corbis Sygma; p. 66, © Elisei Shafer/Shutterstock; p. 67, © Simone van den Berg/Shutterstock; p. 69, © Lorraine Swanson/Shutterstock; p. 73, © Kolesnikov Sergey/Shutterstock; p. 76, Daniel Deme/epa/Corbis; p. 77, © Michele Trasi/Shutterstock; p. 80, © Losevsky Pavel/Shutterstock; p. 83, © photo researchers/Science Photot Library; p. 84, © Mary Evans Picture Library/Alamy; p. 87, © RJ Lerich/Shutterstock; p. 90, courtesy of Richard Kanaan; p. 96, © Markus Gann/Shutterstock; p. 99, © iofoto/Shutterstock; p. 101, © Jupiterimages/Creatas/Alamy; p. 107, © Terekhov Igor/Shutterstock; p. 109, © Ramona Heim/Shutterstock; p. 112, © Jason Grower/Shutterstock; p.112, © Oliver James, www.selfishcapitalist.com; p. 116, © Sebastian Kaulitzki/Shutterstock; p. 120, © Christine Boyd/The Daily Telegraph; p. 121, courtesy of Nathan Klein; p. 123, © Eric Isselée/Shutterstock; p. 124, © Weim/Fotolia; p. 125, © Gustoimages/Science Photo Library; p. 126, © Catherine Pouedras/Science Photo Library; p. 127, © Content Mine International/Alamy; p. 129 (top), © Oxford University Press ; p. 129 (bottom), © GreenGate Publishing; p. 133, © Andi Berger/Shutterstock; p. 140, © Andrew Syred/Science Photo Library; p. 143 © Reuters/Corbis; p. 146, © Jean-Claude Revy, ISM/Science Photo Library; p. 152 (top), © Living Art Enterprises, LLC/Science Photo Library; p. 152 (bottom), © Neil Borden/Science Photo Library; p. 153, © Emilia Stasiak/Shutterstock; p. 160, © Juan Manuel Ordóñez/Shutterstock; p. 163 (top), © Mary Evans Picture Library/Alamy; p. 163 (bottom), © Pictoral Press Ltd/Alamy; p. 164, © Robert Trachtenberg/Corbis; p. 165 (left, right), © Psychology Archives/The University of Akron; p. 166, © Pictoral Press Ltd/Alamy; p. 167 (right), © Manuscripts and Archives/Yale University Library; p. 172, © Julia Russell; p. 177, © William Casey/Shutterstock; p. 180, © Julia Russell; p. 181, © 2007 Getty Images; p. 182, © Albert Bandura; p. 186 (top left to right), © Sudheer Sakthan/Shutterstock, © Gelpi/Shutterstock, © Diego Cervo/Shutterstock, © Vallentin Vassileff/Shutterstock, © Lisa F. Young/Shutterstock, (bottom left to right) © Vallentin Vassileff/Shutterstock, © Vallentin Vassileff/Shutterstock, © Anne Kitzman/Shutterstock, © iofoto/Shutterstock, © Vallentin Vassileff; p. 189, © Jeffrey Smith/iStock; p. 191, © Todd Pierson/Shutterstock; p. 192, © Julia Russell; p. 194, © Content Mine International/Alamy; p. 195, © Photos 12/Alamy; p. 196, © Robert Gooch/Shutterstock; p. 167, © Losevsky Pavel/Shutterstock; p. 200, © Oliver Suckling/Shutterstock.

Every effort has been made to contact the holders of copyright material, but if any have been overlooked the publishers will be happy to make the appropriate arrangements at the first opportunity.